GENERATION F

WINSTON SMITH

Monday Books

A CIP catalogue record for this title is available
from the British Library

ISBN: 978-1-906308-18-6

Typeset by Andrew Searle
Printed and bound by Cox and Wyman

www.mondaybooks.com

http://mondaybooks.blogspot.com/

info@mondaybooks.com

Contents

Dedication

I would like to thank my family and friends for their continued support through hard times and good times alike.

I'm also grateful to the judges of the Orwell Prize for Blogging for recognising me with their award in 2010.

Foreword

Liam often assaults staff. He spits, punches, regularly smashes up the house and cars outside. I can take care of myself, but he's a big lad and at times like tonight, with that vacant, angry look in his eye, he's very dangerous, very scary. As I stand there, weighing my options, Edwin and the pregnant Becky come out of their rooms and start pleading with him to turn his stereo off. Instead, he turns it louder. Myself and the other staff spend another 20 minutes talking to him, cajoling and encouraging him to 'make the right choice' and praising him for the few hours during the week when he wasn't causing mayhem. None of this is working; it rarely does.

Edwin and Becky are now losing their tempers. The pleading of earlier turns to threats and insults. Suddenly, Edwin rushes at Liam and hurls a 4kg dumbbell. Liam ducks. I know that when he stands up there's going to be serious trouble. Edwin runs back to his room and locks the door, taking Becky and the two female members of staff. Liam, apoplectic with fury, charges after them and starts kicking the door, maniacally.

There's not much I can do to stop him. As calmly as I can, I ask him please to stop trying to break the door down — always with nice manners, of course, it's good for their self esteem.

'Fuck off,' he snarls, 'or you're going to get it!'

'There's a pregnant girl in there, Liam,' I say. 'She's terrified... listen to her crying.'

He doesn't even hear me. 'I'm gonna mash you up, Edwin!' he yells, eyes bulging, spittle flying from his mouth. 'I'm gonna shank you, blud! I'm gonna mess you right up!'

'I'm gonna mash you up,' comes the muffled reply from Edwin, safe for now behind his locked door.

Liam races off and returns with a frying pan: I don't think he's planning make Edwin an omelette with it. Over all the banging and screaming and crying, I hear the phone ringing in the office along the corridor. I run to pick it up. 'Winston?' says the voice. 'It's Louise.'

'Louise?' I say, momentarily confused. 'Louise who?'

'Louise-stuck-inside-Edwin's-room,' she says, practically sobbing. 'I'm ringing on his phone but I can't get an outside line. Can you call the police? I'm really scared. He's nearly got the door off its hinges.'

A BRIGHT COLD DAY IN JANUARY

IT IS A BRIGHT COLD DAY in January, and the clocks will soon be striking nine.

I am walking along a dank, grey pavement towards The Emmanuel Goldstein Project, a new 'supported housing' venture run by the Oceania Housing Association. I'm employed by the Talbot Social Care Agency, which supplies staff to places like this, and I've got a six-month contract as a support worker.

Today is my first day.

Emmanuel Goldstein is located in a quiet residential street in a pleasant suburb of a small English town. As I walk, I look at the houses on either side – semi-detached Victorian or Edwardian villas which would cost a million pounds in Fulham. One or two have been divided into flats, but most are family homes, with 'Neighbourhood Watch' and 'No callers' stickers on the doors, pot plants in the windows and neat little front gardens.

I notice the litter. An empty cider can stuffed into a privet hedge here, a screwed up chip wrapper in the gutter there, cigarette butts everywhere on the cracked, grey slabs. As I draw nearer still to the Project, the quantity and variety of this detritus grows. An abandoned shopping trolley half-on and half-off the kerb; fast food cartons; crushed-up fag packets. Beer cans: mostly cheap, strong lager, some stamped flat, others skittering and rolling around in the breeze.

I stop at the driveway.

The Project is an imposing building: three storeys high, it has ornate brickwork, a high, sloping roof and large stone gateposts. Long ago it would have belonged to some wealthy factory owner or industrialist; more recently, it was a 3* hotel. Now it is a supported housing scheme.

In my experience, most people have never heard of supported housing; until I signed up with the agency for which I work, I hadn't either. It's run by the Department of Communities and Local Government via the 'Supporting People' programme. This scheme was launched in 2003 with an annual budget of around £1.7 billion and the remit of providing 'housing-related support services' to 'vulnerable client groups'. Some of this is really excellent work – helping deserving groups like the elderly and those with learning disabilities to live easier lives. However, it also means providing accommodation for young people 'at risk of homelessness'. Between the ages of 16 and 25, they are too old to live in care but unable, for whatever reason, to live with their families. The idea is that we give them a roof over their heads, some freedom and responsibility and a little help in making the transition to living as an adult.

In theory, and occasionally in practice, this is a fine thing (although I quibble at just how much 'support' a 25-year-old 'young person' should require to sort out his or her life). Unfortunately, in my experience, it is widely abused. Some of the residents in supported housing are great kids, trying to make a go of their lives; the rest are mugging the taxpayer for billions. (When I talk about 'taxpayers', by the way, I'm not on about bankers, businessmen and other high earners, who could easily afford to pay in a bit more. I'm on about bin men, and dinner ladies, and people who clean loos and work in chip shops and sweep the streets for a living.)

The Emmanuel Goldstein Project is home to 66 young people: 58 of them live in single rooms in the main building, and the other eight live in a small block of one-bed flats at the front of the building. These latter are ex-residents of the Project who have moved on to what is described, slightly misleadingly, as 'independent living'. It's misleading because the word 'independent' here means, in most cases, that they have just about worked out how to sign on for themselves.

I will later discover that they are on a kind of rolling programme of eviction. This is because after spending a long time being, effectively, babysat in supported housing, they are unable to maintain a tenancy on their own.

I walk down the drive to the Project, stepping to one side to allow an ambulance to leave. Tall rows of mature yew trees, planted a century or more ago, whisper on either side of me; a purple hooded top hangs from one of them, and I count two more shopping trolleys and a couple of bin bags-worth of discarded tin cans, plastic boxes and paper wrappings lying around the place. There is more of this stuff beneath each of the ground floor windows.

The door is recessed into an open porch. It is metal, functional, with safety-glass windows, and firmly locked. To the right, there is a flat, silver panel with a 10-digit keypad, a small fish-eye camera lens, a grill and an intercom button. I press the button.

After a few moments, an electronic voice appears and says, 'Can you wait a sec?' before disappearing.

It's a few minutes before 9am, but somewhere overhead I can hear several stereos competing with each other. I'm not sure which is worse: drum 'n' bass, speed ragga and death metal on their own, or in this weird aural cocktail. I look up: a large CCTV camera stares balefully back at me.

I look down at my wrist and watch the second hand tick round through two minutes. Then I press the intercom button again.

A few seconds later, the same voice says, 'I said, *Can you wait?*'

I lean forward to speak into the grill.

'Hi,' I say. 'It's just that the agency sent me. I'm the new support worker, so I wondered if...'

'The new what?' says the voice.

'The new support worker,' I say. 'From the agency.'

'Christ,' says the voice, which now sounds thoroughly exasperated. 'Don't they tell you anything? We don't use support worker any more. It's *keyworker* now.'

'I'm sorry?' I say, but the buzzer is already sounding and the door has clicked ajar. I push it open and walk inside.

The reception lobby is white-painted and functional, with a blue nylon carpet over what I guess are the original flagstones. There is a table to the left of me and a table to the right, and piled upon each is a bewildering variety of leaflets: most seem to concern human rights, racism, drug helplines, benefits helplines, complaints procedures and stern warnings about HIV-AIDS, Hep B and the other dangers of unprotected sex.

On the walls are a number of garish posters. One advertises the benefits of the world's top 10 religions, and a few others that are bubbling under, like Zoroastrianism. Another celebrates diversity and features huggy group shots of happy, smiling people from every corner of the earth. They all look like they're having a whale of a time.

Sitting on one of the tables, smoking insouciantly underneath a large 'No Smoking' sign and another CCTV camera, is a youth of about 17. He clearly has nowhere pressing to be, despite it being a condition of living in these projects that you have a job or are looking for a job, or are attending school or a college course.

'Hey, mate,' I say, 'can you tell me where the office is?'

'How the fuck should I know?' he says, slipping off the table and out of the door.

'Thanks for that,' I say, but it doesn't matter: the office is clearly straight ahead. Through a long glass wall I can see a man of about my age sitting at a desk. A couple of teenagers are standing in front of him. The three of them appear to be arguing. I walk towards the door, knock and pop my head in. No-one seems to notice me, so I lean in the doorway and listen.

'As I say, Kenny,' says the man. 'I'll get you another key, but there's a £12 charge.'

'For fuck's sake,' says the youth, who I take to be Kenny. He is stereotypically skinny and ratty-faced, and is wearing a 'No Fear' baseball cap and a chunky gold sovereign ring. 'It's not my fault I lost the fucking thing. Just give me another one, will you?'

'If it's not your fault, whose fault is it?'

'Like I told you, I lent it to Perry and he gave it to Marina and she got pissed and lost the fucking thing, not me. I need a fucking key, else I'm going to complain about you for this, because it ain't fair.'

The man at the desk sighs. I sense he is struggling internally with the question of whether or not to prolong this by asking why on earth Kenny gave his key to Perry, when he knows to a certainty that Perry is an idiot, and anyone could have predicted that he would lose it within the hour. In the end, the line of least resistance is breached. 'Christ on a bike,' he hisses, under his breath. 'Right, I'll give you another key but next time…'

He reaches into a drawer, pulls out a box of keys, hunts through for a moment, and then hands one of them over.

'You're sound, you are, Brendan,' says Kenny, with a wink and a sort of clenched fist gesture in the man's direction. 'Wicked!' Then he and his accomplice are gone in a swish of Kappa's finest polyester.

After a moment, I say, 'Hi, I'm Winston. You buzzed me in? I'm the new… keyworker.'

'Yeah,' says the man. 'I'm Brendan Blair. Pleased to meet you. Grab a seat. I'll just fill out the form for Kenny's new key, and then I'll take you on a quick tour of the place.'

'What was the ambulance doing?' I say.

'Sharn,' he says. 'She takes an overdose most weeks, or claims she has. Obviously, we can't take any chances, but it's just attention-seeking stuff – it's never serious.'

I sit behind the other desk and look around me. The room is about 15ft long and 12ft wide, painted light beige and lit by harsh strip lights hanging beneath the polystyrene ceiling tiles. An Oceania Housing Association calendar is pinned on one wall; a small grey clock and a series of health and safety notices on another. Behind Brendan's desk sits a CCTV monitor, its screen split up into 16 discrete pictures. There is a door marked 'Manager' leading through to the inner sanctum, the nerve centre, of the Project. The only other furniture in the office apart from the desks is four metal filing cabinets. On each of them, and on each desk, are several stacked files, all bulging with sheets of paper, forms and folders. I know from experience that the cabinets, too, will be groaning under the weight of the paperwork they hold.

Brendan has his head bent as he scribbles furiously on the form, so I look at the nearest file stack to me and idly pick up the topmost sheaf of A4 – a dozen or so sheets stapled together in the top left hand corner.

'*Emmanuel Goldstein Project – Supporting People*', says the legend on the first sheet. '*QAF Principle Objective Blue 1.6: Assessment Toolkit*'.

QAF – the Quality Assessment Framework – is a hugely bureaucratic way by which we in supported housing measure everything we do against a set of centrally-dictated benchmarks and metrics to prove beyond all possibility of challenge that we're doing a good job. The truth is that it proves nothing of the sort; on the contrary, I think our slavish compliance with QAF pretty much ensures we *don't* do a good job. Now, the very sight of those three letters fills my brain with a sort of irritated buzzing, like I've got a giant bluebottle stuck in my skull somewhere: I've seen countless hundreds, even thousands, of sheets of paper like this, and they drive me to despair. Part of me – a big part – wants to get up and walk out, there and then, never to return to the Emmanuel Goldstein Project or any other supported housing scheme anywhere in the country. But I need the money: £18,700 *per annum* is hardly a king's ransom, but I've got bills and half a mortgage on a tiny flat where I live with my girlfriend, and it's better than nothing.

I turn the page. I can only imagine that this stuff is produced by some sort of random sentence machine, a computer programmed with words and phrases like 'stakeholder', 'service-user', 'proactive approach' and 'inter-agency liaison'.

'Objective Blue Key Outcome 3, QAF target' has the following header:

> *Personal support plans are regularly examined and, where necessary, revised to reflect outcomes of reviews.*

Underneath this header are four boxes, each with space for notes, ticks, signatures and counter-signatures (and possibly counter-counter signatures). I choose one of the boxes at random.

> *Support workers* (I notice the 'keyworker' edict has not yet been fully 'cascaded' through the organisation) *are able to explain how wider support needs will be (or are being) met, including details of ongoing co-ordination with partner agencies concerned.*

The boxes alongside have been neatly filled in, with annotations and remarks and approvals and suggestions and notes, endless notes, in several different pens and two or three hands. I flick through the pages and marvel – though I'm no stranger to any of this – at the sheer number of hours, not to mention the waste of paper and ink, involved. I put the papers back on the top of the stack, looking forward to adding a few kilos of my own in the course of the forthcoming six-month secondment.

Brendan puts his pen down and looks up at me. 'Done,' he says. 'Right, come on, I'll show you around.'

* * * * *

It takes a good three-quarters of an hour to get round the place. We walk up lots of sets of stairs, along various corridors, past rows of identikit doors. Brendan points out certain of them in particular as belonging to residents who are especially interesting, for one reason or another; he opens one to show me a room.

It's big and bright, and smells of fresh paint and new carpet. There's a fridge humming away in the corner, two tall windows and a door leading to an en-suite bathroom. The bathroom is sparkling. I wouldn't mind living here myself: it's bigger and better than my own flat.

'I assume they all have en-suite bathrooms?' I say.

'Yep,' says Brendan.

I look around the room. 'Nice,' I say.

'For the time being,' he says. 'We've got someone arriving for this one later today. I'll show you one that's just been vacated.'

We walk back down the corridor and stop outside another room.

'This one's empty at the moment,' he says, opening the door. 'We've just evicted Casey.'

'What for?' I say.

'You know,' says Brendan. 'The usual. Took ages to get rid of him, but he went in the end.'

In my experience of supported housing, 'the usual' could be taking or dealing drugs, being arrested for a serious crime, threatening staff or fellow residents or falling significantly behind with rent payments. The fact that it took a long time to evict Casey doesn't surprise me, either.

This room is in a different state from the first. There are indeterminate stains and cigarette burns all over the rose-coloured carpet; a window pane is smashed; the paint has been pulled from the walls in many places where Sellotaped posters have been torn down; the inside of the door has been spray-painted with a large cannabis leaf; and the electric light switch has been wrenched or hammered from the wall. Brendan leads me through to the bathroom; it stinks of urine and worse, and something has been smeared all over the mirror.

'Do they all end up in this sort of state?' I say.

'To be fair, we do have some decent residents,' says Brendan. 'You know what it's like – there are those who are grateful for what they get and respect the place. There are just more who don't, for whatever reason. I'd say a lot of them end up smelling like this. I can't see how they can stand it personally, but there you go.'

This chimes with my own experience working in a number of projects.

'It's going to take some cleaning up, all this,' I say.

The carpet will probably need replacing. With the electrics, the window and the redecoration, I can't see us getting much change out of a thousand quid – not to mention the cleaning bill.

We go back out into the corridor and pause at another doorway.

'This is one of the kitchens,' says Brendan. 'We have 54 rooms, and 18 kitchens, so each one is shared between three rooms.'

I poke my head inside. The bin is overflowing, the sink is full of filthy dishes and pans and the cooker covered with congealed fat. It smells rank, and there are flies everywhere.

'They're on a warning to clean this place up,' says Brendan. 'Actually, a number of the kitchens are on the same warning.'

We head back downstairs, through the lobby and into a laundry area full of washing machines and tumble driers. It smells damp, and there are piles of wet, mouldering washing on the floor and every other surface.

'That's the laundry,' says Brendan, leading me back out into the lobby and then into a large rectangular room, 'and this is the residents' lounge.'

A handful of youths are sitting in armchairs or on sofas, watching the biggest flat screen plasma TV I've ever seen. I hate to stereotype, but they are actually watching *The Jeremy Kyle Show*.

'Guys, this is Winston,' says Brendan. 'He's the new keyworker.'

No-one looks up. Brendan shrugs, mutters *Don't get up*, and we walk through another doorway in the far wall.

'And this is the computer room,' he says. 'We've hooked up the internet for the residents, and this is also where they come for in-house courses and things like that.'

There are half a dozen nice new PCs sitting at desks. Like everything else in this place – the kitchens full of flies, the en-suite bedrooms and the huge communal television – they are provided free of charge. It occurs to me that I wouldn't mind a brand new telly and computer in my own flat, but unfortunately I'd have to pay for them myself and I don't have the cash.

We head back out through the common room and the lobby and into the office.

'That's about it,' says Brendan. 'There's a couple of other meeting rooms out the back which we rent out to local groups and stuff and sometimes use ourselves. There's the grounds, obviously. But basically, you've seen the lot. Any questions?'

'There seem to be a lot of people hanging around,' I say. I look at my watch. 'It's nearly 10 o'clock... are they not supposed to be working or at college or something?'

'Most of these you've seen today are on JSA (Job Seekers' Allowance),' he says.

'Well, they don't seem to be seeking jobs,' I say.

'Welcome to the Project!' says Brendan.

INTRODUCING MYSELF

I SUPPOSE I SHOULD introduce myself.

My name is Winston Smith, I'm 34 years old and I'm a support worker – sorry, *keyworker* – in the supported housing sector. When it's offered, I also take on extra, part-time work in residential care homes with children between the ages of 12 and 17. To work in care homes is to inhabit an extra circle of hell beyond the limits of Dante's imagination, but I'm broke so I don't have a lot of choice. More of that later.

I've explained the basic idea behind supported housing, but here's an excerpt from the 'service definition' at the Emmanuel Goldstein Project which gives you a fuller flavour – at least, as far as this sort of strangled officialese allows – of what the place does.

> Our project exists to help disadvantaged young people aged between 16 and 25 who are homeless, or at risk of becoming homeless, and who need support to develop independent living skills. With each young person we have a binding contract, known as a licence agreement, which outlines the conditions of the young person's stay at our project. This agreement will enable the young person to achieve independence. Failure to consistently adhere to the agreement adversely affects a young person's right to accommodation at the project. Licence agreements last for up to two years.

On the face of it, this all sounds very noble and laudable. We've all seen homeless people sleeping in wet shop doorways and on bare park benches; in a civilised and (still) wealthy country like this, who wouldn't want to give them a temporary roof over their heads while they sort their lives out?

The devil is in the detail of how we go about it. When I started working in the sector, I was a true believer. Given that I am a *Guardian*-reading liberal vegetarian, with a first-class degree in Politics, Philosophy and Sociology and a Masters' in International Relations, perhaps that's not too surprising; you don't get too many paid-up members of the Conservative Party in my end of the public services.

The thing is, I got mugged by reality. I learned that the rhetoric doesn't match the facts – in fact, it *obscures* the facts. Phrases like 'disadvantaged young people', 'at risk of becoming homeless' and 'develop independent living skills' sucked me in for a while; 'binding contract' was another good one. The trouble is, these words turn out to be meaningless, or worse. In fact, this project and many others like it create and perpetuate the exact problems they're ostensibly designed to eradicate. This is hugely costly and destructive to society but, above all, it's a tragedy for the kids involved.

Here's what the service definition has to say about my role as a keyworker:

> All of our clients at the project have their own keyworker, with whom they must meet regularly to comply with the conditions of their occupancy. The keyworker, through action-planning, will offer guidance and assistance in a range of areas.

What this means is that when a new resident arrives and is allocated to me, I'll have a meeting with him and discuss his current position vis à vis employment or education, benefits, paying his rent and the future in general. Together, we'll draw up a 'support plan' – a document which will lay out his goals and how he aims (with my support) to reach them. Over the weeks and months that follow, we'll meet up regularly to ensure he's hitting his targets.

Once again, this doesn't sound too bad: let's take these homeless youngsters off those park benches and get them into jobs or training, or even benefits. What could possibly be wrong with that?

Unfortunately, plenty. Obviously, it will involve a lot of paperwork. This is a given; the British State sector leads the world in the production and infilling of forms. But this is really just a minor pain in the arse, not the main problem. After all, if the goal was 'Become a rocket scientist', there would be a lot of stages to be passed through along the way, and you'd expect to have to write a few things down. But it's when you consider that the goal is 'Sign on the dole' that you begin to wonder how difficult that is, and how many meetings you need to have to discuss it. As you'll see, the answer to these questions seems to be, respectively, 'Very' and 'A lot.'

As well as Brendan and myself, there is Olive, the part-time receptionist, and eight other employees. Margaret, Steve, Posy and Nigel are full-time keyworkers (Posy and Nigel are night-workers, who rotate their way through a four-days-on, four-days-off shift pattern). There's also a part-timer, Abigail, who does three days a week, a tutor called Gene who comes in twice a week, and a project manager, Martin, who oversees the running of the place. Mostly, this means that Martin ensures that we keyworkers are filling in all those support plans correctly, in accordance with government regulations on form-filling, as well as dealing with a whole additional layer of bureaucratic requirements set by both the Department of Communities and Local Government and Oceania Housing Association which runs the Project (Oceania is one of the leading housing associations in the country, employing a large number of people nationally).

The project manager has the theoretical power to terminate any troublesome resident's tenancy, but this power is constrained by the resident's right of appeal to the manager's manager, the area business manager (ABM), Tessa (a former Manager of this project, as it happens).

The ABM oversees the work of all the project managers at various individual sites throughout the county. As far as I can tell, this seems to involve ensuring that the project managers are filling in *their* forms correctly, as well as overseeing and double-checking the project managers' supervision of the keyworkers' filling-in of *our* forms.

Above ABM Tessa, at head office down in London, is another layer of management – the manager's manager's manager (and, no doubt, a manager's manager's manager's manager, too), as well as various people working in public relations roles, policy development, human resources and finance.

The people at the top earn hundreds of thousands of pounds. The people at the bottom, like me, sadly don't.

A bit more about me. I'm originally from Ireland and, as a youngster, I dreamed of becoming a journalist. I actually signed onto a journalism course to learn the trade but unfortunately I was a very heavy dope smoker – I'd start the day with a giant spliff, and carry on from there, spending most of my waking hours absolutely mashed, lying around listening to old soul records. Perhaps unsurprisingly, I flunked my first year because I kept forgetting to turn up for lectures. I signed up a second time, but when I noticed that I was forgetting to turn up again I started to wonder whether journalism was for me. At the end of that year, which I flunked again, I decided that it wasn't and went back to live with my parents in Ireland – their firm condition being that I sorted out my drug use with some counselling.

For a while, I knocked the gear on the head, and got myself a job washing dishes in a restaurant. Of course, the one thing places like that have is plenty of booze, so I really just swapped one chemical distractant for another and became a serious pisshead instead. It got to the point where the only things I spent my wages on were alcohol and rent (I ate free at work); when I lost my door key one time, Kenny-style, I remember spending every evening for two weeks sitting outside my flat waiting for my flatmate to come home and let me in. This was because it would have cost me the price of a pint to have a new key cut, and I didn't want to be down a pint.

Along the way, I somehow took up the dope again, and other drugs when I could get my hands on them. I also picked up a criminal record for possession. A counsellor told me I had an addictive personality – no shit, Sherlock – and although they say you can't get addicted to cannabis, I certainly did. I was psychologically dependent on both weed and booze, and my life was going nowhere. I was getting depressed, I was suffering anxiety attacks and, eventually, I reached a crossroads: I could either carry on killing myself slowly on a barstool or I could pull myself together.

I followed John Hodge's advice from *Trainspotting*, and chose life. I quit drinking and smoking altogether – I've been teetotal and drug-free for a decade now – and went to university, got my head down and achieved the aforementioned results.

Why am I telling you all this? For two reasons.

Firstly, to show that I am not someone who has lived a sheltered existence. I experienced personal problems in my own youth, including addictions which affected my mental health and my education. So if I sometimes seem a bit hard on some of the kids we'll meet throughout the book, it's not because I'm some kind of ideological reactionary, coming from a position of ignorance or naivety.

Secondly, I want to stress that my own experience shows that no matter how low you get – and I got very low indeed – you can bring yourself back through hard work and a bit of tough love from those who care about you.

After uni, I spent a bit of time teaching in Spain, and then I came to England to take up a position as a teaching assistant in a tough comprehensive school in the north. My initial plan was to spend a year in that role and then take a Post Graduate Certificate in Education. But the mayhem that I witnessed in the school, and the failure of senior management to deal with troublesome and often dangerous students, or protect the weaker and more vulnerable from extreme bullying, shocked me. Those kids who wanted to learn were all but ignored, while the classes were filled with unruly students on account of the then government's policy of inclusion. I took the advice of some curmudgeonly teachers nearing retirement, and decided the world of bog standard comprehensives was not for me.

But I still felt attracted to the public services, and thought that I had something to give. So I went on to seek what I thought would be more meaningful work with young people in the social care sector.

HOW SHOULD WE APPROACH
YOU IF YOU'RE ANGRY?

A COUPLE OF WEEKS have gone by, and I'm starting to feel I've got my feet under the table at the Project. The staff are a decent bunch and I know most of the residents by sight and name. I've already got half a dozen of my own clients to support, or keywork (if that's a verb), and my own little corner of the third filing cabinet set aside.

Today, most of my colleagues are away on holiday or on courses down in London so it's just me and Margaret in the office. We're at our desks working on some files when a group of four or five young men of about 18 just push open the door and walk in, ignoring the house rule printed on the prominent sign which says they should knock and wait to be invited. (Actually, we're instructed to call this a 'policy' because 'rules' are 'authoritarian' and 'oppressive'.*)

It's not like they can't read – though a shocking number of the young people at the Project are functionally illiterate, given that they're supposed to have 11 years of compulsory education behind them.

---

* At my first Project, I asked for a copy of the house rules. The manager Dave said there wasn't one.

'From a policy point of view, the senior management of the Housing Association feel that the word "rule" is unhelpful,' he said. 'Most people don't have to live by rules in their own homes, so neither should our residents.'

'So they can do whatever they like?' I said.

'Well, we do have clauses in the licence agreements which the clients sign up to, and there are various policies about behaviour and so on.'

'But are they supposed to abide by these licence agreement clauses and our policies?' I said. 'And are there sanctions for failing to do so?'

'Oh, yes.'

'But they're not rules?'

'No.' After a few moments, he cleared his throat. 'I suppose there is one way that we could create a list of house rules and have it put up on the notice board,' he said.

'How?'

'If at one of our consultation meetings with the residents they agree to having certain rules, and calling them "rules", then we can print them out and put them up.'

They crowd around the postal box and start rummaging through the day's mail. It's gone 11am, but they all look like they've just got out of bed. Missing Key Kenny peels off with an envelope in his hand and a grin on his face. 'Fucking great!' he says, waving his benefit cheque in the air. 'Payday!'

One after the other, they all follow suit, dropping the empty, screwed-up envelopes on the floor or stuffing them back into the box, and wandering back into the reception area where a group of their mates is assembling. A loud techno tune blasts from a mobile phone. Then they head off out of the building. I'm not sure where they're going, but I wouldn't mind betting – based on the litter around the place and my experience with them and similar youths – that it involves either an off-licence, an amusement arcade or a vendor of deep-fried chicken. Possibly all three.

Olive the part-time receptionist clucks at them in a motherly way.

'That annoys me,' I say to Margaret. 'Just walking in like that. They're supposed to knock.'

Margaret's in her late 40s and is a lovely woman – she's kind-hearted, thinks the best of everyone and is coming from a really good place. But I do feel she's a bit naïve: I'm sure she'd happily spend a couple of hours working on a support plan for Pol Pot. ('What's your Goal, Pol? Restarting civilisation at Year Zero? That's good. Now, how are we going to achieve your Goal? Shall I put, "Agrarian socialism achieved by relocating city-dwellers to collectivised, forced-labour farms?" OK, excellent. Now, let's have a look at your Housing Benefit claim…')

'Do you seriously expect them to queue up outside?' she says, fondly watching the group leave. 'We have an open door policy here. The young people need to feel that they can talk to us about anything at any time. We don't believe in barriers. We're not authoritarian.'

'It's hardly authoritarian,' I say. 'I mean, I've heard about the thin end of the wedge, but I can't see how asking people to knock and wait is the slippery slope to Franco's Spain. Anyway, surely the whole point of this project is to assist young people to move to independent living? Out there in the real world, once they leave here, they can't just barge in to a bank manager's office, or a lawyer's, or a doctor's, can they? They need to learn the basics, and one of them is queuing and knocking and all that stuff. Plus, if we don't even enforce the simplest, most basic, rules, what kind of message does that send to them?'

I don't think Margaret is listening: she has a faraway look in her eyes.

A couple of minutes later a young woman of about 19 wanders into the office.

'Hi Margaret,' she says, toying with a gold pendant around her neck. 'Just to let you know, I've got that housing benefit application form that you filled in for me down to the council like you wanted me to.'

'Oh, well *done*, Kelly,' says Margaret, beaming. 'Good for *you*! Great stuff getting that sorted, you're doing *really* well, I'm really impressed with you.'

It's as though Kelly has dropped by to announce she has discovered a cure for cancer, rather than walked five minutes to the local authority offices to hand over a form to claim some free money for her free flat – a form, let's not forget, that she didn't even fill in herself. I take a closer look at her: perhaps she's missing her legs, which might explain the strange ratio of effort to reward. No, she's an able-bodied young woman.

Margaret and Kelly walk out of the office together, and I go back to my file.

After lunch, Martin – the project manager – calls me into his office. He's been on paternity leave and then a course since I arrived, so I've not really spoken to him much before now. He seems a nice enough guy – a bit older than me, cheap suit, greying hair and a slightly worried look on his face. It's a look, I'll learn, that he always wears.

'How's it going, Winston?' he says. 'Settling in OK?'

'Yep, it's all good thanks, Martin,' I say.

'Had the Health and Safety brief, tour of the building, *et cetera*?'

'Yep.'

'Got your keys and ID card and stuff?'

'Yep, thanks.'

'You live quite a way away, apparently?'

'About an hour or so.'

'Finding it alright getting in?'

'Yeah,' I say. 'It's not too bad. There's a direct train so…'

'Oh, OK,' he says. 'You're going to be OK for weekends, then?'

The daytime keyworkers cover Saturdays and Sundays, one person at a time, on a rota basis – not something I'm really looking forward to. It's always better to have some back-up around.

'Yep, sure,' I say. 'The train runs on Saturday and there's a bus service on Sundays. It'll take me a bit longer but it'll be fine.'

'Good, good,' says Martin. 'Right, look, we've got a potential new resident coming in at 2pm for his interview. Can you handle it for me?'

He hands me a thin file.

'Sure,' I say. 'No probs.'

I take the file and leave.

Craig Jones is his name: I read through the papers, make a few notes and then a couple of calls to various relevant people. This kills half an hour, by which time he has arrived and is standing in reception. I go out to meet him.

* * * * *

'Craig,' I say. 'Nice to meet you, I'm Winston.'

He has a shaggy Mohican, and is dressed in jeans and a green Rockport t-shirt and a thick gold chain.

He says, 'Alright.'

We shake hands and head into the interview room, where I make us both a coffee before sitting down.

'So,' I say, 'tell me about yourself. How old are you, where are you living at the moment, that sort of stuff?'

'I'm 17,' he says. 'I'm kind of sofa-surfing.'

'Why can't you live at your mum's anymore?'

'She's got too many kids,' he says. 'Like, she ain't got the money to look after me as well.'

'Why did she have more kids if she couldn't afford them?'

He shrugs, and I don't pursue it as it's not technically within my remit. But I do wonder how having children you can't support has come to be seen as morally or socially acceptable. My girlfriend is very keen to have kids, but we simply can't afford it right now, not on the kind of wages we earn. It's becoming a source of friction between us.

I move through the various sections of the interview procedure until I arrive at the page related to 'offending behaviour'.

'I see on your application here that you're currently carrying out a Community Punishment Order and a Community Rehabilitation Order,' I say.

He nods. 'Yeah, that's right,' he says. 'But they was a long time ago.'

'How long ago?'

'Like, when I was 16.'

Six months back, I think. *Is that a long time ago?* I'm not sure.

'And them sentences is nearly finished now. These days I just keep my head down, I don't get into no trouble.'

This is not true (unless you take the double negative literally). Prior to the interview, I telephoned Craig's probation officer; she informed me that he is in breach of both of these orders and that, because of this, his case is being referred back to court. He also has a pending court case for affray with a police officer and could well be looking at jail time for that.

'Craig, I see you have quite a bit of an offending history,' I say. 'Tell me about all the incidents… what happened, how long ago, all the details, please.'

'I done a few burglaries over the past two years and I also got done for one criminal damage,' he says. 'Them are the ones I'm on them orders for.'

'Nothing else?'

'Nah.' He shakes his head and looks at me, wide-eyed, the picture of innocence.

'Are you sure? Because we do talk to probation, you know?'

'Oh, yeah, I forgot. There is one other thing that I'm waiting to go to court for, which is assaulting a police officer, but I swear I never done it. They're setting me up because they don't like me.'

'Would you like some support from the staff in order to help you stop offending if you came here?'

This is a routine interview question for those with a history of offending. I don't know enough about Craig to make a firm judgment on him yet, but with his history of burglary – and based on previous experience with young criminals – I'm pretty sure the only sure way to stop him 'offending' would be to lock him in his room or cut off his hands. We can't do this, though, so the 'support' I'll actually be able to offer him will involve writing in his support plan that he is not to commit any more crime, getting him to countersign this, placing the note on his file and keeping said file somewhere safe as evidence of our 'support' when the pen-pushers from the Department of Communities and Local Government come out to inspect us and review our services. Oh, and I'll also accompany him to his meetings with the Youth Offending Team and Probation Service, at which he will be further told not to commit any more crime, and will solemnly agree not to do so. I'd say a total of five or six people will be involved in all of this, and that it will have zero impact on whether Craig does or does not decide to break into an old lady's house and steal her purse next week.

'Yeah, I would like some support from the staff in order to help me stop offending, as it goes,' he says, scratching the back of one hand and leaning forward in his chair.

He's clearly not as daft as he looks: who wants it on his file that he refused help?

'I tell you what,' he says, 'actually, if you see me with anything you think isn't mine could you please take it off me? But I don't think I will be stealing from now on, anyway, because I don't want to go to jail, but I might be going anyway, but it depends on what happens with that assault charge against the copper.'

Far too many 'buts' there. I decide not to go into the thorny question of how I'll be able to determine whether things in his hands belong to him.

'What happened with the copper, Craig? Tell me about that?'

'I was at the train station with my bird,' he says. 'I was having a row with her. I mean, I'd had a few beers and I was upset about something, you know what it's like. Anyway, some fucker rang the Old Bill, didn't they, and I was nicked for drunk and disorderly, but the police claim I hit one of them and spat on them when they was trying to arrest me. Which is bollocks. All that happened was, they had me on the ground when they was arresting me and I only dribbled on the copper's shoe, and he claims that was spitting on him, yeah, and that I also assaulted him when I moved my leg and it touched his.'

I raise my eyebrows involuntarily as I imagine him trying that defence in court. He is not slow to spot this and takes immediate umbrage – 'I'm fucking telling the truth!' – before realising which side his bread is buttered and calming down.

'The police are only supposed to restrain people on the ground if they're being aggressive or resisting arrest. Were you?'

'No, they just hate me.'

'Why?'

'I dunno, they just do.'

'Let's move on to the section of the interview related to alcohol, Craig. How much do you drink, and how often?'

'Not much these days, as it goes,' he says. 'Only at weekends and only beer nowadays, no spirits, maybe six or seven beers, once or twice at the weekends.'

'How does alcohol make you feel?'

'With beer I feel good, with spirits I get very aggressive so I don't touch it now at all. But I can row a bit with my bird no matter what I drink.'

He stares into the middle distance for a moment, a fond smile on his lips.

'Do you think you ever had a problem with alcohol?' I ask him, reading from the set interview questions.

'I wasn't an alcoholic or nothing. I'd do a bottle of vodka a day, like.'

'A bottle of vodka a day?' I say, though I'm not *really* surprised. This is standard-ish stuff. 'That's an expensive habit. Where did you get the money for that?'

'I used to either sell things I had robbed or I would just go into supermarkets or off licences and steal it.' He looks at me for a moment, suddenly worried he's said the wrong thing. 'But I don't do that no more. Like I said, I stopped the spirits. They used to make me aggressive and I couldn't remember things.'

'That's called a blackout,' I say. 'That's pretty serious for a young lad of your age.'

He nods. For a moment, I remember my own heavy drinking years; not good.

'The next section of the interview is related to drug use. Do you use, or have you ever used, drugs, Craig?'

'I used to smoke a lot of weed and take coke now and again, but I don't take drugs at all now.'

I must confess, I'm a little sceptical about this. As a pretty serious former dope head myself, I can usually see the signs and I'd bet my next week's wages he's still smoking. Mind you, you wouldn't need to be Nostradamus or even Mystic Meg to make this wager; most of our potential residents happily confess to previous drug use in the distant past, like a brutal South African policeman wiping the slate clean before the Truth and Reconciliation Commission. Then, within a week of their being accepted, you find yourself knocking on their doors in the mid-afternoon, asking why there's a smell of skunk drifting out into the hallway.

'How old were you when you started on the coke?' I say.

'About 14,' he says. 'This lad at school used to get it for me.'

'OK, moving on, then... the next section is related to mental health. Do you have any mental health problems we should be aware of, Craig?'

'Well, I had ADHD when I was a kid.'

I know some people doubt the existence of Attention Deficit Hyperactivity Disorder. Personally, I tend to think it's a legitimate condition – I just don't think it can possibly be as widespread as it seems. Every second or third person who comes through our door claims to have it, along with dyslexia and, not far behind, some problem somewhere on the autistic spectrum. Maybe they are all just very contagious.

'Were you self-medicating with the coke and the vodka?' I ask, innocently.

'No,' he says. 'They was nothing to do with it. Anyway, I don't really get the ADHD so much any more. I've, like, cured myself.'

I'm speculating here, but I suspect that Craig's diagnosis of ADHD probably excused all kinds of negative, disruptive and troublesome behaviour at school. But now his schooldays are behind him, I'm guessing that he has discovered – to his surprise – that it's no longer the get-out-of-jail-free card it once was. ADHD may get you off the hook for swearing at a teacher, or ripping up textbooks; it won't work the same magic with burglary, criminal damage and assaulting the police. So hey presto! Having served its purpose, it disappears. Call me a cynic.

'OK,' I say. 'Anything else?'

'I think I might be schizophrenic,' he says. 'The YOT are trying to get me an assessment.'

This is no laughing matter – if he's right.

'That's a very serious condition, Craig,' I say. 'Why do you think you have it?'

'I get voices in my head.'

'Do you actually hear a voice that to you appears that it is coming from outside of yourself – I mean, literally, someone is standing behind you speaking to you, but when you turn round there's no-one there – or is it more like intrusive thoughts you would rather not have?'

'More like the thoughts I don't want.'

'Can you give me an example?'

'Well, if you weren't in the room right now, the voices would be telling me to take that TV and video and run out the door, and I might. And you'd never see me again. I mean, I really wouldn't want to do it, because I'm not doing crime now, but the voices can get very powerful.'

'Craig,' I say. 'I have some good news for you. Obviously, you need to get this officially from the YOT people and maybe a doctor, but I'm pretty sure you're not a schizophrenic. You're just being tempted to steal.'

'No, I reckon it's schizophrenia,' he says, a little defensively. 'There's something wrong with me. I'm pushing for an assessment.'

I agree with Craig, in that there *is* something wrong with him: he is a thief. He'll probably grow out of it, as most burglars do, but before that can happen he needs to take responsibility for his own actions. Unfortunately, thanks to his upbringing and education, this concept is almost alien to him. I say 'almost' because he knows, deep down, that stealing TVs is wrong – that's why he's so keen to tell me those days are behind him, and to invent this cock-and-bull story of some external, medical cause outwith his own control to exonerate him for what are actually his own conscious choices. I don't say any of this to Craig; I don't think there'd be much point.

I proceed with the interview, coming to the bit where I explain the rules of the Project to him and gauge his response and then I move on to the most ridiculous part; I like to call it the 'catering to your every whim' section of the whole spiel.

'OK, Craig,' I say, 'I need to ask you a few little questions about you like to be dealt with. So first, how would you like us to approach you if you're angry?'

To be fair to him, Craig is as baffled by this nonsense as I am embarrassed.

'Er... I dunno,' he says. 'I s'pose... give me a bit of breathing space?'

I follow that one up with this: 'How would you like us to speak to you if you break a rule?'

As I say the words I can't quite believe they are coming out of my mouth; more to the point, I can't believe someone is being paid, handsomely, to sit in an office somewhere and dream up this lunatic rubbish. Do they not see that questions like this undermine the very rules – policies – we are supposed to be trying to implement in the first place? Or do they just not care, being as they are never the ones who have to ask the questions or do the enforcing?

Craig thinks about this one for a moment.

'I don't like people to be too in my face,' he says. 'I'd rather be spoken to nice, like, without anyone having a go at me or hassling me.'

Needless to say, although once I might have taken a different view, I don't subscribe to these stupid questions, even though I have to recite them. These days, if people break the rules, they hear it from me in as direct a manner as I can get away with in here.

'OK, looking at your situation, you're unemployed so you'd be entitled to full housing benefit,' I say. 'Assuming you're successful in your application and we allow you to move here, that is. How would you pay the additional £7.50 a week that your housing benefit won't cover? Because obviously your JSA is mostly going on paying court fines at the moment.'

Currently, you can receive £83 a week in Housing Benefit and further £50.95 JSA. Many of our residents are on other benefits, such as income support and disability living allowance which pay a lot more.*

'I have a fair few stereos and other things I can get my hands on and flog,' he says. 'Not stolen though, I swear.'

'That's not a very secure income,' I say, 'and to be honest it does sound a bit dodgy. What do you mean by "get your hands on"?'

---

* The current government has plans to overhaul the benefits system and to replace the existing extremely complex system of multiple benefits with one single payment. If it happens, one major advantage of this will be to make life easier for keyworkers like me.

'I've just got lots of stereos and things around my mum's. I can sell 'em.'

This still isn't a clear answer. Given that he has never had a job, and on the basis that few people get given more than one stereo, he has either found or stolen this property. I know where my suspicion lies, and I make a note of it.

And that's the interview pretty much over.

'OK, I think we're done, Craig,' I say, closing the file. 'Thanks for dropping by. We'll let you know within a week whether your application has been successful. That decision will be made after assessing the results of this interview and the information we receive from the background checks that we always do.'

I show him to the door, shake his hand and watch him wander off. Based on the discussion we've had, a little voice in *my* head says that he will not receive a place. He has trouble written all over him. If he was complying with his court orders, and if it appeared he was genuinely willing to give up crime, things might have been different. But it seems pretty obvious to me that his inner criminal is still alive and well. If we let him stay here, it would probably only be a matter of days before he was breaking into other residents' rooms and taking what few possessions they have.

At going-home time, my route to the train station takes me through the park two streets down from the Project. It's a sunny spring day, the cherry blossom is out and there's a young couple sitting on a bench. They're both dressed in chav chic, both are smoking and they're sharing a can of Kestrel Super. I pick up a lot of empty cans of Kestrel Super in and around the Project. It's 9 per cent alcohol. Sitting in a buggy to the side of the couple, ignored, is a toddler.

I can't help but think I am seeing both Craig's past and his future.

LIVING INDEPENDENTLY DIDN'T WORK OUT FOR HER

FIRST THING TODAY I have to sit through three hours of training gobbledegook entitled 'An Introduction to Supported Housing', delivered by a senior manager called Stephanie from the area office.

I have tried to get out of it by pointing out to Martin that I'm already well-acquainted with the supported housing sector, having worked in it for years with other housing associations. My interest might have been engaged if the course had been entitled 'A Conclusion to Supported Housing'.

Unfortunately, Martin pointed out that Oceania Housing Association needs to ensure that all of its own boxes are ticked with regards to me. There is no box marked, 'Winston Smith already knows pretty much everything he needs to know about the sector, and thus it would be a waste of several hundred pounds and half a day to explain it all to him all over again', so I receive the appropriate training, even if it is wholly redundant.

There's another staff member in the session, a girl called Sally who works at another Oceania project across town. When the trainer gets to the bit where she stresses the importance of our roles 'in helping young people to gain life and social skills, so that they can move on to independent living', and asks if we have any questions, Sally sticks her hand up.

'Many of the residents at our project keep their rooms in a terrible state,' she says. 'I mean, used condoms and sanitary towels on the floor, soiled underwear lying around, plates encrusted with food, flies everywhere. I don't think its fair for the maintenance workers to have to go in there when the rooms are that sort of state, or that I should have to go in to do the health and safety checks every two weeks. Now, I've tried to raise this with them and threatened some of the worst offenders with action, but it's actually been me who's got into trouble with management. How is that helping them to move to independent living, exactly?'

It's a picture I recognise: sometimes the bedrooms in the building make you heave. But Stephanie isn't on the same page as us.

'Well, Sally,' she says, patiently. 'I can see how this would be frustrating, but unless there is an obvious health and safety issue – such as an exposed electricity socket, or a faulty smoke alarm – then we have no right to tell our residents how to keep their rooms. We need to be very careful here as there is a danger of imposing our own value system on them. What *you* perceive to be tidy and clean is subjective, and their living standards, as long as they don't impinge on anyone else, are also valid.'

'I'm not sure I get you,' says Sally. 'Dirt is dirt, surely. It's not subjective, is it? A plate of rotting food or a floor covered in unwashed clothing is objectively unhygienic. You say that part of our job is to guide young people to develop life and social skills. Isn't cleanliness a pretty basic life and social skill? So, on the one hand we're encouraged to impose values and on the other we're told not to.'

'I can see some of your points, Sally,' says Stephanie with a smile that verges on the patronising. 'But at the same time, we have to respect that the rooms are their homes. You wouldn't want anyone coming in to your home and telling you how to live, would you?'

I speak up. 'Can I just say that I agree with Sally? Firstly, we don't live in supported housing which, by its very definition, makes a value judgement that the residents are not fully functional individuals, and that they need to be guided. Secondly, it's not like the rooms belong to the residents. They rent them from the taxpayer and, in most cases, the taxpayer also pays the rent. The rooms are supposed to be passed on in good condition to a new young person after each resident's two year stay. Currently, we spend about a week deep cleaning each room after it gets vacated.'

'Yes,' says Stephanie. 'I hear what you're saying but I think you need to consider the bigger picture.'

Sally looks at me and raises her eyebrows. Stephanie moves on to a lengthy and highly tedious explanation of the Quality Assessment Framework, in which I contemplate faking an epileptic fit in the hope of being led out of there on a stretcher before settling on daydreaming of having a job in which I can actually achieve something meaningful.

At the end of the session, Stephanie wraps up by thanking us for the job we do.

'I must admit I couldn't do what you lot do,' she says – she having long since moved on from having to work directly with any residents.

'And we really appreciate all of your efforts. I don't think I could last a day in your roles with all you have to deal with. Anyway, I hope you both have a great weekend.'

Sally and I thank her. She's another well-meaning soul who's just been indoctrinated by the waffle of Supporting People and the QAFs. As I watch her leave with her briefcase and her beatific smile, I can't help but wonder what it is about the role of the keyworker that she wouldn't be able to abide? Would it be the verbal abuse? The threat of a complaint being made by a resident should you speak in a forthright manner when required, or even the fear of a physical assault? Perhaps it is none of these things – after all, who is to say any of this behaviour is bad? If I've learned anything by now it's that this behaviour is perfectly normal, and that to expect anything else is to oppress people with one's subjective value system.

* * * * *

After lunch, an ambulance comes to collect Sharn after she takes another overdose, and we have a management meeting to discuss Laura Miller.

We kicked her out a while back for non-payment of rent, but now she has applied to return and we're actually thinking of letting her back.

The Project often does this, and it beats me why: it's nothing more than the triumph of a very distant hope over long years of bitter experience. And no-one has ever satisfactorily explained to me why people who have drunk-driven a coach and horses through our rules should get a second chance when so many (potentially) deserving applicants haven't even been given their first.

Laura's 21, and has a son about two years old. We don't allow children, so while she was living with us her boy was with either his father or Laura's mother, I can't recall which.

After she got pregnant, Laura had put her name down on the local social housing list – her status as a single mum giving her high priority on the waiting list.

Around that time, she stopped bothering with the rent at the Project, running up a debt of several hundred pounds, being simultaneously not arsed to claim housing benefit and keener on going out than paying her bills. This is not unusual, and need detain us no longer.

Eventually, we served her with an eviction notice but it didn't trouble her because the same week the council found her a nice little flat with a registered social landlord and she left us to be reunited with her child.

A life of domesticated bliss stretched ahead of her: she would exist in maternal contentment with her son, and they would live happily ever after.

Except that this was never going to happen in reality.

The shining allure of motherhood soon tarnished. As soon as summer's first swallow swooped by, Laura was off: who wants to be stuck indoors with a toddler, when you could be having a laugh with your mates in the West Country? Down she went to Cornwall to hang out by the sea and have some fun. (I don't know, but I'm pretty sure the kid got dumped on his dad or his granny again.)

Unfortunately, the allure of Cornwall soon began to wear off, too. As the autumn set in, it dawned on Laura that Cornwall isn't as exciting in November as it is in July. Back home she came.

However, there was a problem. The registered social landlord, having received no rent for three or four months and assuming she had abandoned the flat, had repossessed it and re-let it to someone else. Laura kicked up a fuss about this, and threatened to go to court, but when the landlord said he'd counter-sue her for the missing rent she backed down and surrendered any claim to the place to avoid the 'hassle'.

She had to move back in with her mother, and now, a few months on, we're discussing letting her come back to the Project.

This bothers me immensely. Firstly, we're supposed to offer housing only to kids who are homeless or at risk of so becoming, and she lives with her mum. Secondly, she only lost her housing because of her own short-termist and frankly stupid approach to life. She ought to stay with her mother, or sort something private out for herself.

We meet to discuss her application.

I make my view known as forcefully as I can, as an agency worker, but Margaret makes much of Laura's persistent and tearful phone calls to the Project, and, to my enormous unsurprise, my view does not carry the day.

Martin decides she is to be given another chance, and will be allowed to move back in as soon as she clears the rent she owes from her first stay. Margaret says Laura has promised to clear those arrears within a couple of weeks as she is now working as a carer in an old people's home.

We wrap up with a discussion about how to get the residents to attend a meeting at which we can discuss ways of giving them more input in the running of the Project.

'It's all about empowering them,' says Margaret.

I make the point that if they care about getting involved in running the Project they'll turn up, but Martin explains that so far three meetings have been held and only four clients showed up. This doesn't look good on the QAF side of things, so we need to 'be more creative and imaginative'. It turns out this means buying in a lorry load of pizza, fizzy drinks and KFC, and bribing them to attend with the promise of all this unhealthy shite. (This is the norm in most supported housing projects in my experience.) They can all sit around talking rubbish and filling their faces, and we can document their mindless suggestions and place it all in a file as evidence. Then another State bureaucrat will use this evidence as part of his or her evaluation of our wonderful service. Ah, well. It'll be happening on my day off, so it's not my problem.

The meeting winds up, my shift is over, so I leave them to it. In the office, Laura gets the good news about her imminent return from Margaret.

I catch some of their conversation; Margaret is basically aiding and abetting the young woman in the mentality that she needs the State to direct her life.

'The fact is,' she says, 'that living independently didn't work out for you.'

'I know,' says Laura. 'It's not like it's easy for me, or I haven't given it my best shot.'

'No, it just goes to show that you weren't ready for it yet. You just need that bit of support an extra while longer.'

She's 21 years old, for goodness' sake: women have managed to rent their own flats by this age before, I think. They've sailed solo round the world, climbed Mount Everest and won Military Crosses in action way before it. Margaret's heart is in the right place, but I think her head is located somewhere that sunshine rarely penetrates. 'Readiness' isn't bestowed upon you by some outside force; it occurs out of necessity. Laura was ready enough to sort out her old rent arrears when she realised it was a condition of being allowed back. She made the choice to get a job and pay off her debts.

I grab my bag, stick on my shades and walk out in to the early spring sunshine. I don't want to think any more about Laura, and whether she will or will not learn from her experiences. I don't want to think about the 'goals' she will set for herself – obvious things which were once a given, but which now have to be written down in a support plan ('Maintain your tenancy by ensuring the rent is paid') along with the steps she must take to ensure this to 'evidence' our 'support' ('Apply for your benefits to ensure rent is paid' or 'Pay your rent from your wages'). I don't want to think about the section related to 'Employment and Education', which will have goals such as 'Maintain your job' and steps such as 'Go to work every day, be punctual'. I don't want to think about the lunacy of the State employing people on twenty grand a year to record on mountains of paper that they are trying to cajole a grown woman into doing things that a 12-year-old could grasp.

I believe that if you treat people like idiots then, in many cases, that is exactly how they will behave, and I don't want to think about that, or the scale of the idiocy, or the numbers of idiots, or the consequences for the future of this country.

I stick in my headphones, turn on my MP3 player, and The Fantastic Four's *Don't Tell Me I'm Crazy* sends me down the road with a spring in my step.

*****

The next day is mind-numbing, spent reviewing support plans and reading official bumf from Head Office.

I'm ready to make my exit in a quarter of an hour or so when Martin the Manager pops out of his office. The worried look on his face is now accompanied by a slight nervous tic.

'Winston,' he says, running his hand through his lank, grey-brown hair and handing me a fistful of files. 'Can you do me a favour? I've got a stack of service-users all late with their rent. I need them chased up?'

'Sure.' I take the file, nod and sit back down at my desk.

People being late with their rent is not an unusual scenario: a large proportion of the residents in all the supported housing projects I've ever worked in are *always* late with their rent. This might surprise you, given that they don't actually *pay* any rent – at least, not personally. It's paid for via housing benefit, which is free money: the only flaw in the system is that you do actually have to fill in a form to get it, and some of our residents are either too uneducated or too lazy (or both) to do this. As a result of this, part of a keyworker's job involves being hassled by the management to fill the forms out for the residents. I resent this a little, for several reasons. Not least among these is that I have to pay the mortgage on my own little flat by working here and taking all the shit that gets thrown at me by people who can't even be arsed to claim their own housing benefit. But the main thing that bugs me is the sheer stupidity of it all. As I said to the oblivious Margaret the other day, our whole *raison d'être* – the purpose of me, her, Martin and the whole bloody Project itself – is to move these kids to independence. Filling in their housing benefit forms for them is not moving them to independence. As such, it's not fair on them; after two years here they'll have to leave, and we're not preparing them for what lies ahead.

I sit down and open the file. It's a series of sheets of paper detailing individuals, their arrears and action taken to date.

The first name on the list is Ciaran Meacher's.

'Bloody Ciaran,' I say, under my breath, shaking my head. Fair play to him, at least he has a job. In fact, he has two: he works full-time as a labourer and part-time in a bar. But when he came to live with us he was unemployed and he failed properly to submit his housing benefit forms. As a result, the payments never came through and he currently owes us £900. According to the notes, he's had a few requests, escalating to polite warnings, but nothing too serious.

I look at my watch: 5.05pm. There's a train at 6pm, and it takes 20 minutes to walk to the station. If I'm quick about it, I can have a word with him now. I hurry up to his room on the third floor and knock on his door. He opens it, a beer in one hand.

'Yes?' he says.

'Hi Ciaran,' I say. 'Can I just have a word with you about your rent situation?'

'Oh, fucking hell,' he says. 'I've told that tool Brendan, I don't owe any fucking rent. It's the Housing Benefit people, they never paid it when I was on the dole, you need to get it off them.'

'Yeah, but it's not like that,' I say. 'The Housing Benefit people don't live here, you do. The fact is, you didn't fill the forms out right, so they didn't pay you, so you didn't pay us, so you owe us. And we need you to pay what you owe. It's not like you're short of cash – you're probably earning twice what I earn.'

He stares at me, his body tense, and then he slumps a little. 'Alright,' he says. 'But I can't pay it all at once.'

'No problem,' I say. 'How about if you pay your existing rent and 20 quid a week on top until the arrears are cleared?'

'Yeah,' he says, looking at his watch. 'OK. Look, I'm going out in a bit so…'

'Right,' I say. 'I'll just write this down in your file…' I scribble down the details of the agreement we've just reached. 'Now, if you sign there under my signature that'll be fine.'

He grabs the file, quickly signs it and then shuts the door in my face.

I have a feeling he's only telling me what I want to hear, but only time will tell.

* * * * *

Next morning, I crack on with the rest of my list of rent-avoiders. Kenny Mulligan, of Missing Key fame, is second on my list of people to talk to. He owes more than £800.

Unlike Ciaran, Kenny only has a part-time job in a pizza take-away, and his low income means he is still eligible for Housing Benefit. However, it is obviously too much to expect an able-bodied 19-year-old man to fill in the forms to claim his free money and then walk the 300 metres to the council office to drop them in, so his previous keyworker allowed him to get away with not really paying us.

I'm made of slightly more pedantic stuff, though, so I track him down to the common room where he is engrossed in *Loose Women* and spend an hour nagging him about it. Eventually, reluctantly and amazingly, he agrees to let me help him fill in the required documentation and then toddles off out of the building to hand it in. This means that a large slice of his rent arrears should be cleared, which is a start.

Another result – maybe.

I work slowly through the file; lots of people owe us something, ranging for a week or two's money to well over a thousand quid. Some of them will never pay and we'll end up – eventually – evicting them.

After lunch, Martin pops his head round his door.

'Alright Winston?' he says. 'Listen, can you sort something out for me…' He passes a yellow Post-it note to me. On it is written the word 'Stella'.

'Er…' I say.

'Stella collared me and wanted to complain about something,' says Martin. 'Her fridge, I think?'

'Sure,' I say. 'I'll deal with it.'

We get a lot of complaints – some verbal, like this one, and others submitted via the complaints box on one of the tables in the lobby. Occasionally, sensible issues are raised – such as people objecting to fellow residents playing music at 4am – but often it's just trivia or abuse.

I check Stella's room number and head up there to see if she's in. As I walk, I visualise her: 20 years old, medium height, slightly overweight. She has a tightly scrunched face, similar to that of a bulldog. I don't know her very well, as yet, but she seems to be a thoroughly unpleasant character: aggressive, foul-mouthed and demanding. I'm not much looking forward to this meeting.

I knock on her door, and it swings open a moment or two later.

'What?' she says, scowling.

'Hi Stella,' I say. 'You made a complaint?'

'Oh yeah, I did,' she says.

'OK, so can you tell me what it is that you want to complain about, and whether you've filled in a complaint form?'

There's a bloody form for everything around here; I often wonder how many perfectly self-sufficient tribes are being driven off their land by the deforestation caused by our mania for documenting the 'support' we provide.

'Yes, I have,' says Stella, with scarcely a moment's thought for the travails of the Ayoreo-Totobiegosode peoples of Brazil. 'I gave it to fucking Martin.'

'Well, he hasn't given it to me,' I say.

'Well, I fucking gave it to him.'

'Well, he…' I stop.

This will get us nowhere.

'So what's the problem, then?' I say.

'My fucking carpet is ruined. Come and have a look.' I walk in, and she gestures at a large wet patch on the floor. 'What are you going to do about that?' she says.

'What happened?' I ask, my eye flitting over the empty WKD bottles and spliff stubs which also litter the place.

'It's the fucking bastard Project's fault, innit,' she says. 'We had them Health and Safety room checks last week, yeah, and they told me I needed to defrost the freezer bit of me fridge, but no one told me that I had to put something by it because of all that water. So all that shit came out of it, and now I want a new carpet. It's not my fault and I fucking pay all my own rent so I should get it.'

I scratch my chin, pondering. 'Well,' I say, 'it's true that you work and pay your rent – so well done for that – but to be honest that doesn't mean this isn't your own fault. I mean, everyone knows that ice turns to water if it reaches even one degree above freezing.'

She looks at me blankly.

'I mean, you *do* know that ice is just frozen water, and that when it's heated it returns to its liquid state?'

Now she's giving me a look that I'm finding hard to read. It either conveys, 'Don't fucking patronise me' or, 'I haven't a clue what you are talking about.'

Surely it can't be the latter? She's working as a trainee chef (the fourth job she's had in the last six months); she surely must understand the basics of refrigeration?

'Of course I know about ice,' she says. 'I just forgot to put something there and I should have been reminded.'

'You'll be asking us to remind you to breathe next,' I say. Her eyes flash angrily, so I hastily add, 'Come on, I'm just kidding. But look, you'll just have to dry this up with some towels and stuff. Open the window, that'll help. You're not getting a new carpet, and that's that.

In life, shit happens and you have to cope with it. There isn't always going to be a fairy keyworker to swoop down and sort things out. The whole point of you being here is you're supposed to be responsible for yourself. We're not here to do everything for you.'

She splutters something, but I don't want to get involved in a debate over this so I'm already on the way out of the room. I leave her standing there, looking decidedly unhappy, and as I head back to the office, I reflect on the truth: actually, we *are* there to do everything for them. We're there to check their fridges for 'health and safety', there to advise them to defrost the freezer, there to explain to them that when ice melts it turns to water, and there to remind them that water is wet.

That is the very point of my job, even though our mission statement claims we exist to 'empower' people.

STATE ASSISTANCE IN ABANDONING YOUR CHILDREN

I'M ON MY own this morning – everyone else is off sick.

I've got a pile of stuff to get through, including a full round of the building to check how many broken windows we have this week.

First, though, I have to deal with a couple of potential new residents, both 16-year-old girls who currently live at home with their families.

They're interesting opposites, actually.

Cerys Stenson is happy to stay with her mum, but her mum is desperate to offload her to us.

Zoe Parker wants to come and live at the Project, but her mum wants her to stay at home.

In neither case would you say that they are either 'homeless' or 'at risk of becoming homeless' – the sort of cases we are supposed to deal with, according to the 'service definitions' I mentioned earlier. But as I've said, words are flexible things around here.

Because they have homes already, in order to stand any chance of getting places here they'll each need what's called a 'Letter of Estrangement'. This is an official document signed by the parent which has to state, first, that the familial relationship has broken down and that they no longer want their son or daughter in the house; and, second, that the parent is not willing or able to support them financially.

The letter is required by the benefits office (we just get a copy): without it, a youngster between the ages of 16 and 17 cannot easily receive benefits, and without benefits they cannot pay for their room.

Once again, you'd surely have to admit that the thinking behind this system is sound enough – there *are* familial relationships where the above is all true, where things *have* broken down irretrievably and mum and dad either don't have or won't spend the cash on a new place for the kid(s) to live. It's not the kids' fault, and we can't let them kip on park benches – in any civilised society, we surely have to help them out.

The problem is that the mere existence of the system of Letters of Estrangement allows – and encourages – some families to split up as soon as things turn slightly fractious. It's also open to abuse – you can drive a coach and horses of fraud through it.

The letters tend (in my experience) to be accepted at face value by the benefits office; as far as I can tell, there is rarely any thorough follow-up or interview with any of the parties to ascertain that the 'estrangement' is genuine and ongoing. Instead, the benefits people get the letter, the young person gets the benefits and then we simply provide them with a free flat.

In many cases, the supposedly estranged parents then help their offspring move in, visit them with goodie bags on a regular basis, take them out for Sunday lunches and then help them move back out and into the familial home within a few months, usually after they are finally asked to leave for anti-social behaviour or for drug abuse and so on.

In the most extreme example of this fraudulent non-estranged estrangement I have yet come across, a resident called Emily at a previous project went on a cruise around the Mediterranean with her family, and spent as much time back at home as she did with us. Basically, her parents were offloading their kid to our care to cut their own bills. The main problem with this, besides the obvious corruption, is that kids who are *really* estranged from parents who are drug addicts, alcoholics or violent brutes and bullies, or kids coming out of care, and who really do need supported housing, end up living in bedsits while people like Emily – often from quite well-to-do families who are smart enough to play the system – suck up the limited number of spaces. (While I'm on the subject, as a 16-year-old in supported housing, Emily was deemed to be both 'socially excluded' and 'vulnerable to homelessness'. That was a laugh: she had more expensive laptops, TVs and game consoles in her room that your average Currys. She was actually a nice girl, but you get the point.)

Anyway, the two cases in hand are about to demonstrate vividly that potential for fraud.

Cerys and her mum are coming in at 11am, so I decide to read her file first. I stare at it on the desk in front of me, willing myself to open it. I've had a trying week, actually, and I'm struggling a bit. I remember that there's a pair of scissors in the top drawer and I wonder, would I be better off stabbing myself in the eyes with them?

I sigh, and focus on the paperwork.

The application looks very much as though it has been filled in by some kind of social worker on her behalf.

It's full of surprises – not.

Reason for applying? Her mum doesn't want her at home any longer, as they don't get along.

For goodness' sake, I say, under my breath. I didn't get along with my mum and dad when I was a teenager. Who does? How is it that this has come to be a matter for government intervention?

Half an hour later, I get up, and drag feet that feel clad in lead boots out to the foyer. Cerys is sitting there happily gossiping with the mum she allegedly hates. There's also a social worker I've met a few times before and a guy from the council who calls himself something like 'Family Involvement Officer'. I ponder the irony of this job title for a moment: then again, I suppose *State Assistance in Abandoning Your Children Officer* would be a bit of a mouthful.

'Hello, Cerys,' I say. 'And you must be Mrs Stenson?'

'Ms,' says her mother. 'But yeah.'

'OK,' I say. 'If you follow me we can get started.'

This is a little bit unusual – we normally only interview the potential resident. However, with Ms Stenson present it allows me to get both sides of the story. And, boy, is she keen to give me her side. Cerys sits there looking a bit glum while mum starts gabbing.

'What it is, right, is me and Cerys don't get on no more,' she says. 'It's like, ever since me and her dad split up, our relationship has totally broke down.'

'Can I ask how this manifests itself?' I say.

'You what?'

'This breakdown,' I say. 'What do you mean? How have things broken down?'

'Well, she just won't listen to what I say, nor what her new dad says. And it's causing tension in the house. Plus, she stays around at her boyfriend's on school nights, even though I tell her she can only do that at the weekends. I'm worried that her sisters are going to start copying her. They're only 12 and 13. So I think it'd be best if Cerys came here.'

I'm not sure I agree – I think Ms Stenson ought to knuckle down, do her duty as a mother and work her way through this mother-daughter relationship conflict thing like 99% of the population do. She's worried about the example elder daughter is setting younger, but it doesn't seem to have occurred to her to consider the example she herself is setting them all.

God, I'd love to tell her all this, but I think the social worker and her mate from the council might see it as a bit 'judgmental'; that's a big no-no in the State dependency sector, and I'd probably be out on my ear.

I turn to Cerys.

'And how about you, Cerys?' I say. 'Are you happy about the possibility of coming to live here?'

'Well,' she says, lifting her eyes for the first time and looking sideways at her mum. 'To be honest, it's not like I really *want* to leave home. I'd rather stay there. I just want my mum to stop nagging me.'

Yep, sounds like a normal teenager to me. Seems a nice kid, too.

'The thing is, Cerys, if you come here you'll have a keyworker like me on your case, and you'll be expected to go to school and complete your GCSEs and do all that stuff just like you are at home, so all you'd be doing is swapping your mum's nagging, as you see it, for ours. It would be down to you to make sure that you got up and went in to school every day. We'll keep an eye on you, but we can't force you. And if you don't... well, your licence to live here could be affected if you drop out of school.'

Could be, note. This is one of the conditions in the 'binding contract' outlined in the service definition above. In the month or so since I arrived at the Project, I've told a lot of prospective residents that if they leave their jobs or quit their courses in favour of sitting around doing nothing they 'could be' asked to leave. But this is an empty threat, and it never, ever happens. We have enough trouble trying to get rid of residents for anti-social behaviour and staff abuse (as you will see), never mind for just loafing about.

'No, I want to go to school,' she says. 'I like it there... I like learning. I'm just a bit lazy at times, and that's why I bunk off.'

I was the same myself. I nod.

'She's been a lot better lately with getting to school,' says her mum.

'So what you're saying is, the stuff you've been doing at home is paying off?' I say. 'You're starting to see some results?'

Mum immediately starts shaking her head. 'No, that's wasn't what I meant,' she says. 'In fact, come to think of it, she's not really getting any better actually.'

I look at her, and can't help grinning slightly. 'Look Ms Stenson, it seems to me that things aren't so bad. I mean, sure, you're having a few arguments, but isn't that pretty normal?'

I'd like to add, *What the hell are you trying to send her here for? She'll be living in the same building as convicted young offenders, drug users, girls who've had abortions at 14 and 15, people with no ambition or aspiration to do anything else with their lives but get wasted from morning to night.* But I think that even that would fall on deaf ears. Ms Stenson's head is now shaking fit to burst.

'No,' she says, vehemently. 'She needs to come here. I can't cope no more. I've got a houseful of kids and I need some space.'

I try one last time to outline, as diplomatically as I can, the possible dangers of such a course of action.

'Ms Stenson, Cerys,' I say. 'I think it's very important that you both realise that if Cerys comes to live here she'll have a lot more freedom than she would have at home. We do our best, but there are more than 50 residents here. And I'll be honest, I'm concerned that Cerys would find it hard to handle that freedom. We have some residents who are not that active [this is the best euphemism I can come up with for unemployed, and frankly currently unemployable, skunk-smokers] and I am just a bit concerned that Cerys may be very impressionable around them. We're not surrogate parents. We simply provide support in the area of accessing benefits and engaging with the young person to set goals and assist them in achieving them.'

'Yeah,' says Ms Stenson. 'I know all that. Don't worry, love, she'll be fine with the goals and that.'

'It might be useful if I just said something at this point,' says the social worker, clearing her throat. 'In my professional opinion, Cerys's needs would best be served by finding her a placement at the Project. I really think she and mum need some space so they can work out their issues together. If she stays at home, I'm concerned that the conflict between them will only escalate.'

The council's Family Involvement Officer gives a reedy little cough, and pushes his John Lennon specs up to the bridge of his nose. Everyone looks at him. 'I would concur,' he says.

That's odd, that, because I think it's the purest bollocks, and, from the look of Cerys, she agrees with me. Her slow, dubious shake of the head is in sharp contrast to her mum, who is nodding so fast she looks like Churchill (the advert dog, not the politician) on speed.

'OK,' I say. 'I'll note down your views too. As you know, it's not my decision. What happens now is I discuss it with the staff team here and between us we decide whether to offer Cerys a place.'

Personally, I'll be voting against; I think Cerys should stay at home, not be palmed off at great expense to a place which was set up to cater for desperate cases. But I don't think I'll be in the majority, especially now the social worker has spoken.

With a heavy heart, I run through the long list of further documentation I will need for the application, including the Letter of Estrangement required for her to access benefits.

'Yep, yep, all of that's not a problem, Winston,' says Ms Stenson, grinning broadly. 'I'll have all that for you by tomorrow, no problem. When will I know if she gets a place? Will I have to wait long to find out?'

I half wonder why she didn't bring all her daughter's belongings to the interview in a black bag, and just dump her here. Maybe this is written on my face: suddenly, without me speaking, she becomes a little defensive. 'I do care about my daughter, you know,' she says. 'I want what's best for her, but I have to think about the impression she is making on the other kids I have.'

'You'll find out sometime during the next few days,' I say.

* * * * *

Next on my agenda is the other 16-year-old applicant, Zoe Parker. This time, however, *she* is the driving force behind the whole thing. She has friends at the Project and wants to move here, while her mum is fighting it and wants her to stay at home: according to the notes on the file, she is refusing to provide a Letter of Estrangement.

Again, I remember the stirring words of the Emmanuel Goldstein service definition: 'Our project exists to help disadvantaged young people aged between 16 and 25 who are homeless, or at risk of becoming homeless.'

This seems like an open and shut case to me: Zoe is *not* homeless or at any risk of homelessness by any honest definition of the words; *ergo* we should not take her in. Sadly, though, I can't make this decision by myself; our formal processes must be observed.

I pick up the phone to call Mrs Parker. Zoe answers, I introduce myself and ask her to stick her mum on. Then I ask mum to give me the low-down on family affairs.

'Things are fine really,' she says. 'And I don't want to write this estrangement letter. For one thing, we're not estranged – not really. It's just stroppy teenage stuff. But mostly I'm worried that Zoe would just end up going completely off the rails. She's in her first year of A levels and she's already in trouble at Lev Bronstein [the nearby college], thanks to her behaviour. She just rebels against any rules I try to impose in the house. If I don't watch her like a hawk, she goes out all night drinking and…' She lowers her voice. *'And taking drugs, I think.'* She raises it again. 'And if she comes to live at your project with all her mates I just think that's only going to get worse.'

'We-e-elll,' I say, noncommittally. I have every sympathy with Mrs Parker – that is exactly what is likely to happen if her daughter comes here. All the while I can hear Zoe talking loudly at her in the background.

'I mean, don't get me wrong, it is difficult living with her at the moment,' says Mrs Parker, 'but I don't think it would be right for me to just hand her over to social services. She's my daughter… I know best how to deal with her.'

Zoe's disembodied voice echoes down the line: *'Why don't you just let me live my life? You're just a fucking bitch is what you are! Just sign the fucking letter! God, I hate you!'*

'Well, I'm not signing the letter, and that's that,' says Mrs Parker, to howls of outrage.

We conclude our conversation shortly afterwards. It's pretty clear to me that Mrs Parker is doing the responsible thing: it's going to be tough, but she isn't happy to shirk her duty as Zoe's mother.

I close down the application; without the estrangement letter there are no benefits, and without benefits there's no free room.

* * * * *

I'm just about to shut up shop for the night when the phone goes. There's no-one else around so I pick it up, hoping it's something simple. If I miss my train, I've an hour's wait.

'The Emmanuel Goldstein Project,' I say. 'Winston speaking, how may I…'

'I need the number of my doctor's surgery.'

'Sorry, who are you?'

'Kyle.'

'Kyle?'

'Yeah.'

'Surname? We have a few Kyles?'

'Kyle Williams. I need my doctor's number. Can you get it for me.'

Not even the hint of a 'please' in this grunted demand.

'Can you hold the line, please?'

I cup my hand over the mouthpiece and turn to Olive the part-time receptionist.

'Olive, some guy called Kyle Williams asking if we know his GP's phone number? I don't know of any resident of that name… Mean anything to you?'

'Yes,' says Olive. 'He used to live here but he left ages ago. Why's he ringing us about his GP?'

Why indeed: especially after spending a couple of years at the Project where he was supposedly helped to develop 'independent living skills'.

I go back to the phone. 'Hi Kyle,' I say. 'You're no longer a resident here, so I don't have your file to hand. It's stored in another part of the building. Surely you can look your GP up in the phone book?'

'I don't even know the bastard's name,' comes the disembodied reply. I can hear what sounds like speed ragga playing loudly in the background. 'Get Margaret. She was my support worker. She'll know the number.'

I love the entitlement in his voice: I can tell he doesn't think there is anything remotely strange about ringing us like this.

'Look, Kyle,' I say. 'Margaret's not here. But even if she was she'd be busy, yeah? You don't live here any more, so you need to deal with this stuff yourself. If you can't remember the name, just walk down to the surgery. The town isn't that big.'

'I don't know the way,' he says. 'Just fucking get Margaret, will you?'

'Hey, listen, Kyle,' I say, 'I'm glad you called, it's always great to hear from former residents like yourself. You take care, now.'

With that, I put the phone down.

Margaret's a bit of a soft touch – she acts like a personal secretary to the people she deals with, and keeps all the important information in a file in the office. This stops them having to remember anything for themselves. Me, I'm a hard bastard: I tell all the people I keywork to get a little address book and keep essential numbers, emails and addresses in it. Not that it makes much difference: most of them ignore the advice completely. As Kenny said to me once, 'Why would I write it down in a notebook when I can just get you to get it from my file?'

I gather up my things, say a quick 'goodnight' to Olive and leg it before Kyle rings back.

As I leave, I pass two 16-year-old girl residents – Siena and Sky – gossiping about a third.

'Millie says she ain't got a clue whether the baby is Jason's or Mike's, and it's causing all kinds of hassle,' says one. 'I told her to ring up ITV and they can get it Jeremy Kyled.'

This is slang for having the infant DNA-tested.

I stick in my earphones, click on The Impressions' *This Is My Country*, and get the hell out of there.

THE EVER-EFFICIENT AND RESULTS-DRIVEN YOUTH OFFENDING TEAM

IN THE MORNING, I'm supposed to be meeting Perry – a habitual young offender who swaggers about the place in a fake Burberry cap, Reebok hoodie and enormous, white, shoplifted Nike trainers. He looks like the stereotypical yob of the type Dave Cameroon was telling us all to hug a few years back. Obviously, he's exactly the sort of bloke that Dave himself would love to live next door to, so he could come round for canapés and G&Ts of a weekend.

He's currently on a Community Rehabilitation Order for stealing a car and driving it whilst drunk. He has to meet the local Youth Offending Team* several times a week – though I or one of my colleagues usually has to remind him to attend, as he often forgets to go.

The funny thing is, if you can get beyond his ridiculous appearance, criminal behaviour and general incompetence, Perry is actually not a bad lad – as long as he hasn't been boozing. When he's drunk, he's aggressive and spiteful, but when sober he's friendly, polite and even – at times – considerate. As long as you bear in mind that he'd steal the eye out of your head, and you steer clear of him when he has a can of Stella to hand, he's bearable.

While I'm waiting for him to show up, I take out his support plan to see what's going on in his life. He came to the Project three or four months ago, and isn't local; I notice that on his first day here he was given a tour of the town – or, at least, shown the Jobcentre and the Housing Benefit office at the local council – by his keyworker.

As Perry is 17, he has to go through Connexions in order to receive his jobseeker's allowance. This is a government-funded youth agency which evolved out of the Careers Service, and which exists to offer advice and practical support for young people aged between 13 and 19. It employs teams of 'Personal Advisers' all over the country, with advice lines open 8am to 2am, 7 days a week. Kids can call in confidence, free of charge to speak to these 'PAs', who are 'specially trained to listen to you… without judging. Whatever your needs.'

---

* Since changed to 'Youth Offending Service', for some reason.

The very existence of Connexions strikes me as a tragedy, because it means that there are young teenagers out there who would rather pick up the phone to a stranger than talk their problems through with their mum or dad. It's an expensive tragedy, too: its annual budget runs into hundreds of millions.

Anyway, Connexions have to sign a document for Perry every week 'evidencing' that he is 'engaging with' them to seek employment. If he fails to do this he can have his benefit suspended. Since Perry has no intention of ever working (he quite happily admits as much), this is really nothing but a farce, though the file reveals that he actually did have his JSA claim shut down on one occasion after he failed to turn up to appointments at Connexions. There's a note to say that Perry's Connexions support worker telephoned Brendan (who used to be his keyworker at the Project before he was passed on to me) to ask him to remind Perry to get in touch urgently so that they can help him reapply for his JSA.

Perhaps it's just me, but I find it a bit baffling that the taxpayer is funding two jobs to help the same person apply for the free money he's too lazy to sort out for himself, and then to chase around after him to make sure he keeps his benefits. I suppose you could call it redistribution of wealth in action.

Brendan comes into the office to make a cup of tea, and noses over at the papers I'm reading.

'Perry?' he says. 'He's a disaster area, that kid.'

'I'm just reading about you and Connexions and his JSA,' I say. 'I don't know why we can't just let people take a hundred per cent responsibility for their own benefits. If they really need the money to survive, they'll be sure to sign on.'

'I couldn't agree more,' says Brendan, taking a slurp of tea. 'It's not like he's old, or mentally or physically incapacitated, or even completely illiterate. He's just bone idle.'

I flick through a few more pages, reacquainting myself with his criminal past – shoplifting, assault, threatening behaviour, possession of cannabis, various vandalisms and breaches of the peace. He's half an hour late by now, and it occurs to me that I haven't seen him about the place for a while.

'When was the last time you saw him knocking around, Brendan?' I say.

'Must be over a week ago,' he says. 'Hey, I hope he's not getting into trouble again.'

Surely not. The ever-efficient and results-driven Youth Offending Team have been working closely with the young man. They must have been successful in rehabilitating him.

After an hour of waiting, I make a note in his file to say he's a no-show, and head off to the park for a lunchtime sarnie.

*****

After lunch, the staff are due to meet up to discuss Cerys Stenson and Zoe Parker, and I'm just reading over my notes of the encounter with Cerys and her mum when the phone goes. I answer it in the approved manner.

'Hello, The Emmanuel Goldstein Project, Winston speaking, how may I help you?'

'Hi Winston,' says a cheery voice. 'This is Charlotte, from Connexions?'

'Hi, Charlotte,' I say. 'How can I help you?'

'It's about Zoe Parker?' she says. 'She applied for a place at your project through us, and I was just curious about her application because she informs us that you guys have closed it down?'

'Yep, we have,' I said. 'The thing is, she's unable to provide an estrangement letter so she's not financially viable.'

'Yes,' says Charlotte, slightly testily. 'I'm aware that the mother has said she won't provide the letter. But you really should have spoken to us about it first before you closed down the application. We can actually write an estrangement letter on behalf of the young person if the parent won't do it. The mother is very controlling, you know, and we feel Zoe is best off out of the family home.'

This is a new – and pretty shocking – one on me.

'I've just got another call coming through,' I lie. 'It's something urgent. Can I call you back, Charlotte?

'Sure.'

I put the phone down. I want to check this business about estrangement letters written by people other than parents, so I ring up the Jobcentre and speak to Janey in the benefits section. Astonishingly, she confirms Charlotte's story.

'That's right,' she says. 'If a young person can't get an estrangement letter from their parent or parents, we will accept a letter from a keyworker or Connexions adviser stating that the young person is estranged from the parent or parents.'

In other words, Mrs Parker's Trojan efforts at effective parenting are being knowingly undermined by the State.

I ring Charlotte back at Connexions.

'The thing about Zoe,' I say, 'is she strikes me as a fairly typical, rebellious teenager who wants to find somewhere to live where she can do what she wants.'

'Somewhere' being a room in our dysfunctional project, where we can watch as she drops out of college and descends into a half-life which involves her sitting around all day eating junk food, smoking dope and drinking blue WKD.

'I'm not sure she'd be best off here. I think she'd be best off at home. Have you spoken to her mum?'

'I haven't talked to her, no,' snaps Charlotte.

'You haven't?' I say, surprised. 'Surely you don't just take the word of a 16-year-old kid on something like this?'

'Her age is nothing to do with it,' says Charlotte. 'She should be listened to and taken seriously.'

'Sure,' I say. 'If there are serious allegations, of abuse or neglect, say. Then you'd want to listen and investigate thoroughly. I'm all for that. But there are no such allegations here, are there? You're just saying that the mum is a bit… well, what did you say she was?'

'Controlling.'

'That's it, controlling. Isn't that just part of being a parent? Isn't she supposed to control her to an extent, until she's an adult? I've spoken to her and she sounded like a pretty normal person to me.'

'Well, I'd like you to reopen the application,' says Charlotte. 'I've written an estrangement letter for her, and she's going to be handing that in to ensure her benefits are paid.'

I'm astonished by all of this, even though I shouldn't be. A mother who is doing her best to keep her daughter on the straight and narrow is being actively sabotaged by a cabal of State bureaucrats who want the girl to move out of the family home and start claiming benefits – a process which any number of academic studies show will dramatically reduce her life chances (and cost the rest of us thousands of pounds into the bargain). To make matters worse, they aren't even bothering to discuss it with the mother, or to make any attempt to ascertain the truth of her daughter's complaints. It's literally crazy. I'm going to dig my heels in.

'The thing is, Charlotte, we can't take her on at the moment even *with* an estrangement letter from yourselves,' I say. 'We've done some background checks on Zoe at Lev Bronstein College and she is currently displaying problematic behaviour there, so we'll need to give that a bit of time to settle down before we could even consider her applying again. If you disagree with this decision then you can always appeal it to my manager.'

I haven't really discussed this with Martin yet, so I'm hoping she doesn't take up my suggestion. Luckily, she doesn't.

'Thanks for all your help and support,' she says, with more than a hint of sarcasm in her voice. Then she puts the phone down.

I replace my receiver and slump back in my chair. On the CCTV monitor at the end of the room, I can see Kenny and one of his mates laughing and joking with each other as they walk down a corridor. They are sharing a can of beer or cider and smoking something, even though our communal areas are non-smoking. I bet they'd absolutely love to welcome a new schoolgirl to the Project; I'll do my damndest to make sure they don't get the chance.

*****

At the meeting, there's me, Brendan, Margaret, Martin and Steve, the other full-time keyworker.

First we discuss Cerys.

I outline the details of my meeting with mum, daughter and the social worker and Family Involvement Officer; I explain how Cerys really wants to remain in the family home, and how her mum is the driving force behind the whole scheme.

'Thing is, Winston,' says Martin, flicking through the pages of my report. 'What we have here is two social care professionals who both think we ought to offer the girl a place. That's hard to argue against.'

I have absolutely no idea what would motivate the two of them to make the recommendation they did: it could be something to do with performance bonuses for moving kids around, it could be down to that weird Marxist ideology which sees the family as a patriarchal and bourgeois construct designed as a tool of oppression, or it could just be that they're fucking idiots.

'Yeah,' I say. 'But the thing is, I think they're wrong.'

'No point having professionals if we don't listen to them,' says Margaret.

'Plus the mum is prepared to sign the estrangement letter,' says Steve. 'That suggests to me that there's an underlying problem you maybe didn't pick up on.'

The fact that Steve has said this suggests to *me* he has been sleepwalking through his time in supported housing with his eyes closed. But I sigh and hold my hands up. 'I'm just saying, personally, I wouldn't accept her,' I say. 'But I know it's not down to me so…'

'All except Winston agreed then?' says Martin. There are a few nods around the table, and he says, 'OK, with all due respect to you, Winston, and taking your concerns on board, I think we'll give Cerys a place.'

He scribbles something on the file and closes it. As he does so, I remember the slightly bewildered look on the young girl's face as she told me she'd rather stay at home, and feel worthless.

'Now, the second applicant,' says Mike, opening a new folder. 'Zoe Parker. You've been handling this one too, Winston?'

Again, I make a brief presentation, outlining the facts, the various phone calls and finishing with my own views on the matter. This time, my position is taken more seriously, though it's not because we're keeping Zoe's interests at the forefront of our minds.

'The thing about this one,' says Martin, 'is a little way down the road I can see a lot of trouble. Zoe's already misbehaving at home, so she's hardly likely to improve here' – knowing glances are exchanged around the table – 'and I can see mum kicking up a fuss if her daughter fell pregnant or dropped out of college or something. Do we need that kind of hassle?'

There are murmurs of agreement from my colleagues.

'No, I think we'll follow your recommendation on this one, Winston,' says Martin, making further notes in this file.

As soon as I'm out of the meeting, I call Zoe's mum.

'Hello, Mrs Parker,' I say. 'It's Winston Smith here, from the Emmanuel Goldstein Project. Just to let you know that we've discussed your daughter's application for a place here and we've decided not to progress it.'

'Does that mean she won't be going?' she says. 'Only she says that some organisation called Connexions is going to sort it out for her.'

'Don't worry about that,' I say. 'Connexions were keen for her to get the placement but we've decided against.'

We chat for a moment or two, the relief palpable in her voice. Then I put the phone down, make myself a cup of tea and start on some paperwork.

* * * * *

I've just opened the first file when Olive the part-time receptionist sticks her head in the office and hands me a fax which clears up Perry's absence from earlier on. It's from someone at the Youth Offending Team, and it informs me that Perry is in hospital with a fractured ankle, a broken nose, ten stitches to his forehead and concussion.

He sustained these injuries when he collided with a wall while driving drunk in a stolen vehicle, again: whatever the YOT are doing with Perry, they're clearly failing in the area of rehabilitation.

'The police came in while you were in your meeting,' says Olive. 'They found some stuff, apparently.'

Looking at the fax, I can see that the officers did indeed find some 'stuff' – a small quantity of amphetamines and several stolen cheques.

I ring the YOT and a contact there fills me in. Basically, it appears that Perry discovered that a local pensioner was in hospital for a few days, so he broke into the old man's home, stole his car keys and nicked his motor. Although he was pissed out of his mind, he managed to make it five miles away before he crashed. He wrote it off and smashed himself up, but luckily no one else was hurt.

It sounds to me like jail time beckons, or should do. Softly-softly certainly isn't working, and at least while he's behind bars he can't burgle houses and steal cars. But what do I know?

Later in the same shift, the phone rings outside and I hear the receptionist answer it. Earwigging, I can tell it's something to do with my favourite car thief. After a brief conversation, she hangs up and I shout out, 'What was that about, Olive?'

She comes in to the office. 'Perry's mum,' she says. 'She wants me to pick up some clothes from his room and drop them around to him in hospital. I said I'd pop out and do it.'

'Why doesn't she come and get them herself?' I say. 'The hospital's only a ten minute walk. It's not our job to run errands for residents' mothers.'

'Oh, I don't mind,' says Olive.

'I hope someone's looking after that old fella who had his house broken in to and his car stolen and wrecked,' I say.

'I'll be back in 20 minutes,' says Olive.

She's returns half an hour later.

'He looks terrible,' she says. 'Poor lad. I took him in some Pepsi, in case he was thirsty.'

I get angry listening to this. I remember a TV news report from the other night detailing how vital support services for the elderly are being cut back in the county because of the funding crisis; yet here we have people running around, catering to the needs of a prolific young offender. Something is rotten in the state of Britain.

I PLAN TO ADVOCATE DRACONIAN MEASURES

CERYS STENSON'S MUM returns the following day as promised with all the required documents and the estrangement letter.

I take a few moments before going out to meet them. I'm not feeling that great, to be honest.

Last night, my girlfriend and I had a major heart-to-heart about our own situation. She can hear her biological clock ticking ever louder, but I just can't see how we can even think about having kids when pretty much every penny we both earn goes on the mortgage, food, bills and travel to and from work. We haven't been out, even to the movies, for a month.

The conversation got quite fraught, and she raised the question of us separating. It all felt pretty heavy, and we agreed to sleep on it. I didn't get to bed until around 3am. Still, that's life. Time to deal with work.

Ms Stenson has brought her partner – Cerys's 'new dad' – with her, along with her other daughters.

I take Cerys's references and then leave them all sitting in the common room for 15 minutes or so while I go to the office to check through them. They all seem in order, so it looks like Cerys is in.

'Right,' I say, walking back to the common room. 'OK. Cerys's references are all fine, she's had her formal interview, so I'm able to inform you that we are going to accept her.'

A broad smile breaks over Ms Stenson's face. 'Oh, that's great,' she says. 'That's brilliant news. Only, me and James' – she looks at the man to her left – 'are hoping to start our own family soon. We've been together a while now.' She slips her arm through his.

I imagine the couple and three kids all crowded into one little house, and I can't help but think this is part of the reason she's so keen to palm her eldest daughter off on us. But I affect an insincere smile as if to say, I wish you luck. The truth is, it's just a mask for the contempt I feel for her – or, at least, for her attitude to her children. She seems to view them as accessories, with new models being introduced to replace the old. When I think of the people I know who are working all the hours God sends to keep their children fed and housed – and those, like myself and my girlfriend, who'd like them but just can't afford it – it makes my blood boil.

'I want to see her room,' she says, clasping her hands together. 'You stay here with the kids, James.'

I lead her up a couple of flights of stairs; she's panting like a walrus by the time we get to the top. When we reach the room, she's not too impressed, despite the fact that it has been freshly painted and is in a generally good condition.

'It's a bit small isn't it?' she says. 'Could she not have a bigger one?'

I suppose it's too much to expect a woman whose daughter is about to be taken off her hands and cared for by the State that she should show a little gratitude. Nonetheless, I still find it amazing how fussy people can be.

By way of an example, Stella's defrosted fridge gave up the ghost and wouldn't start again, so we replaced it with a perfectly acceptable second-hand one. When we carried it to her room, she kicked up a huge fuss, demanding a brand new one and further saying that she would be writing a letter of complaint to one of our many layers of management. Given that she's surrounded with leaflets exhorting her to complain – it's her right! – at the drop of a hat, that's not surprising. It's also not unusual for a staff member to offer to write letters of complaint like this on behalf of the complainant, thereby allowing them to 'evidence' their 'support' for her in our extensive filing system!

Back to Ms Stenson, and her eyes – which, now I come to think about it, are slightly piggy and acquisitive in character.

'I'm sorry,' I say. 'There are no other rooms available at the moment. It's first come, first served, I'm afraid. And to be honest, I don't think it's that small, myself. I mean, it's hardly a box room. It's got its own en-suite bathroom, too.'

If I sound unsympathetic, that might be inculcated in me by the distinct feeling – after those late night discussions with my girlfriend – that in a week or so's time I'm going to find myself sleeping on my friend Tony's sofa bed, in the spare room of the tiny flat he rents.

'Well,' she sniffs. 'I suppose it will have to do. But when someone with a better room leaves I want her to get their room. After all, she's a teenage girl and they have loads of stuff.'

'Sure,' I say. 'But there are also people ahead of her in the queue who have requested a room change and we have to take them into consideration, too. Not to mention, how she's getting on in school and other stuff like that will have a bearing.'

'Well,' she says, with an air of finality, 'that ain't my problem any more, is it?'

As soon as we get back downstairs, Ms Stenson has a quick conflab with James and then the entire brood hurries off, without even saying goodbye. I assume, correctly as it turns out, that they have nipped home to collect Cerys's things and do a bit of shopping; not a moment to waste when it comes to offloading your offspring.

A couple of hours later, I see a nice lady of about 50 struggling up the stairs with several heavy Tesco bags. Cerys is following her, empty-handed. It's too late to offer to help, but when she reappears half an hour later, I go over, introduce myself and ask who she is.

'Oh, I'm Cerys's intensive support worker from Connexions,' she says. 'Social services referred her to us after they found her the accommodation here. They don't work with her any more, so I'm providing Cerys with support whilst she settles in to living away from home. I'll be helping her with her shopping, giving her advice on cooking cheaply and nutritiously, showing her how to do laundry herself, budget her money… all the basic independent living skills really.'

While she's talking, I remember the intensive support worker I had myself – a woman who taught me how to wash behind my ears, eat my greens and brush my hair. I called her 'mum'. Plus I had a fella called 'dad', too; most kids I knew did back then, and we're only talking 15 years ago. There were no keyworkers, youth workers, tenancy support workers, family involvement officers, play co-ordinators or supported housing workers like me. What the hell is happening?

On the train home, dreading the further chat I'm going to be having with my girlfriend, I pick up a discarded copy of a certain middle England newspaper. Time was when I'd not have soiled my hands with it – sure, everything in its pages was lies. But then, I didn't know then that the State was actively involved in breaking up families. I can't blame the unwitting: if someone had told me this a few years ago, I'd have dismissed them as Tory reactionaries. Since I have been working in supported housing, I have seen evidence of this kind of thing every week, and I cannot argue with the facts when they are staring me in the face. Sometimes – just sometimes – the reactionaries are right.

*****

The conversation with my girlfriend didn't go well.

If I wasn't prepared to try for a baby, she wasn't prepared to put up with my sorry ass anymore. I wasn't, because we can't afford it, so she decided to implement the nuclear option, namely separation.

This means I will indeed be moving in with my friend Tony, and taking nothing with me but my clothes, my books and my small collection of sixties and seventies soul records. Thankfully, my now-ex is just about able to meet the mortgage repayments on our flat on her moderately better salary, though if interest rates go up we could both end up repossessed and bankrupt. We want to sell up as soon as possible, but in the current climate it's just not that easy.

So I'm sitting in the office, wading through kilos of meticulously-filed shit and feeling sorry for myself, when an ironic slap in the face wanders past the door, in the tracksuited shape of Kenny Mulligan.

He knocked up his girlfriend a while back and parted from her immediately afterwards: she'll soon provide the world with his third child, and I suspect he'll adopt the same approach to this one as he does his other two, namely that he will neither support it nor see it. Moral qualms and dilemmas are not Kenny's bag.

'Hey, Kenny,' I yell. 'Can you pop in for a sec.'

He does, plonking himself in Brendan's chair and slapping a copy of *Zoo* on the desk.

'So you'll be a dad again in a few months,' I say, conversationally. 'How do you feel about that?'

'Not really thinking about it too much,' he says, flicking through the mag, mostly concentrating on the photographs. 'I'll be there for the baby when it comes, and I'm trying to stay friends with the mum. Kirsty [his current girlfriend] can get a bit jealous at times but, like I say, she's got to understand that I'm gonna be a part of my kid's life.'

I'll believe it when I see it; he isn't really even part of his *own* life.

'So, was it planned, this baby with your ex?'

'Nah, course not,' he says, tearing his eyes away from some woman in a lacy white bra. 'It was an accident. They happen, don't they?'

You're not wrong there, Ken, I think. I'm looking at one, and the whole bloody building seems to be full of them.

'How do you mean, an accident?' I say. 'Did you just somehow fall in to your ex-girlfriend and ejaculate?'

He looks blank, so I try a less sarcastic tack. 'I mean, did the condom split and you couldn't get access to the morning after pill?'

'I never had no condoms with me,' he says.

Given that the Project makes free condoms available to all residents, this was remiss of him.

'Did you think she was on the pill?'

'No, I knew she wasn't, but it was just, like, the one time and I thought it would be fine.'

'That's not an accident, Kenny. It only takes one time. Please tell me you knew that?'

He is giggling now, as if he's a kid who's just been admonished for a trivial matter like eating too many sweets. It's impossible to dislike him: he's a bit of a rogue but is basically a nice kid – at least, he's never violent or threatening, and he's usually cheerful enough. But he is bloody irritating at times.

'Yeah, I knew,' he says. 'I just didn't think it would happen. Like I said, it was an accident.'

I watch him studying his magazine, and I think ahead 18 years; I'll be long gone from here by then, I hope, but I wouldn't be surprised if Kenny's sons and daughters are sitting in this office with a different Winston Smith.

'Anyway,' I say, 'I'm glad you popped by. Saved me the trouble of coming looking for you. Why haven't you paid the rent from your wages and started paying off your arrears like we agreed a week or so back?'

You'll recall that he owes the Project more than £800.

He looks up from the magazine with dead eyes. 'Ah, I left the pizza place a week or so back,' he says. 'And I've spent my last dough, but I've just been approved for a loan before I left my job and the cheque's in the post. So I'll sort out my share of the rent with that.'

'Why did you leave your job?'

'I shagged the manager's ex-girlfriend,' he says, with a grin. 'She's up the duff with his baby and he wants to kill me.'

Maybe he'll ask the manager for a reference.

'Why did you do that?' I say.

'To piss him off, he's a wanker.'

I wonder whether he used this as his chat-up line when trying to charm the young woman in question out of her undergarments. Though knowing the weird and wonderful lives some people seem to lead, it's entirely possible that she herself was using Kenny to get back at the ex-boyfriend. I guess it's none of my business.

'Well, look,' I say. 'You'll need to access full housing benefit now. You're entitled to it if you have no job.'

I have to admit, the word 'entitled' sticks in my craw a bit as I say it. I think benefits should be for those who want to work, but can't – of whom there are plenty. Even though he had a job and jacked it in of his own accord, and is an able-bodied young adult, and there are – even now – still jobs on offer locally, the State is happy to feed and house him. The State, by the way, being funded by people who carry on turning up to shit jobs in places like Domino's, who don't shag the manager's girlfriend and who have to hand over a quarter or more of what they earn to keep guys like Kenny in dope and lager.

'Basically, you need to fill in what's called a "Change of Circumstances" form and submit that, along with your P45 and your final wage slip. Then they'll be able to re-adjust the amount you can claim.'

Pause.

'You *have* got your final wage slip, right?'

'Yeah, sure,' he says, airily.

I press on. 'I've got all the forms in the office, so I can give the right one to you.'

I don't know why we keep all the various benefit forms here – the benefits office is only five minutes away – but we do.

'You need to make sure to get all that documentation in, or your rent won't be paid.'

And you will almost certainly not be evicted, despite our empty threats.

'It couldn't be simpler.'

'Oh, mate,' says Kenny, rolling his eyes, sinking deeper into his chair and finally giving up on *Zoo*. 'Can you do us a favour and fill it out for me? I hate forms. If you fill it out, I don't mind walking down there and dropping it in.'

'That's big of you, Ken,' I say.

This is his second stay in supported housing; his previous keyworker must have filled in most of his paperwork for him, and he thinks we'll all be an equally soft touch. To be fair, most of the other project workers here, apart from Brendan and myself, would probably oblige. Unfortunately for him, I don't think it's 'supporting' him if we do this; apart from anything else, he's able to read and write to a fairly decent level.

'But I'm not your secretary, you cheeky so-and-so. I'm not your servant, either. You can fill it in yourself. And if you screw it up, it's official warning time. OK?'

'OK, OK,' he says. 'Can I borrow a pen though? I'll do it in my room.'

I've learned that the verb 'to borrow' has a different meaning for Kenny and some of his mates than it does for the rest of society. It means, *Can I take something from you and lose it, or at best return it only after you spend several days asking me for it, days during which I will complain and whinge about being 'hassled'*. Still, he needs to fill in the form, and he hasn't got a pen.

'Here you go,' I say, handing over a Bic biro. 'And just out of principle, can you return it when you've finished?'

'Whatever,' says Kenny, as he gets up and lopes out.

* * * * *

After lunch, Martin sticks his head round his door. The nervous tic has now developed into a full-on head shake, a bit like the Colonel in that *Fawlty Towers* episode where Basil decides to run a gourmet night.

'Hey Win,' he says. 'Brendan did a tour of the kitchens a while back and sent out some warning letters about the state of them. They improved a bit, but I've noticed they're slipping back again. Can you do a tour for me this afternoon?'

'Sure,' I say.

'Great, thanks,' he says, and vanishes back into his office.

I grab a notepad and a pen – Kenny didn't return my precious Bic, after all – and head out.

About half of our residents are total strangers to hygiene, which is most unfair on those who don't choose to live like Stig of the Dump.

Nowhere is this ambivalence to filth, encrustation and general soiling more in evidence than in their kitchens (though I confess that I avoid their toilets), and lately, as Martin suggests, it has become particularly bad.

As I expect, a few of them are neat and tidy and smell of bleach; most (because half of the inhabitants does not equate to half of the kitchens) are messy, untidy and smell of ageing fast food detritus.

The vinyl floors are dirty and sticky to the touch; the white fridges and microwaves are covered in greasy fingerprints; the sinks are filled with unwashed pans and crockery; the oven hobs are spattered with fat and lumps of what I can only describe as *stuff*; maggoty, fly-blown bins overflow everywhere with beer cans, pizza boxes and chip wrappers. These places smell of rancid oil, mould and essence of don't-give-a-toss.

In the worst, I find a sink full of brown, putrid water, and end up throwing out every pot, pan and plate standing in it. Of course, all of that has to be replaced at the expense of taxpayers who get up every morning and go to work, rain or shine, to earn the cash to pay the tax that bought the initial set in the first place. I'm pretty sure that the residents who ruined this kitchen have now abandoned it and are presently turning another into a similar state. It is hard to prove this, though; they move around the building with some fluidity, and all deny causing any of the mess.

Later, I decide to bring this up at our staff meeting. I plan to advocate draconian measures.

So we're all sitting in the long, low, khaki-painted staff meeting room, and just like last week, and the week before that, and again back another week, and probably all the way back to the dawn of time, we fall to discussing the same problems we always discuss, with the familiar failure to get to grips with any of them.

I've asked for the kitchens to be the top item on our agenda, and I speak first.

'We've tried writing letters to the residents,' I say. 'We've tried reasoning with them and we've tried threatening them with official warnings. None of this has worked, so I say we lock the kitchens and we only open them when they come to us and agree to clean them, and then we go and supervise them doing that immediately. If they start to leave rotting food and overflowing bins again, we just lock the kitchens again. Eventually, it will sink in with them that access to a kitchen is dependent on keeping it clean. It's not going to be fair on those people who already do that, but then neither is it fair that they have to live like pigs because of a minority.'

Margaret doesn't like this idea. 'I hear what you're saying, Winston,' she says, 'and I understand your frustrations, but it would be against their rights to lock their kitchens. I remember someone checked this with the policy department at head office a while ago, because it was suggested before.'

'But those kitchens don't belong to the residents,' I say. 'They belong to the housing association. What's more, the worst culprits are the same people who are always in rent arrears, so they're not even paying to rent them. Surely that has some bearing on their rights?'

'Hmmm,' she says. 'I don't think so. Rights are rights, really.'

'I think it's a problem of communication,' says Steve. 'I think we need to be clearer in what we want them to do.'

'How can you get any clearer than a piece of A4 paper with "Please clean up this kitchen" on it?' says Brendan.

'Yes, but sometimes the way you ask things is as important as what you're asking,' replies Steve. 'We've got some very vulnerable people here and we need to bear that in mind.'

Given that the real problem cases are teenage burglars and car thieves like Perry, who swagger about like they own the place, 'vulnerable' isn't a word I'd use.

Martin calls us to order. 'I think we're agreed that the main immediate problem is the bins overflowing in some kitchens? So what I'll do is ask the cleaner to go into those kitchens and collect the rubbish. In the meantime, I suggest we issue warnings to the persistent offenders.'

In other words, he wants us to do again what we have already done, and which hasn't worked before. We find it hard enough to evict people for staff abuse and rent arrears; our harder nuts are not going to feel threatened by letters asking them to clean up once in a while – especially when we're arranging for someone to clean up anyway. I think this is called 'a result' (for them); we've just given them a maid (in fact, they actually have two, as whoever's on nights often gets bored and goes and cleans up the residents' kitchens to pass the time). We'll get to 'evidence' our 'support' for them, though, so every cloud etc etc.

'I thought we were supposed to be helping them become independent,' I say. 'How does cleaning up their rubbish after them do this?'

Martin ignores me and moves on to the next item, and I sit there thinking that it's no wonder so many of our people struggle even to sign on for themselves. The Project consistently refuses to set firm boundaries and deliver consequences for breaches; we're helping to sustain our residents in their feckless irresponsibility even though we're paid to do the exact opposite.

* * * * *

The day ends with another ambulance coming to collect Sharn after another overdose, and a confrontation.

I'm turning my mind to the thorny question of rent arrears, and Ciaran in particular. When he agreed to pay his rent and twenty quid a week on top to clear his debts, I had my doubts and, from the looks of his file, I was right. From the figures, I can see that in the first week after our agreement he paid the full rent and £10 off the arrears. The following week he paid no rent, and no money off the arrears. He's 21, this bloke, and it's not like he can't afford it: there are lads his age and younger dying in Afghanistan for about half the money that he's on.

As I sit there, wondering what to do about this, Ciaran actually walks into the office. I wonder at first if maybe he has come in to pay some rent or at least to discuss the situation, but in fact he's actually looking for money from *us*.

'Winston,' he says, holding out his hand. 'Here's that spare key I borrowed to get in my room. I need the £5 deposit back that I gave Brendan for it yesterday.'

I look at him for a moment, wondering what to do. I decide I have to be adult about it, so I get up and go over the petty cash box. Unfortunately, there's only a twenty pound note in it.

'I've no change,' I say. 'Sorry, you're going to have to come back tomorrow.'

Instantly, he flips into an almost manic rage. His eyes bulge and he spits as he speaks. 'For fuck's sake, if I owed *you* money I'd never hear the fucking end of it,' he yells. 'This stupid shithole treats me like I'm a kid, telling me what to do and hassling me. You owe me that money and I fucking want it now!'

He's pacing frantically up and down the office, flailing his arms about and gesticulating wildly as he continues to swear about the Project. I wait until he's blown himself out a bit and then talk to him, calmly.

'What do you mean, *if* you owed us money?' I say. 'You owe us in the region of a thousand pounds. We talked about this not that long ago. I'm glad you're here, actually. If you miss one more week of that rent and arrears repayment plan we discussed, you will be getting 28 days' notice. In fact, we should just keep that five pounds and take it off your debt. You have no excuse for not paying rent. You have two jobs and you currently earn more money than most of the staff working here.'

This is a simple statement of the facts, but it only serves to enrage him further. He is a big enough lad and he starts moving towards me, his shoulders pulled back in an aggressive stance. He shouts in my face, 'How fucking *dare* you throw that at me? Who do you think you are, threatening to throw me out of here?'

He is literally three inches away from me now, and I can feel his spit landing on me as he rants. I have to step backwards twice to retreat from his verbal onslaught. I decide to be straight with him, trying to stay calm and confident as I do so.

'Ciaran, just look at your body language,' I said. 'It's very intimidating and threatening, and this kind of behaviour can lead to eviction as well. I advise you to calm yourself down. Now, here's how things actually stand. I should have written you up your notice today, but I didn't, I decided to give you one more week to comply with your rent arrears agreement. I'm now seriously reconsidering that decision, in light of your aggressive behaviour, and I would strongly suggest you get out of my physical space immediately.'

It's a gamble to play this card; he could easily just headbutt me and leave me on the floor. Instead, he backs down.

'Aaaah, look, Winston,' he says. 'It don't have to be like this. I'm sorry man, I was completely out of line there. Look, mate, I'm not worried about the five quid, but do me a favour and don't write me up to get kicked out, eh?'

'All you need to do if you want to stay here is start paying your rent on time with 20 quid a week to clear the arrears,' I say.

He doesn't seem convinced by this, and spends the next ten minutes begging me not to have him evicted. Eventually, I think I get through to him and he leaves. As I sit back in my chair, I find I'm shaking slightly.

Later, I relay these events to Martin, our twitchy project manager.

His response astonishes me.

'You shouldn't have reminded him about his rent arrears if he was already agitated about the money we owed him,' he says. 'That's what caused the escalation of the confrontation, and it could easily have led to him hitting you.'

'But in the real world, employers and bank managers and people don't give a monkey's about your mood,' I say. 'How is that…'

Martin cuts in. 'I'm just saying, you need to think carefully about how you approach people.'

Let me get this straight: the management hassle us to chase up the rent arrears, but they want us to check in with the residents as to their moods first, just to see if they're up to discussing the situation?

WE CAN ONLY ENCOURAGE THE GIRLS TO EAT HEALTHILY

IT'S A WEEK OR SO ON and, being single again, I'm slowly getting used to flat sharing. I'm sleeping on a sofa bed in my friend Tony's small spare room; it's OK as far as it goes, but I do miss having my own place. Unfortunately, I don't earn much and rents in this area are quite high, even for a dingy bedsit. I need to save up some cash, so to this end I take on agency shifts at residential care homes for teenagers.

I mentioned the hellish nature of these earlier: in my experience, the word 'care' in care home can be slightly misleading, in that there often isn't any – not beyond the absolute basics of food, shelter and Sony Playstations. Moral or spiritual guidance, or even common sense: not so much.

Many of the residents at the Emmanuel Goldstein Project have come through the care system, and plenty have had bad, even horrific, childhoods. Given this, I can't deny that some of them are a real inspiration. They prove that you can overcome parental neglect, State incompetence and modern bullshit if you work at it.

However, I also can't deny that some of the kids in the care homes are absolutely terrible to work with.

I've got a week off, and a lot of extra work lined up. This is good for my bank account, but bad for my sanity.

The first place I find myself at is Tom Parsons House – a large, five-bedroomed place which is home to three young girls, aged 14, 15 and 16. I flick through their files as part of the preparation for my first day. Of the three, one has already had an abortion, all have criminal records and two are currently tagged and are supposedly being monitored by the youth justice system for various offences. Chelsey – an extremely wild 14-year-old – is constantly running away from the home for days on end, and I hardly ever see her. Sammie, 15, is nearly as bad; 16-year-old Rachel, although not averse to a night on the tiles, seems to spend most of her life sitting down, channel-hopping on the TV and gorging on junk food. Both she and Sammie are grotesquely fat; this is a tragedy for them, with life-altering consequences.

But what really baffles me is the ease and regularity of the absconding. After all, there are always three members of staff – and sometimes four – in the house, 24 hours a day, seven days a week. I wonder why they don't just put a stop to this, and say as much to Jenny, the senior support worker, as we sit in the living room watching Rachel glued to the telly, cramming salt and vinegar crisps into her maw like a starving man.

'Jenny, I'm just curious,' I say. 'Do the staff not notice when these young girls are leaving the premises?'

'Well, sometimes they just run off without telling us,' she says, 'but often they tell us they are going out and don't know when they'll be back.'

'But why don't we stop them?' I say. 'I mean, why don't we lock the doors, or something? After all, they're supposedly in care. They're only 14 and 15, and very vulnerable. God knows what could happen to them and what they could get up to.'

'Look, I agree the whole system is mad,' says Jenny. 'But as you know we're not allowed to touch them, physically. We can't grab them and pull them in to the house. That could be construed as assault and we could get in trouble.'

It seems to me that it's an odd kind of system that believes it's better to allow 14-year-old girls to roam free about the area for days on end without supervision, rather than grab them by the arms and scruff of the neck and bring them back into a home where they can be properly supervised.

'Do they usually stay away for long?' I say.

'Usually it's only a couple of nights at a time,' she says. 'Sometimes it's longer, though. Once they were away together for four nights. What happens is the cops find them, or they get fed up and run out of money or places to stay and then they telephone us and ask us for a lift back to the home. It's a bit of a pain, because it can often be at three or four in the morning, and we have to get up out of bed and drive and collect them.'

'Really?' I say. 'That *does* sound like a pain.'

'We have a duty of care towards them, you see.'

They may well end up in a secure juvenile unit, should they continue to abscond and be involved in low level crime. However, seeing as the youth justice system fails to deal effectively with more serious youth crime, I'd say a tag is as bad as it will get for these two girls, which is a shame because to my mind they need protecting from themselves.

Rachel tears herself away from the telly for a moment. 'Stop flirting with Winston, you fat fucking slag Jenny,' she says. 'He'd never fuck a dog like you.'

We weren't flirting, and for Rachel to abuse Jenny in this way is a bit like every pot in the northern hemisphere abusing one small kettle. Jenny just ignores her, of course; nothing ever happens for verbal abuse like this, beyond toothlessly asking the teenager to 'not speak like that in future'.

Another support worker, Shane, is sitting nearby. He's usually based at another home nearby, but is with us for the day.

'It's even worse at our place,' he says. 'At least these girls are mostly only gone for a few days and then come back. There's three 15-year-old lads in our home who all absconded a month ago and we have no idea where they are or what they're up to. Me and the other support workers still have to turn up there every day for work and monitor the place 24/7 in case any of them come back. Technically they're all still in care, and the care has to be there for them should they come back.'

'God, you must be really bored sitting there all day with no residents and nothing to do,' I say.

'Not really,' says Shane. 'We have a laugh with each other and spend a lot of time playing on the residents' Xbox to pass the time.'

Later on, when she leaves the room, I ask about Rachel's background. Has she had a tough and 'challenging' childhood, full of physical or sexual abuse, or neglect? No. In fact her parents are (if the definition means anything) middle class and not at all poor. Rachel has been voluntarily put in care under Section 20 of the Children's Act 1989, at a cost of something like £2,500 a week. Meanwhile, in a few weeks' time, her parents are jetting off to India with her little brother on their annual family holiday (they also have at least one other foreign holiday each year). One reason for Rachel's current 'anger issues', Jenny explains, is that this is the first time she has been unable to go.

For a moment I feel a twinge of sympathy for her: despite her unpleasant behaviour, she is still a child and must feel very rejected by her parents. Being dumped in a care home has made her behaviour worse, not better.

There are loads of kids under Section 20 care orders – most of them dumped when mum and dad split up and shack up with new partners who don't fancy raising the existing kids. The only people whose interests this serves are the private sector care homes (paid for with tax money) and the social services bureaucracy that maintains and monitors this system.

A couple of days later I find myself being sent to another care home, Syme Place. It's supposed to house three residents but a week ago one of them absconded to God-knows-where, leaving a 14-year-old lad called Wayne and a 15-year-old girl, Kate. There are two members of staff on duty at all times and a manager, nine-to-five Monday to Friday, to ensure all the required bureaucratic bullshit is being adhered to, and with one of the full-time staff off sick I'm there to make up the numbers.

It's a week day, but both of the kids are upstairs asleep until about 11am – we call them for school, but if they tell you to get stuffed there's nothing you can do to make them go. Then Wayne – a small, skinny youth – surfaces and shovels Coco Pops into his gob. He spills them everywhere, and leaves the bowl on the table in a puddle of chocolatey milk when he's had enough.

'Hey, Wayne,' I say, conversationally. 'How's about clearing that away to the dishwasher?'

'We don't fucking do cleaning up,' he says, dismissively. 'We're not skivvies. That's the staff's job.'

He starts smirking, and although I've never clapped eyes on him until 15 minutes ago I think I recognise the type: he's hoping to get a confrontational reaction out of me.

I ignore him, clear away the bowl and wipe the table. He shrugs and goes outside for a victory fag, where he stands smoking next to a staff member who is also having a nicotine break. Given that he's under the legal age for cigarettes, and that everyone surely knows how bad for you they are, this is highly unprofessional though, in my experience, it's very common. It's pretty much impossible to stop them smoking, but we could at least show disapproval.

Kate gets up, has some brekkie and goes back to her room. Ten minutes later, as I'm mopping the floor, Wayne's back.

'I'm fucking bored,' he says.

'Perhaps if you'd gone to school you wouldn't be so bored,' I say.

'Oh, shut the fuck up,' he says. 'I hate school, it's full of pricks telling you what to do. I'd rather go down town and get stoned with the lads.'

He picks up a broom and starts spinning it around. It almost hits me, so I say, 'Hey, watch yourself there, Wayne.'

By way of a reply, he lunges at me and shoves the dirty bristles into my face. I back off, wiping my eyes, and he lunges again, grinning. I grab the brush by the handle.

His expression changes from one of glee to anger.

'Let it fucking go,' he says, pulling at the broom.

'Wayne,' I say, 'that's just not going to happen. I'm a good ten inches taller than you and several stone heavier, and I'm a pretty fit bloke. You're not doing that again, and if you try it I'll restrain you.'

This little speech is like a red rag to a bull: boys like Wayne don't like submitting to authority. He spends a good ten minutes trying to yank the brush from my grip. He's livid with anger but although I'm ready for it he doesn't lash out violently. This surprises me; these power struggles often escalate. Eventually, he tires himself out and admits defeat and I lock the brush in the office, with a friendly grin in his direction.

The next couple of hours pass reasonably peacefully, though Wayne does expend a lot of nervous energy in glaring and swearing at me every time I come within half a dozen paces of him.

At around 4pm, he announces that he's going out 'to get pissed' and just leaves the building. We can't stop him, because as we've seen that might constitute an assault, so we watch him stroll off into the afternoon sun to destroy his immature liver, which obviously does not constitute an assault.

Kate appears again.

She's actually worse than Wayne – she's a violent young offender devoid of manners or respect for others, traits in which she is indulged, and even steeped, by the care system. She is tagged and on a curfew set by the youth justice system after she took a knife to a foreign student a few years older than herself and mugged her for a mobile phone and money. Well, at least the foreign student can go home knowing that she experienced a genuine slice – if you'll excuse the pun – of modern British street culture.

At 5pm sharp, the manager makes his getaway and the other staff member, Rhona, gives me the task of cooking Kate's evening meal – a roast dinner. There's obviously no question of Kate being asked to help, not even to wash the dishes or peel the spuds. I watch Rhona and Kate as the shift progresses; they're gossiping and smoking cigarettes together.

Later on, after I've finished acting as butler, waiter and chef to the teenager, she starts insulting me. 'Did you know you're going bald?' she says. 'Plus, you talk funny. And you wear funny clothes.'

She laughs and points at my chinos and Hush Puppies; to be fair to her, most of the males in her life wear tracksuits. She is looking for a reaction, but she isn't going to get one. A few minutes later, she gives up trying to taunt me and a slightly uneasy silence settles on the room.

I break it by enquiring about her plans for the future.

'I'm going to get a flat when I'm 18 and do whatever I want,' she says. 'They've got to give me one because I've been in care. It's the law.'

She's right: the law (I think it's the Homelessness [Priority Need for Accommodation] [England] Order 2002, but don't quote me) will give her a priority status in obtaining social housing above that of other individuals, due to her history. Granted, as there is a shortage of social housing, she will not be guaranteed a place immediately, but she will be given a flat long before – say – a hard-working couple on a low income. It's not her fault she's in care, of course, and we do need to look after damaged and screwed up kids like her. But somehow this seems wrong. She's not yet 16, and she is already fluent in her entitlements and what she is owed by society by virtue of her position; I can picture her in a few years, with several unruly urchins at her feet, demanding her entitlement to an even bigger flat. This almost always all ends badly for the people concerned. Although she's not a pleasant person, I feel sorry for her.

She goes back to her room, and I'm sitting in the office putting together my generic paperwork for the day when there's a knock on the door. Foolishly, I open it fully – as opposed to using the partial lock – and I'm greeted with the dirty water from the mop bucket. I stand there, dripping wet and wiping my face, and Wayne scurries off, hooting to himself. The balance of power has been restored.*

* * * * *

On Thursday evening, I'm back at Tom Parsons House working a night shift.

Chelsey – the 14-year-old – is nowhere to be seen, and 16-year-old Rachel is kicking around somewhere upstairs. I sit and watch 15-year-old Sammie – about 5ft 5in tall, and weighing around a stone for every year of her age – eat a large fish-and-chip supper which has been bought for her by the staff. She gets up, leaving the plate on the floor for me to clear away, and wanders off.

An hour later, she's back. 'I want some ice cream,' she says to me.

'I don't think we have any in,' I say. 'I'll check, but…'

That's enough to set her off shouting and swearing. In order to placate her, and for an easier life, Lucy – the shift leader and senior care worker on duty – drives her to a shop, where she is bought a box of six Magnum-type ice creams.

I watch in some horror and quite a lot of disgust as she is allowed to scoff them all, one after the other. This can't be right, can it? Sure, it keeps her quiet, which means she isn't abusing the staff or storming into the office and ripping up files, as she is wont to do. But we are letting her kill herself, slowly, with fat, sugar and E numbers: the Magnums suit the staff's needs, rather than the child's.

---

* If you think Wayne sounds like a common-or-garden feral brute, you'd be wrong – and not just because he'd been diagnosed with 'conduct disorder' (or maybe 'oppositional defiant disorder' or 'school refusal disorder', I forget). The funny thing is, with the right guidance, discipline and boundaries I'm sure he could actually make something of his life. I ended up spending a few weeks working with him on and off, and when he wasn't pretending to be hard or acting the yob there emerged a teenager with a very curious mind, particularly in regard to history and geography, with a vocabulary much more advanced than many of his peers. It's an awful shame that none of the services involved in his life had at that point been able to assist him in developing his obvious potential.

An hour or two after Sammie has gorged herself on a week's recommended limit of saturated fat in one sitting, she goes outside with a packet of Marlboro Lights. A few seconds later, she is joined in the yard by the shift leader and another member of staff, plus Rachel, who has consumed a bricklayer's portion of KFC while channel-hopping.

Later, I confront the shift leader.

'Lucy,' I say, trying but probably failing not to sound po-faced, and possibly even slightly priggish, 'I'm a bit shocked that you openly allow a 15-year-old girl to smoke on the grounds of the home, and that you smoke with her. And while I'm on the subject, I've just watched her eat a family box of bloody choc ices. She's obviously got serious weight problems. Don't you try to control what the kids eat? I mean, give them choice, sure, but limit it to healthy food with the occasional indulgence?'

'Well, Winston,' says Lucy, adopting a slightly patient tone. 'We can only *encourage* the girls to eat healthily, but they do have the right to choose their own meals. We can't *dictate* what they eat. With the smoking issue, if we were to try to stop Sammie from smoking she would simply go somewhere else and do it. We'd rather she did it here in a controlled environment, where we know she is safe.'

Sammie and Rachel are both back inside now, and are settling down for a late night (and early morning) in front of the box. Only one telly, and two young ladies with differing opinions as to what to watch: now that's a recipe for disaster, if ever I heard of one. Sure enough, within a few moments it all kicks off.

Sammie's trying to grab the remote off Rachel, Rachel's yelling at her to fuck the fuck off, hair's being pulled. Lucy moves in; I think about helping her, but it's 1am and I've been at work since 10am yesterday morning. My shift is long over and, frankly, I can't be arsed. It's time to head off to bed. At the foot of the stairs, I meet Spencer, one of the full-time support workers, hurrying in the direction of the screeching.

'Hey, Spence,' I say. 'Can you just help with something that's confusing me? I'm just wondering, how is it that these two girls' social workers don't kick up a fuss about the state they're in and all the shit they eat? I mean, social services are always in here visiting them and inspecting all the paperwork.'

'Simple,' he says. 'The weekly care logs get written in such a way as to stress the healthy food they eat now and then. What else are we supposed to do? If we don't give them what they want they complain and we're in the shit.'

He legs it towards the lounge, and I start climbing the stairs. The social workers must be turning blind eyes of Nelsonian proportions, I think to myself, because there's no way that anyone could believe that those two hippos are living on a diet of mung beans and spinach.

To be fair, the company responsible for housing Rachel and Sammie – which does run some very good homes – isn't to blame for all of this, and neither, in my opinion, are the staff. It's really down to the luck of the draw, kids-wise: you can have effective managers and staff who really care and try to give the children consistent and sensible boundaries, but if the kids don't give a toss what you say and think there's not a great deal you can do. It's really difficult for good care homes to flourish within the care system, because the system is set up to allow the children to dictate the agenda. There's been a profound and disproportionate shift in power away from adult forms of authority to 'empowerment', the sector buzzword for allowing youngsters to live pretty much as they wish irrespective of the objective damage they are doing to themselves. It's a tragedy, really.

I get my head down. I'm knackered so I fall asleep pretty quickly, and I'm dreaming of nothing much when I'm jolted back awake by a massive banging on my door.

I turn on the bedside lamp, momentarily disorientated, and struggle out of bed.

The banging comes again.

'Alright, alright,' I say. 'Give me a minute.'

I climb into my trousers, pull on my shirt and open the door, rubbing my eyes and squinting in the harsh light.

It's Spencer.

'You need to come downstairs, Winston,' he says. 'The police are here.'

It turns out that the fight over the remote control degenerated a bit after I left. Thankfully it didn't turn properly violent, but it all culminated in Sammie picking up a can of deodorant and hurling it at Rachel. The can brushed her arm, so – despite the fact that she is herself more than capable of hurling cans of deodorant and anything else within grabbing distance at anyone, anytime – Rachel called the cops to make a complaint of assault against her younger housemate.

And despite the fact that absolutely no injury has been suffered, and that Rachel has a history of being arrested and charged with making false allegations in the past, and has a host of other convictions, two uniformed officers have arrived. They're downstairs taking statements from the 'victim', and they want witness statements from Spencer, Lucy and myself, too. It all takes almost two hours. At one point I say to one of the police constables, 'As far as I can see, there's not a mark on her. The can didn't actually hit her.'

'Yeah,' he says, 'you're probably right. But the throwing of the can itself is technically an offence and now that a complaint has been made we're duty bound to investigate it.'

'What's likely to happen?' I say.

'Depends,' he says. 'We might get the younger girl to admit to it, and that will probably mean a caution.'

'Surely there's better things you could be doing than getting embroiled in a teenage squabble where no one was hurt?'

'I couldn't agree more,' he says, with a sigh. 'There's only four of us on call at the moment for the whole town. But like I say, once that call is made and logged on our computer system we have to respond. We don't have a choice, particularly where kids in care are concerned. We're not able to use discretion. We have to deal with the allegation and bring it to a conclusion, or "detect it" as we say.'

It's nice – in a way – to see that the bureaucratic, tick-box madness isn't confined to my job.

At around 3am, the cops leave when a more pressing call comes in over the radio. They tell us that someone else will be back to interview the perpetrator in the morning

I crawl back into bed at 3.15am, with my alarm set for 8am. I struggle to get back to sleep. Mainly I'm wondering how things got this mad. Do the politicians who set our laws not get it? We all want a police force that protects the law-abiding and the vulnerable, but I think we tend to think this means lonely old ladies, not giant teenagers surrounded by care workers.

WHERE ARE THE MARCHES PROTESTING AT SCHOOLING?

AS IT'S THE WEEKEND, I'm lone-working, which I hate – as most of us do. If anyone decides to take a pop at you, or subject you to a barrage of abuse or threats, or make a baseless allegation of some sort, you're on your own and you have to deal with it all by yourself.

Luckily, most of our more volatile residents tend to spend the majority of Sunday sleeping off Saturday. I make myself a cuppa, tune the radio to Jazz FM and sit at the desk. I'm planning to put my feet up with the *Observer*. At times like this, alone with my thoughts and a good read, I almost like this job.

At least things are *slightly* more sane here.

Kenny comes into the office and hands over £250 in notes. It's a down payment on his rent arrears.

I carefully count the money, write him a receipt and make a note in his file. As I'm doing this, I ask, 'Where did you get this cash then, Ken?'

'You know I said I'd got a loan sorted?' he says. 'I got five hundred notes, but I wanted some for the weekend.'

I shake my head. 'I thought the days of cheap and easy credit were over,' I say.

Who on earth would be stupid enough to lend money to Kenny? And I know I ought to be pointing out to him the sheer stupidity of taking out a loan on a credit card and blowing half of it on booze and drugs, but it would literally be a waste of my breath.

'While you're here,' I say, 'I've had a call from housing benefit. They say they still haven't got the Change of Circumstances form and the other required documentation to re-assess your claim, and until you submit it they're suspending your benefit.'

'Yeah, yeah,' he says, airily. 'That's all cool, man, it's gonna be sorted tomorrow.'

It's always tomorrow.

'You have to get it done within the next week,' I say, 'or they're going to go from just suspending the claim to closing it, and you'll have to reapply all over again. Now look, because of this I'm going to have to give you a second official warning for your rent arrears. I'm making a note of it here in your file, yes?'

I'm hoping, almost certainly in vain, that this will motivate him. He nods. 'Sound, mate,' he says, and walks out.

If push came to shove, he could always return to live with his mum, so he probably doesn't care too much about paying his rent here. As I watch him leave, I ponder the money paid to me, and thousands like me, to run around after the Kennys of the nation.

* * * * *

June is mooching around the place at lunchtime.

I've heard she's been having problems at college, so I grab her for a quick chat. It turns out she has been kicked off her course for smashing a window in the classroom.

'What did you want to go and do that for?' I ask.

'I was being wound up by Mia, innit?' she says, her accent and syntax belying her middle-class background (her dad drives a BMW and the family live in one of those detached 'executive' houses on the outskirts of town; I'm not sure what she's doing with us because she was certainly not at any real risk of homelessness). 'She was, like, riling me, man. I got, like, angry, so I punched the glass, innit.'

'You're lucky they didn't ring the police and have you arrested for criminal damage,' I say.

'Pah,' she says. 'What they gonna do?'

She has a point: lots of our residents have received precisely no punishment for smashing up bus shelters and similar nonsense.

'I never meant to break it, anyway,' she says. 'I was just hitting it.'

June is either quite seriously stupid, and really doesn't know that hitting a window hard with your fist will smash it, or she is a liar. She *is* a liar, but I tend to think she's probably telling the truth in this instance.

June isn't alone in her stupidity. When you consider that our residents have attended compulsory primary and secondary schools for 11 years, the level of education that most of them have reached is literally scandalous. A million people marched against the illegal Iraq war, which is fair enough. But where are the marches protesting at the abysmal schooling many British kids get?

Some of our clients can barely read their own names, and a lot of them are unable to multiply anything more complicated than the ten times table (some can't even do that). I have honestly seen dolphins and chimpanzees on nature programmes display more evident signs of intelligence.

It's not that they're all inherently stupid, even June; it's just that their parents and teachers have been unable or unwilling to instil any personal discipline or self-control in them, and without these qualities it is impossible to be educated even to a minimal standard. They don't seem to be able to think ahead, and don't seem to understand the concept of actions having consequences.

Having spent time working as a teaching assistant with 'emotionally and behaviourally-challenged' kids in a shambolic comprehensive school, I have some insight into this, but don't just take my word for it. I read in *The Observer* the other day that between 1997-2007, almost 60 percent of school-leavers failed to achieve five C grades, including in the core subjects of English and maths. A further million left without even five Gs, the lowest grade possible (grades E, F, and G are now considered to be passes, by the way).

Since employers tend to view five GCSE Cs as the minimum benchmark, failing to hit even that low target means your working life is pretty much over before it has even begun.

Our residents often fall into the 'five Gs or less' category, and one of our jobs is to find a way of dragging them through a further two years of study to give them a second shot at getting their GCSEs.

These 16- to 18-year-olds don't go back to school to do this, but instead enrol on what's called an e2e (Entry to Employment) course*.

The idea is that it will act as an entrée to the arenas of employment, further education or training, and we require many of them to take this

---

* The e2e scheme has recently been replaced by a new scheme called Foundation Learning, administered by Connexions – though the chances are that it will be replaced by a different one between me writing these words and the book appearing in your hand. I'm sure one of the main reasons for the constant churn of rebranding and renaming all these schemes is to make it harder for people to work out how much money is being spent, and how useless they are.

course as part of their 'licence agreement'. (As opposed to a tenancy agreement, most people living in supported housing have a licence agreement which stipulates the conditions by which they are allowed to live in a given project. The conditions of these agreements are more than often ignored and are only inconsistently and arbitrarily enforced by the Project.)

It's crazy, really. The country has already coughed up tens of thousands of pounds apiece for these kids to get a free education – the kind of thing poor people in Africa walk a dozen miles a day to receive. Now it has to pay again. It makes more sense, to me, for some way to be found to ensure that our children get a decent basic education the first time around. But that's by the by. Given that these e2e courses exist, do they succeed where the formal education system has failed?

Er, no, not really. The scheme is funded by the quango the Learning Skills Council, the budget of which, for 2007-2008, was £197.8 million; during that year, 54,400 teenagers were enrolled and 26,000 ended up finding work or going on to further education or training. Even if you believe that success rate of less than 50 per cent, that's still akin to flushing almost £100 million down the toilet. Not to mention, every student received an Education Maintenance Allowance of £30 a week for attending – money that is not included in that £197.8 million.

How about locally? Well, my slice of the national picture isn't any better. I can't remember any of our residents successfully completing e2e courses, much less entering work at the end of them. The only thing that they have subsequently come close to entering is the penal system.

Dawn is another 16-year-old who was recently asked to leave her course for repeatedly arriving under the influence of drugs and alcohol. She would kick off the day with a can of Stella and a couple of strong spliffs, and was thoroughly intoxicated by the time she arrived to be educated. Within a few weeks of being kicked off the course, she was arrested for shoplifting. Her case is pending. Meanwhile, the Stella and spliff are taking a hammering.

Dave is 17, and isn't actually one of our residents, but he is going out with a girl who is, Alicia. When he was thrown off his course for making physical threats to the staff, she dropped out in solidarity.

Their union means an additional layabout at the Project, as he visits her every day. It won't be long before we have to ban him from the building, as there have already been several incidents of him verbally abusing Posy and Nigel, the night staff, whilst out of his head on amphetamines.

Of course, I know I'm only seeing part of the picture. I arrange to pop out to meet one of our local e2e co-ordinators, Jasper, on my way home the following day. I tell him I want to discuss June's case, but really I'm engaged in what you might call an open-minded search for the truth.

The first thing I ask him is what kind of students they get on the course.

'We deal with young people aged 16 to 18 who didn't thrive in a traditional education setting,' he says.

This is what you could describe as a bureauphemism.

'All our young people are referred to us through Connexions or the local Youth Offending Team – they send offenders to us via Connexions as part of a court order.'

'So what does the course entail?' I ask.

'Well, there are several elements – some of it is stuff like personal and social development, but probably the most important section of the course is numeracy and literacy skills. Most of our students are functionally illiterate when they arrive. We aim for them to leave here with a grade C GCSE equivalent in maths and English.'

'Do you manage to achieve that?' I say.

'To be honest, no. Most of those that complete the course leave with a D-grade GCSE equivalent in maths and English.'

'So what's the success rate of getting them into jobs or further education or training?'

'I'm not sure of the exact figures,' says Jasper. 'But I'd guess about 50 per cent of the young people that come through our doors in this locality go on to further training or get jobs. The rest just don't even complete the course or fail to do well enough to get a job or progress in to further training.'

'What would you say are the biggest problems that you face with the kids?' I say.

'Mainly their attitude,' he says. 'The majority of them don't want to be here – lots of them only *are* here because of a court order to do with a conviction, or because it's a condition of receiving income support or jobseeker's allowance for under 18s that they have to register with Connexions and either evidence that they're looking for work or enrol on a course. So most of our young people are here to ensure they can get benefits and/or keep out of jail.' He sighs. 'There's also their attitude to the course. A common expression I hear from students is "I don't do education".'

I hear this kind of thing often, too; it baffles me how so many kids can revel in their own ignorance. There was a time when people were ashamed of failing at school, or not having a job. There is an underclass of people – and I don't mean people defined by their class origins or financial situation – for whom those days have long gone. They see failure as a badge of honour, and the 'three Rs' have been replaced by the three Is: ignorance, indolence and illiteracy. Generation F, you might call them: failed, failing and fucked up.

'It must be very frustrating,' I say. 'I mean, you're only trying to instil a basic level of literacy and numeracy. Without those, they won't even get a job in McDonald's or Tesco.'

Jasper nods in agreement. 'Most of our students say that the reason they can't get work is because the Eastern Europeans or the Africans are taking all the jobs,' he says. 'I challenge that view. I say, "No mate, the reason you can't get a job is because you can barely read or count your own fingers and have no skills whatsoever." I point out that you can't expect employers to take on uneducated and basically lazy British teenagers when there are other people out there from other countries who are generally better educated and have a much stronger work ethic. After a while, some of them do accept that and they do try to improve themselves. But as I say, it's only about half of those who come through the door.'

'I was talking to June Stevens today,' I say. 'I don't know if you know, but she's been booted off her course. In fact, I think a few of our residents have been a bit of a nightmare?'

'Yes,' he says. 'That's putting it mildly. *I* don't know if *you* know this, but we believe a lot of the students who *don't* live in your project go there during lunch breaks to get stoned with your residents who are either on the course or have been kicked off. That's a big problem for us, people getting stoned on weed or taking other drugs and then turning up to the class in no fit state for anything. If we spot it continually in the same person we eventually ask them to leave the course.'

'Yeah, I did know that,' I say. 'Unfortunately, there's not much we can do about it. If we catch them at it we kick them out, but we can't stop people coming back to the Project and bringing mates with them, and we can't go into their rooms without permission so if they're reasonably discreet about it…'

Another problem he failed to mention is absenteeism, and students turning up late. Jasper and his fellow teachers are constantly ringing the Project to ask us to remind those of our residents who are on the course to turn up on time, or just to turn up. OK, not all that long ago I was a teenager, and as you know I also smoked a lot of weed. I know all about how hard it can be to get up in the morning. But getting people like me up used to be the job of parents – 'controlling' people such as Zoe Parker's mum.

Now it's been outsourced to people like me.

IT'S PROBABLY JUST CANNABIS-SCENTED DEODORANT

MARTIN'S IN EARLY THIS morning, twitching like Bill Oddy on crystal meth.

'Have you seen the biscuits?' he says, holding out an empty tin and breathing hard.

'No,' I say.

'The tin's empty,' he says, superfluously. 'There was a pack and a half of Boasters and some Highland Shortbread in it when I left.'

'Strange,' I say. 'Perry's back from hospital and I saw him hanging around on his crutches…?'

Martin snorts himself into, and then out of, quite a major spasm, and makes to go back into his office.

'Martin,' I say. 'While I think about it, I was talking to Jasper over at e2e yesterday…'

I relate the conversation I've had, majoring on Jasper's concerns about residents and non-residents using the Project as a cannabis den during the day, with the adverse educational effects that ensue.

It's clear that the mysterious disappearance of his biscuits has stiffened Martin's resolve.

'I'll get the drug dog in,' he says, and vanishes into his inner sanctum.

From time to time, we call our local cops and they send round an Alsatian and it walks around the corridors for a bit (with a handler). They've never found anything – not least because Martin insists on us putting up notices giving everyone three hours' notice of a visit – but it freaks some of our problem cases out slightly and lets them know we're on their cases. Personally, I'd prefer it if we did it without the warning notices, but I suppose the notices do at least let those who weren't here know the dog has been in. Plus if we didn't give advance warning, the large number of subsequent evictions would reveal the scale of the drug problem on the premises, whereas maybe we'd rather hide it.

Don't get me wrong, I'm not really into making people homeless for smoking weed. I certainly wouldn't kick someone out of a flat I personally owned for smoking – to me, it's a less harmful drug than alcohol – but I don't own the Project so I don't make the rules, and part of what we're supposed to be doing here is habituating people to rules (or 'policies').

In my experience, there's two kinds of potheads. There are the thinkers and philosophers who wear trench coats or shroom t-shirts, read a lot and listen to slightly leftfield music on their iPods, and think about stuff; and there are your chavvy scum who just like smoking dope. We have both sorts in abundance.

I flatter myself that I can spot each and every one of them a mile off on their first day at the Project. I tend to take the more cerebral ones to one side and say, 'Right, just to let you know, you can't smoke weed in here. We'll be walking around and if we smell it you'll get one warning. If we smell it a second time, you'll get evicted.'

Then I look up and down the corridor, to see who's in earshot, and say, 'OK, that's the *official* chat. Now here's the unofficial line. I know you're stoned all the time, I've been there myself, you might as well have a cannabis leaf tattooed on your forehead. Now, there's a great big park two streets over. I'm not saying you should do this – in fact, I think you *shouldn't* do it, it's destructive to you, the amount of drugs you obviously take – but you seem like a nice enough fella, I wouldn't like to see you sleeping in a doorway, so if you *have* to smoke weed, why don't you take a walk through the park there and do it discreetly? And we didn't have this conversation, right?'

The thinkers, 90 per cent of the time they just listen quietly and they get it. They respect the fact that you've been there and done it yourself. Of course, they're still smoking in their rooms at 3am, but they're not going to get caught then, as long as they keep it low key.

Then there are the other types – the guys in the Kappa and Fila tracksuits. (I'm stereotyping, but, honestly, it's true.) With those guys, I give them exactly the same chat. The difference is that, unlike their more thoughtful brethren, they immediately go on the defensive and deny everything, even as they continue to smoke weed on the premises. Inevitably, you find yourself evicting them a month later, at which point they get all stroppy.

* * * * *

The drug dog comes and goes without a collar, so to speak. Half an hour later, I'm up on the top floor, walking along to Kenny's room to stick something under his door, when I notice the unmistakeably fruit scent of skunk emanating from June's room.

I know it can't be June smoking it, as I saw her leave the building earlier. I'm presuming that her boyfriend Jackson must be in there getting toasted, watching some of his peers on the afternoon edition of *The Jeremy Kyle Show* or *Booze Britain*. He's already on his first drug warning, and if he's caught a second time he should be evicted; then again, he should have been evicted long ago for a wide variety of offences, and he would have been if management adhered to their own rules and supported the staff a bit more.

Jackson is one of our worst residents and has been ever since he came here. He is regularly drunk and threatening to us and to other residents, he plays terrible music very loud at 3am, he has brought worse people than himself into the building and he is in significant arrears, due to failing to apply for housing benefit when he should have and regularly failing to pay his share of the rent from his jobseeker's allowance.

I knock on the door, and he opens it, pupils like saucers. He really *is* toasted. The smell is overpowering now, but he's not holding a spliff.

'Hey, Jackson,' I say. 'That smells like some good weed you have there.'

'It's wicked, man,' he says.

'Thanks,' I say, with a grin. 'Catch you later.'

I walk away, and he shuts the door. I hear it open again after I've walked about 10 paces. It occurs to me that this is a pretty good measurement of the speed of Jackson's brain, particularly when wasted: *10 steps per thought.*

'Hey Winston!' he shouts. 'It smelled like this when I got here.'

How noble of him to shift the burden of guilt on to his girlfriend.

'Anyway, it's probably just… er… cannabis-scented deodorant.'

'I'm just going to write up your second and final warning Jackson,' I call over my shoulder. I'm already imagining the conversation we keyworkers will have when his eviction is mooted. Margaret and Steve will argue that none of this is really Jackson's fault, and will suggest that his problems are related to his 'low self esteem'.

I will acknowledge that there might be something in this, and suggest that if I sat around on my arse all day, watching *Trisha*, playing on my Xbox, smoking dope and failing to sign on when I had to then I'd probably feel a bit useless myself. This will be described as 'unhelpful'.

Brendan will suggest that we are failing Jackson, not because we haven't given him the right kind of support plan but because we have failed to help him understand that life is tough and that you need to take personal responsibility and work hard if you want to get anywhere.

Jackson is following me now, chuntering to himself. As I get back down into reception, I see our local PCSO, George, walking in through the front door. He looks about 16, with a uniform that's two sizes too big and a dopey grin and has high hopes of one day graduating to the police proper. He certainly likes to adopt their mannerisms and modes of speech.

He and his mates drop by a lot and ask us if there's anything we need to tell them, or whether we have any concerns. Sure, we have concerns, but none they can deal with: the only concern that I have which is relevant to them is how long they're going to stay and waste my time. They *really* like to chat: it's either that they have nothing much to do, or that they have lots they'd like to do but are statutorily incapable of doing any of it (not having any powers of arrest and so on).

'Alright, Winston,' he says, thumbs hooked into his stab vest like the real cops on the news do as they stand outside 10 Downing Street, or guard a murder scene. 'I was in the area, just patrolling and that, and thought I'd look in and check you're all OK.'

'Hey George,' I say. 'Good to see you. Listen, can you have a word with Jackson Barnes here, please? Only, I suspect he's very recently been smoking cannabis on the premises.'

The PCSO draws himself up to his full height (about 5ft 3in) and looks the teenager up and down.

'Well?' he says to Jackson.

'Well what?' says Jackson.

'I can smell cannabis on you,' says the PCSO. 'Have you been using drugs?'

Gene Hunt or Dirty Harry he isn't. *The Famous Five* would be more help.

'What the fuck has it got to do with you, you little twat?' growls Jackson. 'You're only a fucking PCSO. You can't do anything to me anyway, so just piss off.'

Ignoring this statement of the bleeding obvious, the PCSO presses gamely on.

'I need your name and address, please,' he says, taking out a large notebook.

Asking for a name and address is just about the only power he has, and in doing so he makes himself look a bit foolish because (a) he already knows Jackson's name, as I've just told him it, and (b) he also knows Jackson's address, as he is at it.

Jackson just laughs at him. 'Fuck off,' he says.

I'm quite embarrassed for the officer. He clearly isn't sure what to do by way of a response; his mouth opens and closes like that of a goldfish as he searches for the right retort. Then, beaten, he turns on his heel and walks away, heading to our office.

'That's right,' calls Jackson, at his retreating back. 'Go away, there's nothing you can do, you don't have any power.'

And I thought that being a keyworker was the only job where you needed almost no dignity or self-respect.

'Clear off, Jackson,' I say. 'You're getting your final warning, and that's that.'

He spits and snarls a bit, but eventually heads back upstairs to seek solace in weed and plot his next move.

I walk into the office. George is sitting at my desk, which irritates me a bit because it means he plans to be here for a while. He's also grinning like nothing just happened, which irritates me even more.

'Anything I can do for you then?' he says.

Well, you have to admire his nerve.

'I don't think so, George, thanks,' I say. 'Everything's… actually, tell you what…'

I get up and walk to the window to look out into the grounds.

'Yep… you see that guy there, the one sitting on the wall smoking what looks to my untrained eye like an enormous spliff?'

George looks, and nods. 'Yep.'

'Well, he's called Gavin and he's not a resident here,' I say. 'He used to be, but we kicked him out – amazingly – because of his behaviour. Ever since, he's been hanging round, abusing the staff and the residents he doesn't like. So… can you get him to clear off?'

'Done deal,' says George, confidently. Off he walks, fingering his radio, his measured tread clearly modelled on the opening credits of *The Bill*.

I scurry back to my chair in my office to watch proceedings unfold on our CCTV monitor. He makes his way over and stands in front of Gavin. Gavin's only response is to take an enormous toke on the carrot-sized joint he's enjoying and then blow the smoke into George's face. The CCTV isn't exactly hi-definition flat screen quality, but it's good enough that I can make out the contemptuous expression on the teenager's face as he looks at the PCSO.

I can see that George is talking to Gavin, and that Gavin is replying – mostly two-word answers which look like they start with 'F'. There's some to-ing and fro-ing for a minute or two, with the PCSO pointing firmly at the pathway leading off the premises, and Gavin doing some pointing of his own. Eventually, I watch as he walks away – the plastic policeman, that is, not the teenaged dope fiend, who continues to sit on our wall, scratching his balls and puffing away on his spliff in a contented sort of way.

Later on, as the sun sinks and the streetlights buzz into pinky-orange life, one of George's colleagues, Julie, wanders in. I like Julie, but she's even worse than he is for overstaying her welcome, and is very hard to get rid of when she calls; she always demands a cup of tea and can then easily spend an hour chatting about any old nonsense or reading the paper, ensconced in the comfort (and relative safety) of our offices. Still, I enjoy teasing her a little; I particularly like asking if she has arrested any criminals lately, knowing full well that she can't. She takes it well enough, though. Lately she has taken to tearing articles out of my newspaper without asking. Perhaps that's her idea of a riposte.

So anyway, here she is again, resting on her laurels and drinking her cup of tea. The fight against crime must really wear her down.

'Hey, Julie,' I say. 'You know Eric Blair Street where loads of our residents and other undesirables tend to congregate drinking and taking drugs and generally being a nuisance to the local neighbourhood? Well, if you were to come across, say, a group of young people who were causing a serious disturbance over there, and you were concerned that they could become aggressive and posed a threat to the public, what would you do about it?'

Obviously, this is a bit of a wind-up, though the fact is that she and her fellow PCSOs are usually the only visible police presence patrolling the streets of this town on foot. They are the first line of defence, if you could call it that, against yobs.

'Well,' she says, helping herself to a biscuit and dunking it thoughtfully in her tea. 'I could approach them and ask them for their names and addresses, but often they'll say their name is Borat and they live in Kazakhstan or something similar, and then they just walk away laughing.'

'What it they're boozing and they look under age?'

'I do have the power to confiscate their alcohol,' she says. 'But there again, I've tried asking them to hand over the White Lightning or whatever and they just tell me to fuck off. There's not much I can do about that, really.'

'Can you not just arrest them, then?' I ask, innocently.

'You know we can't arrest them, Winston,' she says. 'Stop taking the piss. Mind you, if they're committing arrestable offences I *can* request that they wait with me for up to half an hour until a bobby arrives. But that doesn't get me very far. They just run off.' She pauses. 'To be honest, if I see groups of youths who are drunk and look quite menacing, I tend to stay away from them and just ring the police, and they come over if they can.'

WE GET BORED AND THEN THINGS LIKE THAT HAPPEN

IT'S 2PM ON FRIDAY, so that means it's our weekly staff meeting.

This is our chance to get together and discuss various issues related to the Project. Items No1 to about No8 on the agenda usually concern the multifarious ways in which the residents are being a pain in the arse.

As I walk in to the office, I notice there is an eerie and sombre atmosphere about the place. The staff are very quiet, and the residents all look pretty subdued.

Brendan catches my eye. 'Have you heard what's happened?' he says.

'No,' I say. 'What?'

He just shakes his head and looks away. 'You'll find out in the meeting. It's not good.'

My imagination runs wild as I walk towards the staff meeting room. Has one of our girls been raped – or one of the lads stabbed? Whatever it is, my heart is beating in dread anticipation; I can't say I'm fond of all of our inmates, but I certainly don't want any of them to come to any harm.

Once we're all seated at the big table, Martin calls us all to order with a cough and a twitch.

'Right,' he says. 'Let's start with the big news. For those of you who are not aware, there's been an incident involving several of our residents. Late last night, at about 11.30pm, there was a big police raid on the Project and two people were arrested for attempted murder.'

There's a gasp around the table from those who hadn't heard, myself included.

'According to the police, Jason and Luke were with two others who came across a young man who had fallen asleep on a bench near the public library. Some of them attacked the man with bottles. He was beaten about the head and body repeatedly. One of the group filmed the whole incident on his phone, apparently.'

He pauses, and looks shaken. He's a very caring man, Martin, and he's obviously struggling to find the words to describe this act of random barbarity.

'How's the victim?' asks Steve.

'It's too early to say if he'll live,' says Martin. 'But even if he does, the doctors say he will remain in a persistent vegetative state.'

I sit, there utterly shocked; for once, there's no joking and banter, or sarcastic cracks. Martin goes on to outline what is happening to the two arrested residents, and what our role is from here on in, which is basically to reassure the other kids in the place and assist the cops in any way we can.

The meeting comes to a close after about five minutes: somehow, the state of the fridges in the kitchens doesn't seem all that significant right now. The run-of-the-mill criminality of lads like Perry has also been put into perspective.

Later, I'm on duty with Steve. He's a good lad in his early 20s who sees the best in everyone, and believes that all of the problems we experience with young people can be solved by listening to them talk about their feelings. Some would say he's your classic bleeding heart; since I used to hold a lot of the views he holds, I think myself that he just hasn't opened his eyes fully yet. We get chatting in a bit of downtime.

'The thing is, Winston,' he says, 'I can't help but feel that we could have done more to prevent this from occurring. I mean, surely we could have spotted some kind of sign and done something?'

'Like what?' I say. 'It's not like the lads in question wandered around the building with crowbars saying, "I'm so bored… I wish there was someone around so I can beat him to within an inch of his life."'

'I just think we should have intervened… somehow,' he says. 'I think… coming from their dysfunctional backgrounds, this sort of thing is almost bound to happen. I just don't think they know it's wrong, because no-one has ever told them.'

'That's horseshit, Steve,' I say. 'With the greatest of respect. Do you think that if someone started whacking *them* about the head they wouldn't think it was wrong? OK, I accept that upbringing and background and that all play a part in everything we do, but there are limits. The decision to walk up to that kid and start smashing him over the head with bottles was theirs and theirs alone. If it's down to the fact that they're from broken homes and haven't got jobs and all that baloney, why doesn't every kid like that do this sort of thing?'

'I don't know,' says Steve. 'I just think we could have done more.'

'I don't think I personally could have done anything to stop them unless I was there,' I say. 'And if I *had* been there I'd probably be lying on a ventilator next to the poor guy right now.'

Steve wanders off, shaking his head. I share his despair at what has happened – just not his sense of responsibility. His position isn't unusual: I regularly listen to other excuses for all sorts of anti-social behaviour from colleagues in the social care sector, and very few of them hold any logical water as far as I can see. I studied sociology, so I'm not unfamiliar with the arguments – they just don't survive contact with life outside the lecture theatre in my opinion.

I lose count of the number of times I've been told that one of our recidivist thieves who has been caught breaking into someone else's house and taking their stuff is only doing it because he is poor but lives in a materialistic and consumer-driven society, and because he is unable to realise the norms of our materialistic culture or achieve the same levels of wealth as others due to an inherent and systemic inequality.

Lots of my colleagues in the social sector actually believe this stuff, too. I don't, for several reasons.

First, the 'poor' with whom I work are not really poor at all. They have free bedsits with central heating and all their bills paid. Depending on the type of benefits they're on, many have more disposable income than the staff who work with them. Most have TVs, microwaves, toasters, DVD players, video game consoles and flash mobile phones. They eat processed food – which is more expensive than fresh – and somehow find the dough for dope, other drugs and drink. They have access to free health care, libraries, sports facilities and education (which would cost tens of thousands of pounds if they had to pay for them). Compare that with the grinding lives of people in the north of England during the 1930s, as described by George Orwell in *The Road to Wigan Pier*: they *were* poor.

Second, almost *all* of us are poorer than someone. I myself earn several thousand pounds under the average UK salary, and have less cash in my pocket than some of my own clients; why are my colleagues and I not out robbing from the better off?

I agree that we live in a grossly unequal society and there are many things I would like to see changed. But when the underclass commits crime, it is usually against decent, working class people or the lower middle classes, often elderly, whom they live beside. They aren't beating up judges, MPs and senior policemen, who can afford to live far away, protected by state-of-the-art security systems.

As I'm ruminating on all of this, in walks Jonny, an 18-year-old lad who was in court today for vandalising a bus shelter. He was acquitted, though he happily admits his guilt in private.

We chat for a few moments about the terrible events of the previous night, and he actually looks quite upset. But when we turn to his own good fortune, his mood lightens.

'You had a bit of a result there today, Jonny,' I say.

'Yeah,' he says, grinning. 'My brief got them to drop the ID evidence from the two old boys who saw me smashing the thing up because he said it was at night so they weren't reliable.'

'Don't you feel a bit guilty, though?' I say. 'I mean, you did do it, and it all costs money.'

'Nah,' he says. 'It's not my fault really. It's the council – they don't give us stuff to do, so we get bored and then things like that happen.'

Another classic excuse, swallowed whole by many of my colleagues: there's nothing for the kids to do, so you can't blame them for getting into mischief. The devil, after all, makes work for idle hands.

Maybe I'm hallucinating as I walk from the station to work each morning, and I pass a skateboard park, an all-weather football pitch, a swimming pool and a youth club. In fact, I used to volunteer at the aforementioned youth club a while back. At one stage we had to close it for several weeks as lots of feral teenagers used to turn up and bully all the decent kids. There was nothing we could do about it – though some of youth workers naïvely thought they could 'reach out to them'. I left after a 16-year-old hoodlum threw a bin over my head and one of his mates lobbed a bottle at me. I was seriously tempted to give them both a shoe in the arse, but I'd have seen the inside of a cell pretty quickly and that would have been the end of what I laughingly call my career.

Like Jonny and our two attempt-murderers, this pack of ferals – who I think would make the Pope reconsider his position on abortion – had all these facilities, and yet they still behaved like yobs. When my dad was growing up poor in the 1950s in a small, rural Irish town – where there were no youth clubs or youth workers – there was next to no youth violence or youth crime. Why?

The truth is, the majority of young people in this country are not involved in crime, and manage to find plenty of things to do with themselves; even the majority of the bored ones haven't taken to shooting or stabbing their peers, setting tramps on fire or robbing, just to pass the time. It's an insult to the millions of well-behaved – if slightly sullen, withdrawn and bored – teenagers up and down the country to assume they are all potential gang members and violent thugs.

*****

Later on, Sharn takes an overdose – her first for three weeks, which is impressive – and I keywork Catriona for the first time. I interviewed her when she applied to come to the Project a couple of weeks back, and I was pretty impressed; despite a very troubled childhood, she seems a pretty well-adjusted kid. She spent her early years looking after her chronic alcoholic mother and a younger sister, before being taken into care when she was 12. The next three years were spent in and out of various foster families, with her school record full of references to problematic behaviour. But at 15, she changed the way she was behaving, realising that if she wanted anything from life she would have to go out and get it. She's now a mature and responsible 17-year-old, who is respectful, polite and considerate.

Today, we're going to work on her main 'action plan'.

She turns up bang on time at 4.30pm.

'Hi Winston,' she says. 'Can I come in?'

'Sure,' I say, gesturing at the desk opposite and opening her file. Once she's settled down, I say, 'So you're currently doing a work placement at a hairdressers' for your hairdressing course?' She needs to complete her placement as part of her qualification. 'How are you getting on with that?'

'It's going quite well, thanks,' she says. 'I'm getting loads of good experience. I don't like the boss much, he's a bit of a bully, but I just stay out of his way if I can and get on with my work. The other girls there are great, really helpful.'

'That's good to hear,' I say. 'Now, as part of the condition of you living here, you need to formulate an action plan as regards employment, your housing situation and your finances, and you need to agree that I'll be supporting you in whatever way I can to help you achieve your goals. Sound OK?'

She looks a little puzzled at this: I'm obliged to read out all this guff about action plans and my support for her in achieving her goals, even though she's already got it all sorted.

'I sort of know what I need to do and I'm doing it,' she says.

The rare sound of common sense being spoken within these four walls.

'I know,' I say. 'The thing is, it's our procedures.'

I need to get these goals written down, just as I will need to record every keywork session with Catriona from here on in; otherwise, how will we receive our funding for giving Catriona the support that she doesn't actually need?

I pull out a sheet with the heading 'Employment/Education' and the sub headings 'Overall Aims', 'Goals' and 'Action Taken'.

'So, what's your overall aim regarding work and your apprenticeship at the college?' I say.

'Er… to pass and become a hairdresser.'

I write her obvious response down.

'OK,' I say. 'What action do you need to take to achieve this aim?'

'I don't understand,' she says, shooting me a confused glance.

I think she thinks it's a trick question, but it isn't; every section must be completed so that the government regulators from Supporting People don't find any gaps when they come around snooping in the file.

'I tell you what, Catriona,' I say, 'why don't I write in the action section that your goal is to go in to work and college every day?'

'Er,' she says, 'OK. But I'm already doing all that.'

She's looking at me as if I'm mad for asking her this stuff. Maybe I am. I also get the impression she feels quite patronised by these questions, and I don't blame her.

I move on to other sections of the action plan, explaining her housing options when she leaves our project after her two years is up.

'You should put your name down on the social housing waiting list with the council,' I say. 'You'll get some priority status because you're a care leaver.'

I record in the action plan that her overall aim is to get her own flat by the time she leaves the Project. I write that her goal is to fill in the application form with my assistance and submit it. She's shaking her head in mild exasperation as I do this; again, I can't say I blame her. She's a motivated and intelligent young woman and this is all blindingly obvious stuff. To make matters worse, I know she's going to have to duplicate the whole process again with her 'Leaving Care Social Worker' – this social worker will need to document everything to access the costs of *her* service, too.

From this point on, I will meet Catriona once a month. I confidently predict that none of these meetings will be necessary, and that there will be nothing new to write in her support plan, because she needs no support. So every month I will write the same thing, that she is doing well and achieving her own goals and aims.

To a certain extent, I feel like I am complicit in a giant, legalised fraud on the taxpayer.

RIGOROUS NON-CUSTODIAL INTERVENTIONS

PERRY'S LATEST DRUNKEN escapade behind the wheel of the stolen vehicle landed him back in Youth Court a few weeks back, once his injuries had healed up enough for him to hobble there.

I'd assumed he'd now be locked up for a while, and was already mentally letting out his room. After all, he was already serving a Community Rehabilitation Order for stealing a car while drunk – an order which he had self-evidently ignored. Just giving him a different kind of order with which he would probably also fail to comply didn't seem to make much sense to me.

It turns out I was being naïve.

At court he *was* given a new order – an 'Intensive Support and Supervision Programme'. In the words of the Youth Justice Board, the government quango which oversees the youth justice system with the help of a budget of more than £500 million, and lots of staff earning £50k or £100k+ a year, this ISSP is 'the most rigorous non-custodial intervention available for young offenders', combining 'unprecedented levels of community-based surveillance with a comprehensive and sustained focus on tackling the factors that contribute to the young person's offending behaviour.'

The YJB says the ISSP will 'reduce the frequency and seriousness of offending… tackle the underlying needs [yes, their *needs*] of offenders which give rise to offending (and) provide reassurance to communities through close surveillance backed up by rigorous enforcement.'

The supervisory aspect of Perry's programme involves him being placed on a curfew between the hours of 8pm and 7am. During that time he must remain within the grounds of our complex; he has been warned that if he violates this curfew he can be brought before the courts again.

Unsurprisingly, this means nothing to Perry. Twice this week to my knowledge he has either walked out of the building after curfew or arrived back hours late, usually quite drunk and stoned.

How can this happen, given the 'unprecedented levels of community-based surveillance' he is under?

Well, that's a bit of a semantic trick, if you ask me. I'd say that being under 'close surveillance' suggests someone is watching your movements, closely. In fact, all it *actually* means is that Perry wears an electronic tag. If he wanders off at midnight (to buy drugs, burgle someone or steal a car – who knows what he gets up to?), nothing happens. No-one swoops to ask him where he thinks he's going. The tag just alerts someone in a security company somewhere. Eventually, he comes back – of his own accord, not under police escort.

Luckily, such breaches 'can lead to him coming back before the court'. Given the 'rigorous enforcement' of his order, perhaps this means he'll finally receive the custodial sentence he needs to inculcate in him the idea that there are consequences for his actions, and which the town's car-owners need to keep him out of their vehicles?

Not so much. In fact, he's breached the conditions of a tag before, was brought back before the courts and nothing happened to him at all (though if you know anything at all about our justice system this will not surprise you).

In fact, he was told that 'overall' he was 'doing well'; if they'd thanked him for not committing any more crimes (that they knew of) it wouldn't have surprised me.

The YJB asserts that these ISSPs and the rigorous enforcement thereof 'provide reassurance to communities'. I haven't asked everyone in my community whether they feel safer now that Perry is on a tag which doesn't stop him doing anything and which isn't enforced, but I suspect that they would say that they did not.

Anyway, he's has been on this ISSP for a fortnight or so now. He pops in to the office today, and we have a chat about it.

'Hey, Perry,' I say. 'How's that court order thing going? What do you actually *do* on it?'

'Well,' he says, 'I've been out picking up litter in the park a few times, but that's only for a few hours. I'm starting a course to improve my reading and writing in a couple of weeks. That lasts a few months. I also get to go paintballing, which is gonna be wicked.'

'What, if you pass the reading and writing course?'

'Nah, it don't matter whether I pass or not. I get to do lots of activities like that. It's all pretty enjoyable.'

Even given Perry's chronic inability to stop taking that which doesn't belong to him, I wouldn't agree with flogging him, say, or chopping off his hands, but I'm a bit disturbed that, as a repeat offender, he should be finding the majority of his ISSP 'enjoyable'.

'How do you mean?' I say.

'Well, last week I got to go on a radio show talking about the dangers of drink driving, which was good,' he says. 'Plus I got to make a video with a few other offenders like myself about staying out of trouble. Basically, we were role-playing, pretending to be causing trouble and then the police pretended to chase us, someone filmed it and then we watched it back.'

'What was the point of that?' I ask.

'To show us we can get in trouble with the police if we are causing a nuisance.'

'Really?'

'Yeah, mad ain't it?' he grins.

'What else have you been up to?'

'We're making a film for, like, the local film festival about young people and alcohol abuse, so I got to go out with this posh bird asking people in the streets about their views on young people and alcohol abuse, and recording it and that.'

I remember reading an article in the local paper about this. The journalist described Perry as 'a future bricklaying trainee': this is stretching the boundaries of the likely, if you ask me, but I suppose it's better than 'current unemployed car thief'.

'There's other activities as well,' he says, taking off his Nike cap and peering at the inside.

'Like what?'

'I've been fishing a few times, swimming, playing snooker. I get lunch bought for me at McDonald's. Today I went on a tour of one of them... what do you call it, where they keep cows and that?'

'Farms?'

'Yeah, that's it, a farm. Fucking stank, it did. But it was alright, like.'

I raise my eyebrows. 'Come on, Perry,' I say. 'You've got to be exaggerating?'

'I'll prove it,' he says, indignantly, clearly irked by the implication that he might be fibbing. He fishes in his back pocket and pulls out a crumpled timetable for the week. I stare at it: almost every day he gets to go on some outing or another. 'Here's me ticket for the farm,' he says, handing over a stub. 'And here's me membership card for the snooker club.'

I look at it; it is dated from last week and has been paid for by the Youth Offending Team.

'Blimey,' I say.

'Yeah,' he says. 'It's barmy really, innit? I thought I was gonna get punished. It don't make any sense.' He laughs, with a hint of incredulity. 'I ain't complaining, like, but I wouldn't have moaned if they'd given me a bit of a stretch this time.'

Obviously, he has more common sense than the bosses at the Youth Justice Board and the magistrates and judges in the courts.

I'm not averse to him doing a bit of litter-picking – bearing in mind that he and his mates drop half of it – and there's a lot of sense in helping to improve his basic educational skills. I don't even mind rewarding him for sticking at his courses. But he's had these sorts of chances before, and I'm not optimistic. There needs to be a balance between carrot and stick, and there's so much carrot here that it looks like the Youth Offending Team have mistaken Perry for a rabbit.

'Do you think you've learned anything from all this?' I say. 'I mean, have they convinced you that it's wrong to get drunk and steal cars?'

'I don't know to be honest,' he says. 'I ain't really thought about it much.'

*****

Cerys Stenson – the young girl whose mum couldn't wait to offload her, and who was angry at the size of the free room her daughter was getting – has been with us for a month or two now.

She's a decent girl, Cerys, though we're experiencing a few teething troubles with her, and her presence here is a total farce. As you know, in order for her to live at the Project and qualify for benefits, she is supposed to be estranged from her mother; we have a formal Letter of Estrangement to say this is the case. In reality, she is anything but. Ms Stenson often picks her up and takes her off up town, doing whatever it is that mothers and daughters do together when their relationships have officially 'irretrievably broken down'. Cerys also spends at least one day a week at the family home.

She is not alone in having an actual family situation which differs greatly from the official: the majority of our age 16 to 17 cohort are in a similar position, vis à vis their parents. We often see 'estranged' youths being driven off for Sunday lunch, laughing and joking with the very ma and pa whom they ostensibly cannot bear. Most end up evicted from our project. The greater personal freedom and inevitable lack of supervision or discipline amounts to the provision of more than enough rope with which to hang themselves. In many cases, the very parents from whom they are estranged help them move back out. As I see them go, I often think that these parents only want to be involved in their children's lives during the good times: Sunday lunch, a quick visit and a chat, the occasional shopping spree. As soon as there is the hint of trouble it's someone else's problem.

Anyway, I'm sitting in the office struggling with a crossword and a cheese and pickle sarnie when the phone goes. It's the deputy head from the local girls' secondary school, Polly Toynbee High.

'I'm just ringing to say we've not seen Cerys in school at all this week,' she says. 'Given her generally poor attendance record, this is concerning.'

'You're right,' I say, 'but I can't say I'm surprised. We had our concerns that this might happen if she came to live here. Unfortunately, there's nothing we can do about it – it's all there in black and white in her support plan, but if she chooses to ignore the plan we're kind of stuck.'

This is another unintended consequence of allowing parents to walk away from their responsibilities.

'She needs to be in school,' says the deputy head. 'She's a bright girl who is wasting her future.'

'I agree with you,' I say. 'Look, I'll talk to her later when I see her. And I'll ring her mum now and see if she can get through to her.'

I put the phone down and dial Ms Stenson's number. After half a dozen rings, she picks up.

'Yeah?'

'Hello, Ms Stenson? It's Winston from the Emmanuel Goldstein Project. Are you free to talk. It's about Cerys?'

'Not at the minute, love, no,' she says. 'I'm just going out.'

'It will only take a few seconds, Ms Stenson. It's really important.'

'Is it about her income support? She hasn't got any money yet. I thought you lot were supposed to help her get that sorted?'

'No,' I say, 'it's not that. Though, I have to say, Cerys only has herself to blame for that really. She missed several appointments to make the application for income support at the benefits office, but we've finally managed to get her claim made. It's being processed at the moment, and that can take about a month.'

'But she hasn't got any money,' says Ms Stenson. There's a sly and obvious suggestion in her voice. Jesus, I would just *love* to tell her to get lost, I really would. Would she be happy if I gave her cash out of my own threadbare pocket? We're getting off topic, though, so I just ignore her remark.

'I actually phoned you to talk about the fact that Cerys hasn't been going to school,' I say. 'I just thought you might like to know and I wondered if perhaps you could have a word with her? I know you see her several times a week and that she sometimes stays over.'

There's a sigh on the other end of the line. I press on.

'As it happens, I'm also concerned that she is drinking quite regularly. In fact she was very drunk last Monday night, which is a school night after all.'

Out of concern that Ms Stenson might not be able to take too much bad news at once, I refrain from mentioning that Cerys also seems to be stoned most evenings, judging by the regular stink of skunk off her clothes and her red-rimmed eyes. Or that she has befriended Perry, which means she has a fair chance of ending up dead or smashed up in a stolen car at some stage.

As it happens, her mum doesn't seem that worried anyway.

'Look,' she says, sighing heavily. 'I have enough problems of my own at the moment.'

This is the same woman who indignantly protested of her concern for her daughter a few weeks ago, following Cerys's interview. The truth is she doesn't give a monkey's: the State now cares for Cerys, and it, too, is doing a crap job.

I end the call quickly, not trusting myself to stay civil.

Later, I see Cerys walking through reception.

'Hey, Cerys,' I shout. 'Hey, could you pop in here for a sec?'

She wanders over. 'Hi, Winston,' she says, smiling openly. 'Alright?'

She's sunny-natured and never rude or abusive, so I suppose that's some credit to her mum.

'Yep, fine thanks, Cerys,' I say. 'Listen, your school rang today to say you hadn't been in all week. And look, while I'm at it, I know you've been drinking and smoking weed, and you know they're both illegal at your age and neither are exactly conducive to getting on in life. Believe me, I know.'

'I know I shouldn't be smoking and that,' she says. 'And I like going to school. It's just, I seem to not get round to going?'

'Will you at least try next week?' I say. 'If I'm on duty I don't mind giving you a knock in the morning to wake you up.'

'Yeah, thanks Winston,' she says. 'That would help.'

I ask her how she thinks she's settled in at the Project.

'You've been here a while now – are you comfortable? Everything OK?'

'I suppose,' she says. 'But you know I never wanted to leave home. My mum just wanted rid of me because of the arguments.'

'Why did you want to stay at home? Particularly, if you and your mum were always arguing?'

'It wasn't always. Just now and then. You just feel more secure in your own home… you know there are people there for you.'

I nod my head in agreement. Her words make me feel quite sad. You can see that the rejection hurts.

* * * * *

As Cerys heads off, I look out of the window and see Perry outside. Having finished his activities for the day with the Youth Offending Team, he is now cycling up the driveway on a BMX bike.

This concerns me for three reasons.

The first is that Perry doesn't own a BMX.

The second is that Perry doesn't have the income with which to purchase a BMX.

The third is that, as we know, Perry is an enthusiastic and recidivist thief.

Perhaps the YOT gave it to him as part of one of their crime reward schemes. I wouldn't be surprised. The only way to find out for sure is to ask him.

'Hey, Perry!' I say. 'Hey, can I ask, where did you get that bike?'

'Yeah, I was in that corner shop over the road,' he says. 'And the old lady working in there asked me if I wanted a bike. She said it had been sitting outside for over a week, so obviously no-one owned it. She asked me did I want it, and I said yeah.'

'Looks a bit new to have been abandoned,' I say. 'Was it not locked up?'

'How do you mean?'

'Well, if it wasn't locked up, I can't see how it would have stayed there outside the shop for a week. Someone would have nicked it.'

'Er, yeah, I mean it *was* locked up,' he says.

'So if it was locked up, that sounds like whoever owned it didn't want it moving.'

'I mean, nah, it weren't locked up,' he says. 'I dunno why no-one nicked it.'

'Did it belong to the old lady?' I say.

'Do what?' he says. 'It's a kid's bike, ain't it?'

'So what gave her the right to give it to you?'

'Yeah, I remember now,' says Perry. 'I think she said it used to belong to her grandson and he didn't want it no more.'

His eyes are flicking wildly from side to side: he is thinking on his feet, and he is not really very well-equipped for that task.

'I think you're being a bit of a Pinocchio, to be honest, Perry,' I say. 'I reckon you stole that bike.'

He squirms uncomfortably, and can't look me in the face. He doesn't respond to my accusation and changes the subject.

'Any post for me?' he says.

I dig around in the pigeonholes and hand him his post.

He takes it, and then blurts out, 'I'll say one thing, I've never burgled a house. It's not my style, I would never do that.'

I look at him, half angry, half despairing. 'Do you expect praise for that, Perry?' I say. 'Do you think we should give people credit for the crimes they haven't committed? In that case, I've never murdered anyone, so I win, because not murdering someone is better than not burgling their house.'

This bamboozles him a bit. 'What you on about?' he says.

'You're lying anyway,' I say. 'What about the old guy whose house you broke into so you could nick his car keys, and then steal his car and smash it up for him? Is he supposed to be grateful that you only robbed his car?'

'Oh, man…' says Perry. 'To be fair…'

'Did the selfish old git forget to send you a *Thank you for not ransacking my home* card?' I say.

'Stop taking the piss,' says Perry. 'That was a one-off.'

As far as we know, I think. One thing is clear, and it is that Perry is still a thief. All those fishing, snooker, swimming and excursions are not having the desired effect on his behaviour. Maybe he isn't getting enough of them: I might telephone the Youth Offending Team and suggest a weekend in Euro Disney.

ALL THESE FOREIGNERS
TAKING OUR JOBS

PERRY WANDERS BACK into the office at around 3pm with Mike, a 20-year-old mate of his who recently left the Project to move to one of the nice, one-bedroom flats in the little block out at the front of the building.

Oceania Housing Association provides them at about half the market rate: I wouldn't mind one myself – it would beat Tony's sofa – but I couldn't afford it. I don't qualify for housing benefit.

Both of them have their hands placed firmly down the fronts of their tracksuits, doing something with their testicles – sadly, not removing them.

'Has our pizza come?' says Perry, jerking out a hand for a moment to scratch his neck, twizzle his baseball cap round on his head and yawn.

'What pizza?' I say, looking at my curling home-made cheese sarnie and feeling slightly cantankerous. Bearing in mind that almost everyone here is on benefits, they do seem to have a lot of spare cash for fast food.

'We ordered a pizza half an hour ago,' says Perry. 'Has it come?'

'Deep pan, spicy pepperoni,' says Mike, helpfully.

I look around the office. 'Er, can you see or smell any pizza?'

'No,' says Perry.

'No,' says Mike.

'We ordered it half an hour ago,' repeats Perry.

'Well, it hasn't arrived yet,' I say.

'We might as well wait,' says Mike.

They shuffle out in to the reception area, nodding at Olive and still idly furgling with their bollocks and twizzling their caps.

I watch them, still slightly testy. These pizzas cost about eight quid apiece, and neither of these fellas work. Perry is an embryonic career criminal and Mike is a small-time drug dealer who flogs dope and pills to all-comers. Despite having left the Project, he's always knocking around, seeing one of the girls or visiting Perry.

Mike heads back to me. 'Hey, while I'm here, Winston,' he says, 'I need the spare keys to my flat. I've lost mine again. I might have left them in there. Give us the spare keys will you?'

'No,' I say. 'I won't give them to you, Mike.' Our residents lose dozens of sets of keys each year, and it actually gets quite irritating. Mike is one of the worst offenders. 'The last time I gave you the spare keys you lost those as well and we had to get the locks changed, at our cost. When the caretaker comes in he can go around with you and let you in, and if you want a new set you'll have to pay for them to be cut.'

'Oh, for fuck's sake...' begins Mike, but he's cut off by the sound of the buzzer. It's the pizza delivery man.

Perry answers the door and the guy walks in. He's called Ondrej – I've got to know him a bit, since he's here most days. A nice bloke, about Mike's age, he comes from the Czech Republic but speaks perfect English. I watch Mike and Perry grab the pizza box off him and chuck the money at him – literally. He bends down to pick up the tenner, fishes for change in his waist bag and then leaves.

Perry and Mike start tearing into the pizza, and I get up and walk into reception.

'Can you take that upstairs and eat it in your room, Perry?' I say. 'Other folks don't want you stinking the place out, do they?'

But he ignores me. 'That bloke really pisses me off,' he says.

'Yeah,' says Mike. 'It's taking the piss ain't it, having foreigners working here like that.'

I've heard this lots of times before – about the African women tasked with trying to make the place hygienic, the Afghan window cleaner and the various eastern Europeans working in bars and shops around the town.

'How do you mean?' I say.

'That Polish pizza guy,' says Mike. 'He's basically come over to steal all the jobs of young British workers like me. I don't agree with all these foreigners coming over here taking our jobs. It's just not right.'

Personally, I'd rather *they* stayed and Mike was stripped of his rights as a citizen, deported to an uninhabited rock in the Outer Hebrides and left to think about it for a while. However, I don't say this, as I have been trained to view Mike as a vulnerable victim of mere circumstance.

'Actually, he's Czech, Mike,' I say.

'Well, they all sound the same to me,' he says, the 21st century Alf Garnett.

'And don't you think that you are being just a little bit hypocritical? With your mum and all?'

His mum came to the UK from Colombia in the '70s, and his parents both now live and work in the Far East, where his dad has a job in the construction. (Mike's a classic of the wealthy underclass: his parents have cash, but stuck him into supported housing as a 16-year-old because they wanted to emigrate.)

The double irony is lost on him.

'Don't be stupid,' he says. 'My mum's got British kids and she's been here most of her life.'

'How do you think the locals in Abu Dhabi feel about your parents working there?'

'That's different,' he says. 'You know what I mean.'

'Sure,' I say. 'Assimilation and integration are fine for some immigrants, like your rellies, but not for Eastern European Pizza delivery men.'

'I just believe that British people should get jobs before foreigners.'

If anything, this bugs me more than his casual racism.

'I wouldn't mind you saying that sort of thing,' I say, 'if you actually got off your backside, walked down to the pizza place and asked them for a job. You moan about the Poles and the Czechs and the Afghanis and the Africans, but they're not taking your job, they're doing jobs you've decided you don't want to do.'

'Them jobs don't pay enough,' he says, 'and they're crap, anyway. If I'm going to work, I want to make good money.'

Like you do as a cannabis dealer, I think to myself. His flat has been raided by the police before; they failed to find anything, but we've seen him dealing outside the Project a few times. It's only a matter of time before he gets caught. As he has a string of other convictions for anti-social behaviour and shoplifting, he might get a few months behind bars. There wouldn't be too many tears from us if that happened: he regularly makes complaints against staff and in one instance these led to a former colleague being suspended for speaking sternly to him over contravening one of our 'authoritarian and oppressive' policies.

She was so demotivated by this experience that she resigned, and Mike openly gloated about it.

'So who would deliver your pizzas to you?' I say, 'Because most young British lads like you don't want to do those kinds of jobs, do they?'

'I just don't like all these foreigners in my country,' he says, with an air of finality. 'And I don't want to talk about this anymore. I'm going up to Kelly's room to eat this pizza.'

He slopes off with Perry in tow, and I go back into the office. From my perspective there are a lot of immigrants who are more active members of British society than the indigenous underclass who expect to be handed benefits and housing without doing a damn thing to contribute to the country they are so vociferously patriotic about.

I bend my shoulder once more to the paperwork wheel, but I'm interrupted within 30 seconds by Josh, one of our less socialised residents, who barges into the office.

'Any letters?' he says.

For someone with limited literacy skills, he is oddly interested in being written to – but then he has us to read his letters for him.

'I'll have a look,' I say. As I rummage in the post box, I notice that his nose is bleeding.

'Did you know that you have a nose bleed?' I say.

'Yeah,' he says, nonchalantly. 'I get that a lot. It's probably the ketamine.'

This is a horse tranquiliser, though it never seems to sedate Josh, who is regularly involved in violent and threatening behaviour. Maybe he needs to up his dose.

'I'd knock that on the head if I was you,' I say. 'That's dangerous gear.'

'Nah,' he says. 'I've been taking it for ages and I'm OK.'

I look at him, with blood now trickling from both nostrils. How do you reason with that kind of thinking?*

'No post Josh,' I say, and he leaves.

---

* When I worked in education, it wasn't at all unusual for 12-year-old boys openly to admit to being on drugs of one sort or another. (Or, for that matter, for girls as young as 12 openly to admit to their sexual promiscuity.) It's extremely sad.

I open his file and make a note of the conversation we've just had. Any chit-chat can be deemed 'support', and it all counts.

* * * * *

It's quiet in the Project for once, and I decide to check through a couple of housing benefit applications.

We have 66 residents, and at any one time around two thirds of them are on full HB. This is 'paid by the council', which actually means it is paid *to* the council by people who get off their arses and go to work every day, in order that the money they earn can then be dished out to people like Mike and Perry (after appropriate subtractions to ensure the continued employment of the council bureaucrats, of course).

A further dozen or so are on partial benefit (because they work part-time), and the remainder either pay their own rent or are young people recently out of residential care and thus have their rent paid by social services.

I don't begrudge the young care leavers, those residents on part-benefits or those who are really trying to find work – the benefits system is supposed to support genuine cases, they're trying to do something for themselves and given the price of buying or renting property in this country – so high it verges on the immoral – they deserve the help they're getting.

I do begrudge housing benefit being paid to those who clearly don't want to work. Even in these straitened times, there is plenty of low-skilled, low-paid employment in the area. It's foot-on-the-ladder stuff, sure enough, but everyone has to start somewhere.

I put my pen down and pick up the calculator.

Let's see… at the moment, 45 of the 66 residents we currently have in the Project and ancillary flats are receiving the full housing benefit and a further 11 are on partial HB.

The full rent at the Project is £91.50 a week, which includes all bills.

Full Housing Benefit is £84 a week, and the residents have to pay the remaining £7.50 from their jobseeker's allowance or income support, depending on which benefit they are in receipt of.

I tap the keys, and come up with an astonishing figure.

Our residents – just those on full HB – cost local taxpayers £196,560 a year.

According to a recent report by the Housing Corporation, there were 10,648 'supported housing units' in the country (as of 2006).

If we multiply that £196,560 by 10,648, we arrive at a total cost of more than £2 billion. (I accept that this is a rough calculation; some projects will be smaller than ours, others larger. But it is indicative.)

Of course, housing benefit only covers the rent. The salaries of the project workers and the layers of management are paid direct from central government, along with the capital costs associated with buying the properties and ongoing maintenance costs. The full figure must be staggering.

One interesting thing to bear in mind is that in 1996 there were 5,392 units like mine nationally. Under the last government, this number increased by 98% to that 2006 figure of more than 10,000.

Why was this?

I can only see two possibilities.

1. For some reason, relationships between parents and children deteriorated at an alarming rate over that decade.
2. For some reason, it became easier for parents to offload their children into State care.

I think it's the latter: the development of estrangement letters and the ploughing of billions into the system allowed, even encouraged, it.

At the same time as there has been this dramatic expansion, social services for the elderly have been cut at a dramatic rate. I would rather we helped old people, many of whom are infirm, many of whom fought to keep us free from fascism, many of whom have paid in to the system, than we accommodated teenagers whose parents refuse to take responsibility for them.

* * * * *

I turn back to the applications. Ironically, one is for Tony Griffin, a 19-year-old with the initiative of a tree stump.

Tony is permanently struggling to find work – if 'struggle' is the right verb. Every time he gets one, he loses it, though it might be better to say *they* lose *him*. This is usually because within a few days he decides they are 'boring' and starts ringing in sick when there is nothing wrong with him. The last-but-one-job he had he just decided he wasn't going back – didn't even write to let them know.

It being my lot in life to be Tony's keyworker, I tried to point out that this would mean he had no reference – not that it would have been particularly glowing – but he ignored this 'support'. He ignores all my support: I'd have more luck getting a stone to absorb water than I would have getting Tony to cop on to himself.

His last job was as a kitchen porter in a busy pub. I've worked as a kitchen hand myself and it's not the greatest thing in the world, but Tony was full-time and earned £170 a week.

I had a long conversation with him at the time, where I congratulated him on finding work but pointed out that, because it would mean he was no longer eligible for housing benefit, he now needed to make sure he paid his own rent.

'It's really important, Tony,' I said. 'You don't want to end up being evicted for non-payment, because it will cost you a lot more to live somewhere else. You'll have to pay your own gas, electric, council tax…'

'Yeah, man,' he said. 'Don't sweat it, I'm on it…'

I remember mentioning it to him again on his second day when I happened to see him heading off to work.

His response: 'Yeah, yeah, the rent, you're always hassling me about that. I'll get it sorted. I can't talk now, I'm late for work. I should have been there at 11.'

At that point, it was one o'clock in the afternoon.

'You only started yesterday,' I said, 'and you're late already.'

'Yeah, I know,' he said. 'I slept in. It's not my fault – I had a few friends round in my room until late. We were celebrating my new job, and I had a few beers. I didn't get to bed 'til really late, and I just didn't wake up in time.'

'Whose fault is it, then?' I asked. 'I used to work in restaurants, and I'm telling you, they'll be letting you go if you turn up late without a really good excuse, like video footage of you standing next to the corpse of a loved one. You need to wake up, or you're going to be out of work again in no time.'

He just shook his head and slammed out of the door.

Over the next few weeks, he was hopeless. Sometimes he would be late by a few hours, and other days he just wouldn't show up at all. I used to listen as he rang his boss – residents are allowed to use the office phone free of charge in relation to work, training or benefits – and gave him some absurd excuse. I reckon he only lasted as long as he did because of the entertainment value.

One day he called and said, 'It's been raining all morning, and I don't want to get wet. I'll be in soon.'

I mouthed, *Move to Arizona if you don't like rain*, but he ignored me.

Another one – a favourite he'd trot out two or three times a month – was, 'I only got five hours sleep last night as my neighbour was up until late making noise. I need to get at least seven hours sleep to feel rested, so I won't make it in today.'

I tried explaining that his employer would be unsympathetic to this, but he didn't like this support. He felt I was 'griefing' him, and hinted that he was thinking about putting in a complaint about me.

Another excuse I heard was, 'I don't get on with the chef. He picks on me and tells me I'm not doing a good job, so I'm not coming in today.'

He only used this one once, as that time they fired him summarily.

I said, 'Is it any wonder the chef picked on you? He's probably ended up washing all his own pots and pans while you're at home having your beauty sleep or worrying about the weather.'

More 'grief' that he didn't 'need'.

Of course, he was by then in big rent arrears; the housing benefit had stopped, as I'd told him it would, and he had just avoided paying his rent, handing over nominal amounts when confronted and 'hassled' about it. I felt, as I often do, like I was appearing in a non-comic version of *Groundhog Day*.

We'll be evicting him soon, but not before a huge amount of hassle. By then he'll have totted up a thousand quid or more in arrears, but we won't bother trying to recover it – we'll get it off you.

To even try to get away with excuses like these displays you might think that Tony is clearly not dialled into the frequency the rest of us are on. But that depends how you define 'the rest of us'.

Kenny Mulligan quit *his* job a few months ago because, 'I'm having a bad day remembering my ex-girlfriend and just feeling a bit down, and I don't want to go in to work.'

He'd only been there a week or two. I asked him why he didn't ring in sick instead, and he had no answer. To be honest, I sort of think he was just lazy.

Stella – having lost her job as a trainee chef for raiding the work fridge – got a new job in an office doing very basic clerical work. She'd obviously refrained from displaying her disdain for any form of authority at the interview, but a few weeks later she was fired for persistently turning up in jeans and casual clothing, despite being instructed that the office had a dress code. Of course, she thought she was being 'unfairly treated'.

If you ran a pizza takeaway and you needed a sparky new person to handle deliveries, who would you take on: Mike, Perry, Tony, Stella, Kenny, or Ondrej?

UNFORTUNATELY, I JUST
ESCALATE THE SITUATION

BIANCA THE BOOZER is one of our most problematic individuals. At 21, she is an emotionally-damaged young person who is very quick to take offence (and also to give it). A lot of it stems from the drink, with which she has major problems. But even when sober she's very rude and spiteful, and treats the staff as if we are her personal servants.

She was evicted last year, after numerous warnings and many months of being pissed and aggressive to other residents and workers. She stayed alcohol-free for several months in a drying-out hostel, re-applied to the Project and was allowed back on the strict proviso that she abstain from all intoxicants.

She was told in no uncertain terms that any deviation from this would lead to her being served immediate notice.

This didn't stop her celebrating her return by doing a late night impression of Amy Winehouse, minus the musical talent: this manifested itself in her running up and down the corridors kicking the doors of other residents and screaming at them when they answered.

She was so out of control that several of them called the police to come and arrest her; given that many of our residents hate the police and abhor 'grasses', you can see that she was putting in quite a performance. According to the conditions of her accommodation outlined above, it should have led to an immediate 28 days' notice to quit. It didn't. No surprises there.

Today she's pulling one of her usual tricks – sitting in the office demanding that I talk to her as she is 'bored'.

'I hate this place,' she says. 'There's nothing to do here.'

'Well, to be honest Bianca,' I say, 'I've got lots of stuff to get on with.' None of it actually worth doing, so I'm actually planning to spend a pleasant half-hour browsing the newspapers online. But that's by the by. 'So if you don't mind, can you leave the office?'

Brendan looks up from a report he has been trying to finish for some time. 'Yes,' he says. 'Please leave, Bianca. We must've spent an hour talking to you already.'

Actually, I've said relatively little. I've mostly been daydreaming about what I'll be doing with the few days off I have coming up. So far I haven't progressed to anything firmer than getting as far the hell away from Bianca and her ilk as my meagre earnings will take me.

'No, I'm not going,' she says, defiantly. 'The staff are here to support us and I'm bored and annoyed and I need to talk to someone. That's support. You can't make me leave the office.'

I decide that being judgmental and condescending might do the trick and allow me to return to the *Guardian* Society section, where some nice man with a beard will probably have written a piece about not being judgmental about people like Bianca.

'Listen, Bianca,' I say. 'You've been in here long enough and it's time to go. Another thing, here's a bit of advice for you. Perhaps you wouldn't be so bored and annoyed with your life if got up off your arse and *did* something. Maybe even looked for a job, or applied for a course?'

She doesn't appreciate this observation, but it does have the desired effect. She gets up, scowling, and stomps out.

My miniature triumph is short-lived, however; I soon discover that my straight-talking approach has merely the effect of 'escalating the situation', in the terminology of management.

* * * * *

Half an hour later, Bianca turns up in reception and sits there swigging from a large bottle of blue liquor.

Brendan's disappeared somewhere and there's no-one else about, so as the only member of staff in the office at the moment it falls to me to remind her that alcohol is not allowed outside of your bedroom. (The word 'remind' here is more than a bit farcical: she is reminded of this rule most days, so she is more than aware of its existence. Enforcement is what is actually needed, but that, sadly, never comes.)

I gird my loins and walk out into reception, wondering what state she'll be in. When she gets drunk, which is often, she travels through two stages. In the first, she briefly exhibits a certain jovial inebriation, and can generally be jollied along. In the second, though, she turns into a foul-mouthed, facially-contorted harpie with matted hair who emits bile and hatred to all who pass her way. She reminds me at times like these of Regan, the possessed child in *The Exorcist*.

'Good evening, Bianca,' I say. 'Bit early for that, isn't it? Besides, you know the policy about drinking and being drunk in communal areas, don't you?'

Unfortunately, the brief window of jollity has opened and shut, and she has morphed into Bad Bianca.

'Why don't you just fuck off?' she splutters.

In my head, I'm asking myself the very same question. Why *don't* I just fuck off? If my ex and I can flog our flat, I might.

'You've never liked me,' she says. 'You're always picking on me. If you don't go the fuck away, I'm going to smash this bottle over your head.'

I doubt that she would – not just yet, anyway. Her bottle of toothpaste-flavoured grog is still at least half full, and her loathing for me, while intense, doesn't match her love for booze.

But there's no point in antagonising her further, and there's nothing I can do to make her move, so I sigh and fuck off to the relative safety of the office. I say 'relative' because a window runs the whole width of the front of the room; Bianca could easily put a chair through it if her simmering rage bubbles over. Whoever designed this place can surely never have worked with violent and aggressive teenagers and young adults.

Outside, Bianca is turning her ire on her peers. They say alcohol brings out the truth and she is certainly displaying a lack of self-censorship in relating her true opinions to her fellow residents.

Overdoser Sharn has just come in to the building and is trying to shuffle discreetly past. She gets both barrels.

'Oi, you fucking loony,' she barks. 'If you want some fucking more pills just call round my room. I'll help you do the job properly. Fucking sad bitch.'

Kenny gets the same treatment a few moments later.

'You're a fucking chav bastard, you,' she opines, swigging more of her blue hatred juice. Bianca is obsessed with 'chavs', and constantly complains that she has to live alongside them. In her eyes, it is a status achieved sartorially, by the wearing of a cheap tracksuit and a baseball cap. Whilst many of our residents do dress in this manner, not all of them are wholly unpleasant. 'You're a right scumbag,' she continues. 'And you're gonna be a shit dad to that kid.'

Well, I never said she wasn't perspicacious.

Kenny shouts something back and scuttles in to the main part of the building, clearly in terror of her wrathful tongue. As I watch his Reebok-d form disappear, it occurs to me that perhaps this is why so many like him dress in sports gear. Whether it be the scene of a crime, or an act of conception, or merely a tirade of verbal abuse from a deranged drunk, the tracksuit-trainer combo is the ideal attire to aid a quick getaway.

Her next victim is poor Patrick, our affable, dishevelled, cannabis-induced psychotic (my amateur diagnosis, admittedly). Patrick is notionally a friend of Bianca's and, as she switches her attention to him, he clearly hopes he'll be able to reason with her. As he hasn't had much success in applying sane judgment to himself for some time, I don't rate his chances.

'Come on, Bianca,' he pleads. 'Let's go to my room and calm down, eh? You're only going to get yourself in trouble, maybe evicted, if you carry on like this.'

'I ain't going to your room,' she spits, swigging more blue crazy. 'I might find a rat in there or worse. You live like a pig and you smell, so fuck off.'

I watch through the window. Patrick's slightly jaundiced face betrays no signs of distress. Perhaps he accepts this as a fair cop: he does seem to enjoy living in his own filth. His room is full of rubbish, he often smells of excrement and he dresses like a scarecrow, with a rope for a belt. He often goes hungry for several days, preferring to spend all of his benefits – roughly £200 a week – on video games, alcohol and pornography. He complains of voices in his head, but the local community mental health team have assured me that he is perfectly sane and that he is mostly just lazy and his apparent psychosis is not much more than an excuse to eschew responsibility. Normally, I'd be the first to be suspicious of people using mental health labels and conditions to avoid taking responsibility for their lives. But I think going hungry, not washing for weeks on end and living in a room full of rotting leftover food is more indicative of not being too well between the ears than simply being idle. (I'm not saying he isn't also idle, of course.) When you lob in the old voices-in-the-head element... I mean, what do you have to do to be considered mad these days? (Am I allowed to use the word 'mad' anymore?)

I sit there, vicariously enjoying hearing Bianca tell it like it is. She may be a horrible little minx, but I have to say that some of her observations are spot on. It dawns on me that I am actually jealous of her freedom of speech. There are several of our residents who I'd take great pleasure in insulting; it would be nice, for a change, to be the insulter, as opposed to the insultee. Of course, in practice I would never do such a thing – not least because my job requires me to 'build constructive relationships' with them – but it's nice to have one's fantasies. They are a form of release.

I hope she has a go at Lee next; if anyone needs to hear the plain and unvarnished truth, delivered in stentorian tones, it's him.

* * * * *

I've been working at the Project for six months on a temporary contract now, and a full-time job has come up after Steve quit to go and do something less insane somewhere else.

After a long chat with Brendan, I decided to apply for the job full time. I'm sure you're wondering why I'd do something crazy like that, given that I've spent the previous however many pages moaning about the place and its denizens, so I'll tell you.

First, there *are* some decent kids here who are making the best of the pretty bad hand life has dealt them, and I like helping and supporting them.

Second, whatever the government stats show there's a big recession on, it's a job with a bit of security and I have to eat.

The application process is gruelling, to say the least. I have to go through two interviews and then make a presentation in order to 'evidence' (which I refuse to accept is a verb) that I can fill in forms and support young people in their indolence, as I have been doing since I arrived here.

There's a nice little humiliation hidden in the interviews, too; four residents are named on a 'resident interview panel', of whom two will be selected to sit alongside the management interviewers.

I could see some sense in this if they selected Catriona, or Steven, or Janie, all of whom are working hard, doing their best and getting on with their lives. But the interviews take place during working hours, when most of the decent residents are at work or college: when I look at the list of people they've selected I see that it contains several of the most dysfunctional and anti-social specimens at the Project.

To my horror, the first name I see is that of Bianca. This is quite staggering: as well as her alcohol problem and general nastiness, she has *never* held down a job. How on earth do years of sitting on your fat arse drinking cider and watching daytime telly make you an expert in human resources? If I get her, I could be in trouble.

Next up is Clyde. Although he is 23 years old, and has thus technically been an adult for the last five years, Clyde cannot keep a job (he generally lasts a couple of months, tops, before being fired), or manage his own finances. In a familiar tale, his rent arrears to the Project are a little over £800. When he was working and entitled to part housing benefit, he couldn't be arsed to make the five-minute walk to the council's office to hand in his paperwork. Since he was sacked and became re-entitled to full housing benefit, he still can't be arsed, because being arsed clashes with sleeping until late in the afternoon. He has recently lost his jobseeker's allowance too, being also unable to find himself arsed to turn up to sign on on several occasions there. Luckily for him, his girlfriend has a job and she buys all his food for him. She must be literally mad – as must anyone who thinks a guy who can't even successfully scrounge off the State ought to be given a voice in staff recruitment.

The third member of the panel is Martina. She is 17, also unemployed and also in arrears. She refuses to pay that tiny slice of her rent – all of £7.50 a week – which is not covered by Housing Benefit because it is 'unfair'. Instead, she prefers to spend all of her benefits on cigarettes and lager. Personally, I don't mind a 17-year-old having a beer now and then – I did at their age. But we have rules about underage drinking on the premises; Martina is repeatedly warned about this, and responds with venomous abuse. She's on another final warning for this at the moment.

Helpfully, I delivered it to her.

She is a regular visitor to the staff office, where she refers to us all as 'cunts', 'pricks' and 'wankers', or other variant terms of endearment. A few weeks back, when she was told that she was not allowed any more overnight guests in the building until she started paying her share of the rent, she walked into the office, yelling abuse, and flung about ten pounds in loose change in the direction of a staff member.

I warned her about that, too.

Maybe management have asked her along to swear and throw loose change at the interviewees to see how much abuse they can take? After all, the ability to take lots of crap off people like her makes up a fair old proportion of the job.

Finally, there is Gavin, another 17-year-old, who has lately taken to calling all of the staff except me 'darling'. He is actually the most functional of this assortment of misfits, but then, to be fair, the competition isn't that stiff. On the other hand, he does have a very bad temper; at least once a month he is to be heard throughout the building (and it's a huge building) arguing with his on-off boyfriend Julian (and often defending himself against Julian's quite serious physical attacks), throwing things around his room and screaming his head off. On the positive side, he does have some social skills; unlike many of the others, including Julian, he doesn't verbally abuse the staff and he does keep his benefits claims active without too much help from his keyworker. His share of the rent is always paid on time out of his jobseeker's allowance. In context of the numpties with whom he resides, he might actually seem something of an overachiever.

So at least two of the four despise me. If you didn't laugh you'd cry, so I chuckle to myself.

If the idea of allowing feckless youngsters who are utterly incapable of running their own lives to get involved in staff recruitment like this strikes you as mad, you're not the only one. But there *is* method in the madness, and it has a lot to do with government regulation and the allocation of funding to the supported housing sector. As I've mentioned, we receive a large portion of our income from the Department of Communities and Local Government's 'Supporting People' (SP) programme. As part of this, under the Quality Assessment Framework, we need to involve residents in the running of the service, and 'evidence our compliance' in this vital area. The key passage in the in-house document at our project reads as follows:

> One of the core values behind the SP review process is that service users should be involved in reviewing and shaping services wherever possible. This goes further than involving service users in choices about the service, or holding house meetings. It's about getting service

users involved in reviewing the nature of the service,
how it is run and delivered. The SP review process also
aspires to involve service users in developing policy.

If we don't 'engage with' this bullshit, we don't get the funding. It's governmental corruption, if you ask me.

After a broken night's sleep on my mate Tony's sofa – at about 3am, I realised I really do want the minimal level of job security a full-time position at the Project will offer – I'm up bright and early for my interview.

I arrive at 9am, half an hour before showtime. I'm nervous, understandably, but to my immense relief I see that project manager Martin has arranged for Clyde and Gavin to do my interview. Other candidates will have to prostrate themselves before Bianca and Martina.

About five minutes to go, and I almost choke on my own shock when Bianca saunters over to me in the reception area and upbraids me for the way I'm dressed.

'Winston,' she says, full of her own self-importance at having been selected for the panel, 'you'd think you would have dressed properly for today. You look very scruffy, and your shoes are inappropriate.'

I'm actually dressed quite well, and I debate whether to stick one of my shoes up her arse and ask her how appropriate she finds that. In the interests of trying to ensure my bills are paid, I keep my mouth shut and just ignore her. She doesn't like being ignored, so she turns the nasty dial up a notch.

'As you know, I've got some say in who gets hired for this job,' she says. 'And I will be stating that there is no way I feel you deserve it. Just thought I would let you know that, too.'

I ignore her again, biting my tongue, and she walks off, smirking.

I get called in for the interview. Martin and area business manager Tessa ask me a few things, and I recite the spiel that I more or less learned off by heart last night. Then Gavin and Clyde put two questions. One is what makes me think I would be good working with young people, and the other is what skills would I bring to the job.

I want to give them the real answers circulating in my head, but that would be counter-productive. Instead, I give them some other answer that I know the management want to hear, in which I use words like 'empower', 'support', 'action plans', 'client involvement and consultation', 'empathy', 'valuing diversity' and so on and so forth.

I feel sick to my stomach at my own complicity in this charade as I recite these buzzwords and phrases. As I talk, I search the faces of the managers for clues, but see none. I do see much movement of their pens, though, and feel quietly confident; I know how to get the right boxes ticked.

At the end, Martin thanks me and twitches. He tells me I'll know in a week or so whether I've got the job.

RACHEL, HER RIGHTS AND OUR DUTY OF CARE TOWARDS HER

IT'S GONE MIDNIGHT ON Friday and I'm back doing an extra shift at Tom Parsons House, one of our local children's residential care homes.

I'm sitting on the sofa in the living room, eyes closed, trying not to listen to the telly that churns out crap 24/7. I feel thick-headed and lethargic, like I'm coming down with something. On top of the supported housing shenanigans, and waiting to hear back about my job application, pulling a late night here is pretty knackering.

Friends often ask me whether I work such long hours for the money. I patiently point out that there isn't any money in this work, which is why I haven't been out in the last fortnight and am existing on a diet of baked beans and past-their-best-before-date Quorn burgers.

Oh, they say, it must be because it's rewarding on some level, then?

Yes, I say, on some level it *is* rewarding. I get to help a few kids who need and deserve my help, and I get to try to inculcate some sense of personal responsibility into the others.

But what really motivates me, if I'm being honest, is the genuine adrenaline rush I often experience when working with wild and unruly adolescents. In a weird kind of way, someone threatening that they are going to kill you is exciting. Of course, it helps that I rarely think they'll attempt to carry out the threat, though serious physical assaults are by no means unheard of in my line of work.

It's really just part of the job – not that they tell you about that stuff at the interview, at least not in so many words. Instead, they say that you will be 'working with challenging individuals', which you later discover is a euphemism covering everything from people who will dish out casual verbal abuse to armed psychopaths.

Rachel has just phoned. She is the morbidly-obese 16-year-old who spends half her life dodging aerosol cans hurled by her friend Sammie, and the other half chucking them. She has missed the last train home and she wants us to go and pick her up from the nearby town, a dozen miles away. I suspect this was not an accident. She knows that we have a 'duty of care' towards her, and that if we refuse her demand we could end up in trouble – possibly even sacked. It's so much easier to call out a chauffeur than sit on a late train amidst *hoi polloi*.

Sammie is still up and about, despite the fact it is well past her bedtime – 'bedtime' being a largely academic concept. (It's also past my bedtime, of course, but my needs are not relevant.)

'I want to come with you,' says Sammie. 'I'm bored.'

I'd like to refuse, but I'm overruled by a senior member of staff. They almost always capitulate to these demands: it's easier.

So Sammie, another support worker called Vic and I load ourselves into the little blue Renault and set off. Rachel has informed us she'll be waiting by the kebab shop near the clock tower, and we find her cramming the remnants of something brown and dripping into her gaping maw as we arrive.

She drops the wrapper on the floor and waddles over, through the crowds of young men squaring up to each other in short-sleeved shirts, and pissed women wobbling about in mini-dresses. Surprisingly, given that we have just driven 20 minutes out to collect her at her convenience, Rachel doesn't look as though she is exactly oozing gratitude. In fact, she looks none too pleased to see any of us, particularly me. I've been an intermittent presence in her life for some time now, and she doesn't much care for my habit of picking her up on her lack of respect for others and her absence of self-discipline. She wastes no time in making this clear.

'Why have you brought this cunt with you to pick me up?' she says. 'I'm not getting in the car with him in it.'

She turns her back on us and lights a fag.

'Come on Rach,' says Vic, pleadingly. 'Winston's alright, he's a good bloke, really.'

She's not having any of that. From time to time, she turns her head to us and spits verbal abuse in our general direction. Sammie gets out of the car to join her in this exotic yobbery. Both then hurl insults at myself and Vic; the main thrust seems to be that I should get the fuck out of the car and get myself a separate fucking taxi back to the care home.

'Do you think you should get a cab?' says Vic.

'No,' I say. 'Do you?'

'No,' he says, resignedly. 'I mean, it would be easier but…'

We sit there, two grown men inside the car, helpless.

'We mustn't escalate the situation,' says Vic, after a few minutes of drumming his thumb on the steering wheel.

Eventually, Rachel cracks first. It's started to spit with rain, and it dawns on her that maybe she isn't going to win this battle. Grudgingly, she stubs out her latest cigarette and climbs into the car, closely followed by Sammie.

My older brother enjoys extreme sports – he's a big one for kite-surfing, and claims that the adrenaline surge from pursuits like that is addictive. Pah! You know *nothing* of adrenaline until you find yourself doing 65mph on a busy motorway, at night, with a huge, deranged teenage girl kicking the driver's seat with all her might and opening and closing one of the back doors.

I'm sitting in the front passenger seat, which makes me a nice target: I receive several slaps across the head, and a clear view of the fear on Vic's face each time his seat is violently kicked from behind, causing him to jerk forward. I can see he's trying hard to concentrate on driving, rather than worry about our potentially imminent demise in a metal fireball at the side of the road.

After half a mile of this lunacy, he pulls over onto the hard shoulder.

'Right,' he says. 'I am not going to carry on driving unless this stops.'

'Sit here, then,' says Rachel. 'Fuck you. You've got to be up in six hours and I can just sleep in all day if I want.'

Actually, I'm not on duty tomorrow, but Vic is. He and I look at each other, and he turns the key. In the interests of getting some sleep, we'll risk dying in a crash: we soldier on with Rachel continuing with her mayhem in the back.

Eventually, we make it back in one piece. We have paperwork to complete now, despite the fact that we are completely head-fried and emotionally drained from driving Miss Crazy.

'Something has to be done about that, Vic,' I say. 'I mean, she could have killed all of us.'

He assures me that there will be consequences for Rachel. I go to bed, and next morning I'm up and out of there as soon as possible.

I return three days later. Rachel has indeed been punished – if you can call it that. It took the form of a two-day car ban – instituted, of course, after much form-filling and discussion. She has served the ban and this very afternoon is being driven here and there by staff.

I ask why the prohibition wasn't substantially longer, and why other privileges were not removed. After all, she put people's lives at risk.

'Rachel has her rights,' says someone, in all seriousness. 'And we have to be careful we don't bring about a conflict with our duty of care towards her.'

I walk away, shaking my head. I have no problem with the concept of 'duty of care'. Obviously, kids like Sammie, at 15, and even Rachel, at 16, need looking after, and there has to be some sort of standard that support staff like me are held to. I do think, though, that there should be a corresponding duty of responsibilities for the teenager to adhere to. To me, this is what real care is about: we should be teaching them to respect others and themselves. This involves sometimes being tough and enforcing negative consequences. But this industry is littered with people who ignore rudeness and aggression and only ever 'encourage and reward positive behaviour'. The trouble is that in failing to tackle the former they rarely get to experience the latter. They never seem to make that connection.

* * * * *

The following week I have off, but, short of cash as ever, I've arranged some more care home shifts – this time at Charrington Place, which houses three 15-year-old kids – pregnant Becky, Edwin and a lad called Liam.

Becky and Edwin aren't too bad but Liam's a different story. It would be wrong to judge him, obviously, and it would also be wholly inappropriate to speculate on his future; but if I were forced at gunpoint to do so I would imagine that it will be as an inmate of our overcrowded prison system. He is 15 years old, but he already weighs in at about 15 stones and stands around 6ft 2in tall. As well as being physically big, he has a generally aggressive outlook on life and is subject to rabid outbursts; in short, he is a nightmare to work with.

Liam came into care under Section 20 of the Children's Act 1989. This means that, unlike with a Full Care Order (Section 31 of the same Act), his mother has some say in his life: she asked for him to be taken into care, and she can withdraw him at any time. The staff live in hope. However, I don't think we should get our hopes up *too* high; this is unlikely to happen anytime soon, if at all.

I don't really blame his mum. He is a semi-feral brute, and the system that cares for him is complicit, along with his mother's lack of parenting skills, in ensuring that he remains one. I don't really blame Liam for the way he is, either: he's still only a kid, after all. I suspect that what made him that way is that his father was never around, and his mother never disciplined him. From a young age, he learned that when he threw a tantrum he would get his way. As he grew into the teenaged giant he is today, his temper tantrums became outbursts of physical violence in which he asserted power to get what he wanted. At first unwilling to deal with him, his mother eventually became literally unable, by dint of his size and strength, to control him. At that point, she palmed him off into the care system.

In a sane world, once in care he'd receive the discipline and strong authority that might sort him out, and give him some chance of becoming a decent and productive member of society, instead of the jailbird he will surely be; instead, obviously, he is indulged at every turn, as if he is somehow the main victim of his own savage behaviour. He *is* a victim of a sort, certainly, but the real victims are those he abuses and attacks – the staff, management and his peers at the care home. During the many shifts I've worked here, he has spat on me, thrown a clock at me, threatened me with a home-made flamethrower (a can of aerosol and a lighter – 'Look at you, you're fucking shitting yourself!' he laughed as he pointed it at my face) and pelted me with eggs. He's done much the same to pretty much everyone else.

This week it is my turn again.

On the Monday morning, he deigns to go to school for an hour. 'School' is actually a classroom at the care home, with a teacher provided one-to-one – expense-wise, this must be far more than an Eton education costs and, extrapolated across the country, it has to cost tens of millions. Meanwhile, good, well-behaved kids are being taught in oversized classrooms by stretched teachers. I wouldn't mind if Liam took advantage of this opportunity, but he usually doesn't. What mostly happens is the teacher turns up and waits to see if he can be bothered to see her, and often he can't. Nothing is done to force him to attend, of course. Instead, we work on a reward system; and because today he 'chose' to sit with the tutor for an hour, in the afternoon he is taken out shopping with his clothing allowance.*

He returns later with lots of new clothes, and is only averagely verbally abusive to staff for the rest of the day.

Later, well past midnight, I'm helping the two other staff on duty, Kerry and Louise, to try to settle the three kids to bed. Liam doesn't want to turn his light off, and is instead playing his stereo at close to full volume. I can only imagine the effect this has on local neighbours, though they must be used to it.

There's a plan afoot to take the trio to Alton Towers at the weekend, and I point out to him that his place on the trip is at risk if he doesn't do as he's told. Used to empty threats like this, he jeers at me.

'Bollocks,' he says. 'I'll be fucking going. I'd like to see you try and stop me.'

'It's not a question of me stopping you,' I say. 'It's a question of me refusing to take you there. You don't drive, and Alton Towers is 30 or 40 miles away. Now, I need you to make the right choice' – we have to talk like this, it's a management diktat – 'so that you get to go on the trip, yeah? I know you can make the right choice and turn your music off and go to sleep. If you don't, then I'm going to have to come in and turn it off for you, because you're disturbing your peers and preventing staff from finishing their work and getting to bed.'

'If you come in to my room, I will fucking smash you right up!' he bellows, grabbing a steel toe-capped boot in his hand.

---

* Kids in care get weekly pocket money and hundreds of pounds in annual clothes allowances, plus weekly visits to bowling alleys, cinemas, gyms, swimming pools and amusement parks. Additional 'incentives' – daily cash bribes – are also available for complying with various behaviours and standards – getting up by a certain time, brushing your teeth, behaving reasonably well, going to school and getting to bed on time. They can be earned Monday to Friday. I don't object to any of this in principle – it's only the kind of stuff many kids receive from their parents. But there is little in the way of gratitude and the money is rarely withheld, even for grossly bad behaviour.

As I've said, Liam is a big lad. He has assaulted staff on many occasions. He spits, punches, throws objects and smashes up the house several times a week and has smashed up several staff members' cars. I can take care of myself – I'm a fair-sized fellow myself, I've boxed – but at times he's very dangerous, very scary. Tonight is one of those times. He has that vacant, angry look in his eye. There may be reasons why he's like this, but at the moment I don't have the luxury of caring what they are. All I'm thinking is, *Do I go in and turn the music off myself, or what?* I know this will escalate his behaviour, and I want to avoid this, if possible, but something is going to have to be done eventually. He could go on like this till 4am, 5am, forever. It's not like he has to get up in the morning.

As I stand there weighing my options, Edwin and Becky come out of their rooms and start pleading with Liam to turn the damned stereo off. For a moment, I wonder if this might work: peer pressure often works a lot better than adult authority. But it doesn't. Instead, he turns it louder. Myself and the other staff spend another 20 minutes talking to him, cajoling and encouraging him to 'make the right choice' and praising him for the few hours during the week when he wasn't causing mayhem. None of this is working; it rarely does.

Edwin and Becky are now losing *their* tempers, and the pleading of earlier is turning to threats and insults. Suddenly, from nowhere Edwin produces a 4kg dumbbell; charging at Liam, he lets the weight fly. Liam ducks, and I know when he stands up that there is going to be trouble. He has wrecked the entire house and assaulted staff simply for being asked politely to go to school. Imagine what he is like now.

Edwin is – for once – ahead of me. Realising that he has overstepped the mark, and is now in line for a good hiding, he scurries back to his room and locks the door, taking the pregnant Becky and the two female members of staff. Liam, apoplectic with fury, pulls on his steel-toed boots, runs to Edwin's door and starts kicking in maniacally.

Pathetic as it sounds, there's not much I can do to stop him. To try to do so physically would certainly end in serious violence, quite possibly with one of us unconscious – and if it's him I'll never work in social services again, regardless of the surrounding circumstances. As calmly as I can, I ask him please to stop trying to break the door down – always with nice manners, of course, it's good for their self esteem.

'Fuck off,' he snarls, 'or you're going to get it!'

'There's a pregnant girl in there, Liam,' I say. 'She's terrified... you can hear her crying. That's not good for her or the baby.'

Liam couldn't care less. He doesn't even hear me. 'I'm going to mash you up, Edwin!' he's yelling, eyes bulging, flecks of spittle flying from his mouth. 'I'm gonna shank you, blud! I'm gonna mess you right up!'

'*I'm* gonna mash *you* up,' comes the muffled reply from Edwin, safe for now behind his locked door.

Liam races off and returns with a frying pan: I don't think he's planning make Edwin an omelette with it. Over all the banging and screaming and crying, I hear the phone ringing in the office along the corridor. I run to pick it up.

'Winston?' says a frantic voice. 'It's Louise.'

'Louise?' I say, momentarily confused. 'Louise who?'

'Louise-stuck-inside-Edwin's-room,' she says, practically sobbing. 'I'm ringing on his phone but I can't get an outside line. Can you call the police? I'm really scared. He's nearly got the door off its hinges.'

I put the phone down, call 999 and the cops arrive pretty quickly. The officers who show up are none too pleased to be there, mind you, and tell me no offences have been committed, and that I should have dealt with the scenario myself. I point out the criminal damage, the threats and the general breach of the peace, and add that we could have had a GBH or worse if I hadn't called them. I thought crime prevention was important?

They refuse to arrest Liam, but they do spent fifteen minutes talking to both him and Edwin and this seems to do the trick. As soon as they're gone, though, Liam refuses to go to bed and starts demanding a lift home to his mother's house (as he's on a S20, his mum still retains most of her rights over him). When we refuse, he demands to talk to the on-call manager – it's his right to have our decision approved by a more senior person. It's now 1.45am and we've been on duty since 8am. Kerry is on her second day straight through. Luckily, his emotional high punctured, Liam is almost as exhausted as we are. Eventually, by 2.30am, tiredness gets the better of him and he goes to bed. It has been a close call. The night could have gone so much worse.

On Tuesday morning, after four or five hours' kip, I'm called into the manager's office. Naïvely, I think maybe it's to ask how I am after the trauma and drama of the night before. This is because I have momentarily forgotten that the care system treats its frontline staff with disdain, and views them as expendable receptacles of abuse. The managers, many of them nice people, some of them not, spend their days in offices filling in forms and ticking boxes. Sometimes, they too can be at the receiving end of abuse but it's rare. The manager is upset because the incident is creating some bureaucratic issues for her.

'Winston,' she begins, 'why were the two female members of staff hiding in Edwin's room with Becky?'

'Well, it might have something to do with a 6ft 2in teenager in steel toe-capped boots running towards them with a frying pan?' I quip.

'Staff should not hide from the young people,' she says, sternly. 'By doing so, the young people learn that they are in charge of the house. Liam should have been restrained in that scenario.'

I'd like to see you try, I think. *In an ideal world he should have been restrained, sure. But then I'd have a couple of blokes my size with me, not two small, frightened women. There also wouldn't be several forms to fill out after the restraint to justify it, three suspensions and the inevitable witch-hunt of a complaints tribunal dragging on for the next three months.*

'Also,' says the manager, 'why did you call the police? There was no need to do so in these circumstances. I am going to find it very hard to justify in my report to OFSTED why the police were called for what was basically a bit of a ruckus. I mean, Liam often kicks off and he mostly never carries out his threats.'

'Yes,' I say, 'but sometimes he does carry out his threats, and in this instance Louise and I judged it wise to call the police. This was close to the worst I've seen him, and we do also have a pregnant girl in this house whose safety we must guarantee.'

'Well, it's going to be a nightmare to write up and OFSTED will not be happy.'

Obviously, the issue here is how this all fits in to the existing bureaucratic templates and the reaction of the State inspectorate, not how we control this boy and make sure he cannot hurt others. Louise and Kerry follow me in to the manager's office and are reprimanded for the manner in which we acted. No-one bothers to ask us how we're feeling.

Liam 'chooses' not to go to school for the entire day, and is weirdly rewarded for this choice by being taken for a walk in the countryside and for a relaxing rowing boat excursion on a lake at a local stately home. This is described creatively as an 'educational outing' in the paperwork at the end of the day. I can understand the teacher's rationale. Sit in a class with a feral and aggressive lout twice your size who throws things at you and insults you, or take him out walking in the fields, where with any luck he might encounter a particularly spiteful bull? I know which choice I'd be making.

Incidentally, let's look at that creative daily paperwork.

In care homes, daily log books are kept, as a statutory requirement. However, what is written in them is often extremely economical with the acutalité.

When he gets back, Liam announces that he wants to go back into town and spend more of his clothing allowance.

'Can you walk him into town, Win?' says the manager.

Liam isn't best pleased at this.

'I don't want to fucking walk,' he says. 'Get me a car.'

'Josie's out in the car,' says the manager.

'Well, get her fucking back here, then,' shouts Liam.

When he's told this won't be happening, he begins rampaging around the house. He tears several paintings off the wall, throws a plate at me and the manager (luckily, he misses), slaps the manager, spits in my face, grabs me by the throat and spends a good hour trying to kick the office door down.

At the end of this, he is solemnly informed that he has lost his £1 good behaviour incentive money for that day. Beyond that, he escapes censure; indeed, he is told that he will be taken on a trip to a nearby leisure centre on Saturday if he manages to behave until then.

Wednesday doesn't start well, when I go to wake him for school. I knock, enter and spend several minutes pleading with him to get up. He pulls the covers over his head and ignores me. It's a welcome change from the usual barrage of abuse and threats.

Eventually, I give up, go back downstairs and make an entry in the daily log book.

It states:

I went in to Liam's room and attempted to wake him. He pretended to be deaf and ignored my requests to get up.

An hour after entering this in the log, I'm called in to the office by the manager.

'What you've written here might be viewed as judgmental by social services,' says the very woman who has just been slapped, sworn at and almost brained with a flying plate by this youth. 'And it's very harsh language. You're making a presumption as to Liam's reasoning, and jumping to conclusions without being sure about the facts.'

I don't bother arguing the toss with her. I know by now that you can't expect simply to record your experiences in a working day in these journals of deceit. Social services object to anything that even hints at criticism of the young people in our charge, and frontline staff are expected to write up daily reports about the events in their respective care homes as if they inhabit some kind of morally neutral universe, where no judgments or standards exist. I was there, and I saw what I saw, but that counts for nothing. The log will be rewritten – as will a remark by another keyworker that one of the other residents was 'sulking' ('oppressive language'). This whole sector is infected with an institutional and ideological form of insanity.

Liam eventually rises at around 11am – he won't be doing school today – and shortly afterwards another worker called Dean and I catch him trying to climb out on to the roof through a Velux window. It's a three-storey house, so although we generally indulge these kids in every way possible this is judged a step too far, even for us. We shout for help, and three of us spend quite some time wrestling with Liam to keep him off the roof, grappling with his flailing legs and dodging flying fists and feet. Eventually, Dean manages to lock the window, and we release the teenager.

He stands glowering at us, and singles me out.

'I know which fucking room you sleep in, Winston,' he says, breathing hard. 'Tonight, when you're in there asleep, I'm going to kick the fucking door in and mash you up, and there won't be anything you can do about it.'

'Whatever, Liam,' I say, wondering whether I could unlock the window later, and spread goose fat all over the roof tiles. I also think about wedging a chair under the handle of the bedroom. I'm not physically scared of Liam as long as I can see him coming, but I don't fancy the idea of being attacked in my sleep.

We go our separate ways, and I don't see him again until the early evening, and Liam is tired of playing his Xbox in the lounge. I'm not surprised: the roof escapade apart, he's spent the whole bloody day on the thing.

He walks over to me. I'm on my guard, though I try not to show it.

'Hey Winston,' he says. 'Play us a game of tennis in the garden will you?'

Maybe he's forgiven me for earlier. I'm pretty knackered, having spent the day cooking him and his peers the individual meals of their choices, as well as washing up after them, doing their laundry and hanging it out to dry. (Now I know why my mum was always so shattered.) But I decide to go along with him in the hope it will tire him out. If he sleeps, instead of kicking off late into the night as he usually does, maybe the other staff members and I will get some kip, too. We badly need it, that's for sure; constantly watching your back, living and working under threat of complaints or violence and being woken up every night at all hours would leave anyone stressed and exhausted.

Out into the garden we go. I take off my shoes and leave them at the edge of the lawn, pick up a racket and knock a ball over the net. It comes back with interest: he's got the power of a young Rafa Nadal, if not the talent. We whack it to and fro for a few minutes. Naturally, Liam is winning – I wouldn't want to dispute any of his line calls, and I'm a lot keener on keeping him happy than beating him. And he is happy, because he's getting exactly what he wants.

Ten minutes into the game, though, I pull a muscle in my shoulder. It's bloody agonising, and I sink to my haunches, waiting for it to subside. Liam stands there laughing at me and generally taking the piss. After a few minutes, the pain eases but it's still pretty sore and I can't carry on.

'Liam,' I say, 'I'm sorry, but my shoulder's killing me. That's it, I'm afraid, no more tennis for me today.'

He stops grinning at my pain, and starts to look annoyed and frustrated at the fact that his plan for the afternoon has been wrecked. But he says nothing, just plonking himself down beside me in the grass, sulking.

After about five minutes, he turns to me. 'I'm sick of seeing you around here,' he says. 'I'm gonna complain to my social worker and the manager that I don't feel safe around you. I'm gonna say you're a bit creepy. Then they'll have to get rid of you.'

This is the lowest card a teenager in care can play – the threat of a false allegation of physical, sexual or psychological abuse. Inside, I'm livid. How *dare* he – how dare *any* of these kids – casually threaten to smear the very people who are paid to care for them?

These threats happen all the time, and they ruin lives. Just the suggestion of a complaint is frightening enough, and if one *is* made against you, however flimsy and ridiculous it may be, you are immediately suspended from work. The evidence is weighed against you, and even if the complaint is subsequently found to be utterly groundless, it stays on your record. It's against all natural justice.

With all this spinning round my head, I have to stay calm. I can't even raise my voice in response: this would merely be to give him ammunition. If other staff see or hear me react, when he goes on to make his bogus complaint he'll have witnesses to say they saw me shouting at him. Working in care has this corrosive effect on the truth. You become hypersensitive to possible misinterpretations of your own words and actions, and some become willing Quislings, happy to collude with lies. Of course, the kids know this and some of them take full advantage.

Instead of reacting to the threat, I call Liam's bluff.

'OK, Liam,' I say, quietly. 'You go ahead and do that if you want to. I've got an impeccable work record [this is true, by the way; I've never had any formal complaint made against me, much less upheld, anywhere] and I've worked with kids for years. I won't lose my job if you say you feel threatened by me. Though the truth is, if you're going to lie about me I'm not sure I want to come here and work with you anyway.'

He blinks at me, and looks a little disappointed. I'm guessing he thought I'd either lose my rag or start crying; he wasn't expecting this relatively robust response.

'In fact,' I say, 'how about this? I'm going to go straight away and inform the shift leader what you've just said, and I'm going to write an incident report to hand to the manager about it. So go ahead and make your allegation. To be honest, I'd rather work somewhere where the kids have manners [there are some homes where the children are great] and if I have to leave here my agency will just relocate me somewhere else.'

This is not true; as I say above, I will actually be suspended, but he doesn't know that.

Liam moves from disappointment to anger in about a third of a second. He grabs the trainers I took off earlier. 'You wanker!' he yells. 'You pussy! I'm gonna throw your shoes over the wall into next door's garden.'

Next door, by the way, is home to an ordinary couple: pray to God a care home is never relocated next to you.

'Liam,' I say, 'give me my shoes.'

'Fuck off,' he shouts. 'If you want them, come and get them.'

I'm still trying to stay as calm as possible. 'Give me my shoes, or I'll ensure that all of your recreational activities are cancelled for the weekend. You're already not getting your good behaviour incentive for today, after this.'

'Why don't you just fuck off, you cunt?' he spits, his face contorted with rage. As he does so, he moves towards me and swings my trainers at my face. I manage to duck back, and avoid the blow. It's bad enough being attacked, but when it's with your own shoes it kind of takes the biscuit. It flashes through my mind that he might pull them on and start trying to kick my arse with them, but I think he lacks the sophistication for an ironic humiliation like that.

'The reason that I don't fuck off, as you put it Liam, is that you have my shoes,' I say. 'In order to be able to fuck off I'll need them. If you give them back to me I'll gladly fuck off. In fact, you can watch me go skipping up the road, because I've had enough of your behaviour today.'

By way of a response, he lunges forward and swings the trainers as hard as he can at my face again. Initially, I dodge back, but then something inside me snaps and I decide I'm not going to take this any more. I switch from a passive acceptance of his abuse, stand my ground and stare him in the eye.

'You're not going to intimidate me any further, Liam,' I say. 'I'm one of the adults in charge around here, and you are *going* to give me my shoes. I'm not going to ask you again. If you don't give them to me, I'll take them from you.'

He steps forward and swings at me again; this time, I grab one of the trainers and, after a few seconds of struggle, I tear it from his grasp. I'm pretty pumped up with adrenaline, and I lunge forward and grab the second from his other hand.

I've backed away, trainers in hand, panting slightly, and I'm now in the living room standing by the patio door that opens onto the back garden.

The other three staff on duty have arrived on the scene.

'Winston, can you just go into the kitchen and let us deal with this from here,' says one of them. This is the classic technique (and management policy) of de-escalation, of dealing with aggression by retreating from it: if I retreat, this will allow my colleagues to calm Liam down. But I'm not going to be bullied any more, and I'm not going to let him win; for his own future well-being, he needs to learn that he cannot get his own way with foul language, violence and rage. If he doesn't learn this lesson here, in safety, then one day he'll either come up against someone bigger and nastier who will hospitalise him, or he'll seriously hurt someone else.

So I don't move. In management terms, this is 'antagonistic behaviour' and, sure enough, it does antagonise him.

He starts bouncing around, frothing at the mouth and screaming at me, 'Fuck off! Fuck off! Fuck off!'

Calmly, though I feel anything but calm, I stand at the patio doors and say, 'I'm not intimidated by you, Liam, you're a child.'

I cross my arms and hold his gaze, and at that moment he runs at me, grabs me by the throat and lifts me off my feet. As I land, he starts trying to push me back out of the house by my neck.

'I'm gonna mash you up, I'm gonna mash you up!' he's shouting, apoplectic with rage.

My three colleagues rush in and drag him away, and are just about managing to restrain him as he bellows more threats at me.

I continue to stand my ground, but suddenly, he wriggles free from the grip of the other staff and comes at me again. I walk backwards, holding his gaze, waiting for the blows to begin. I boxed as a teenager, and I'm hoping to use those skills to slip his punches, but I'm seriously worried about what will happen if he connects. At his size, he'll pack a jaw-breaker of a punch, and I don't want to spend the next three months eating through a straw. But as he comes forward, he spots a heavy potted plant sitting on the ground. He stoops, picks it up and hurls it at me. I manage to dodge it and it smashes behind me, spraying terracotta and compost everywhere on the wall and floor. If he'd caught me with it, I could have been knocked out or blinded or worse. This is getting out of hand. Luckily, the other staff have regrouped and regrabbed him, and now his fury seems to have blown itself out a bit. He's huffing and puffing, and if looks could kill I'd be a dead man, but the real anger has abated.

His anger, that is. For me, this is the final straw. Here and now, I make the decision that I'll not work in residential care homes any more.

No more assaults and threats, no more watching kids like Liam receive cash bribes and other rewards for the few minutes or hours a day they aren't misbehaving, while their violent and dangerous behaviour goes unpunished (a policy known as 'positive reinforcement', where all 'negative behaviour' goes unremarked: you can see how well this works).

It's only a matter of time before he seriously injures me, or I respond instinctively and smack him one. That might be satisfying, but it would lead me straight to court.

I've been in court before as a youth, and I didn't like it.

Skint or not, I don't need this any more. I'm out of here.

WE'RE ACTUALLY A COVER ORGANISATION FOR A SECRET GANG OF WHITE SUPREMACISTS

I'M BACK AT Emmanuel Goldstein on Monday, and Martin walks in to the office just as I'm annotating Ciaran Meacher's support plan to reflect the fact that that he is now even further behind with his rent than he was before.

'You got the job, Winston,' he says, handing over a letter. 'Congratulations. And can you have another look at the kitchens?'

I put down my pen, and look up at the grey ceiling tiles and the greeny-yellow strip lighting above his head. I feel pretty flat. A full-time job is better than agency work, especially nowadays. But there's no salary increase, and on less than twenty grand a year I'm struggling to keep my head above water financially.

'Thanks Martin,' I say. 'I'll get on it later.'

He walks out and I carry on with Ciaran.

Before lunch, the staff all get together for a big meeting to discuss our 'Valuing Diversity' policy. Like all public organisations, the Department of Communities and Local Government and the Supporting People programme both have very strong policies in this area.

To an extent, that's all good, but it does kind of get on your tits when you spend your whole life labouring under the suspicion that you're actually a cover organisation for a secret gang of white supremacists.

Martin's had to go out for some reason, so Margaret – his *de facto* No2 – chairs the Diversity Compliance meeting, kicking off once we're all settled around the long black table in the grey conference room.

'I'm quite concerned that we are currently not demonstrating a high-enough standard of compliance with this QAF,' she says.

Part of the Quality Assessment Framework supposedly measures the degree to which we are complying with regulations on diversity and anti-discriminatory practice in the workplace. Our organisation is required to demonstrate 'that there is a commitment to the values of diversity and inclusion and to practice of equal opportunity (including accessibility in its widest sense) and that the needs of black and minority ethnic service users are appropriately met.'

Once again, on the face of it this diktat sounds fine (if a bit trite). But it's also unnecessary: at a conservative estimate, I'd say that 99.99% of people working in my industry are fully signed up to it all anyway. You just don't seem to get racists and bigots applying for jobs in the social services. Bores, idlers and incompetents, yes, but not racists and bigots. Of course, no-one's going to take it at face value that we're all decent folks, because you don't get a £150,000-a-year salary and a fancy office by taking things at face value. So a huge bureaucracy has been created, to the point where the best way to prove you're not a Ku Klux Klan Grand Wizard is to make sure all your paperwork is in tip-top order. I'm not kidding, Josef Mengele could keep a job in the British State sector as long as his QAF boxes were all ticked (which they would be, of course – say what you like about the Nazis, but they were meticulous).

But since our paperwork *is* Mengelean in its tip-topness, Margaret's problem must be elsewhere.

'Not demonstrating a high-enough standard of compliance in what *way*?' says Brendan.

'Well, in particular, our project rarely houses any people from an ethnic minority background,' says Margaret, leafing through sheaves of paper, looking for something. 'I've been going through our stats, and we really need to be able to demonstrate more that we're doing all we can to ensure that ethnic minorities have fair access to our service.'

It's true that we don't have many non-white British users. In fact, we currently have only one resident from an ethnic minority background, an Iraqi refugee called Tariq.

Given that he fled a war zone and arrived here with nothing, Tariq ought to be gold dust to us – God, you could build a whole career on the back of a bloke like that! Unfortunately, he doesn't really play the game in terms of 'support'. Not for him the indigenous life of sitting around all day getting stoned, drinking cider, procreating and playing video games. Instead, he gets on with his studies, works part-time and is basically doing fine in his adopted country without spending half his time being cajoled and threatened by us. Perhaps having friends and relatives tortured by Saddam and then seeing his country descend in to internecine conflict and chaos have given him a bit of perspective.

'Ah!' says Margaret. 'Here we are. The local ethnic minority population is about two per cent, but we don't consistently have two per cent of our residents coming from an ethnic minority background. We need to be able to explain why this is the case and evidence that we have tried to turn it around. So… any suggestions?'

'Well,' says Brendan, 'we could always not beat ourselves up about a non-existent problem?'

'That's not very helpful,' says Margaret, irritably. 'I've just told you the figures, haven't I? We're non-QAF-compliant… that's hardly non-existent, is it?'

'First of all,' says Brendan, 'if our target is two per cent, then we only need – what? – 1.2 of our residents to come from an ethnic background. Assuming we can round that down, Tariq's from Iraq so it's like I said – there's no problem.'

'We can't round it down,' says Margaret.

'So how do you propose we get that additional 0.2 of a person?' says Brendan, looking slightly mystified.

'There's Zara,' I say. 'Her granddad was a Hungarian Jewish refugee during the war, so she's kind of *partially* a foreigner. Would that do?'

For a moment, Margaret seems to be considering this. Then she realises I'm being facetious.

'Now that you've been taken on full-time I think we're all expecting you to take important things like this much more seriously, Winston,' she says. 'What I propose as a plan of action is that we get in touch with various ethnic community groups and provide them with information about our service. We need to document and record the contact with these organisations as evidence that we are trying to promote fair access for all in the community. I really want us to consistently reflect the ethnic diversity as well as the gender make-up of the community.'

I sit there, grinning inside at the lunacy I'm hearing. How in the hell are we to 'reflect the ethnic diversity of the community'? Are we to descend upon the local Indian restaurants in the evening with brochures promoting our project and suggestions that the owner consider sending some of his children to live with us when they turn 16, in order that we can prove that our organisation isn't run by Nick Griffin (and justify all that lovely funding which keeps us in work)?

Margaret waffles on for a while about 'best practice' and 'gold standard' and 'inclusion' and 'paradigm shifts'; I look at Brendan and Sally (who replaced me, after I replaced Steve), who are both thinking about beer or doing the washing or which film to watch at the pictures on Friday night, and decide to speak up.

'Has it ever occurred to the people who draw up all this diversity bollocks,' I say, 'that one reason we don't get many ethnic minority residents is because lots of the ethnic minority groups in the UK today are quite traditional about family stuff? I mean, that's the nature of diversity, right? Some people see the State as the central unit of society and don't give a toss about their kids, so they're happy to palm them off to places like this where they can live surrounded by rampant drug and alcohol abuse, casual sex and STDs, domestic violence, inertia and criminal activity. On the other had, other people aren't. I know there are social problems and pathologies in all communities, but I suspect a few folks might wear it as a badge of honour that their communities are not using this place, rather than an indication that they're being discriminated against.'

Margaret is staring at me. 'I don't think any of this is very helpful,' she says.

'Maybe I'm wrong,' I say. 'But I wonder, who's going to be the next person to leave here and get themselves into a flat of their own, paid for by themselves, a proper start in life? Ciaran? Well, he's too busy getting pissed and getting into fights. Kenny? Too busy getting stoned and getting sacked. Stella? Too busy getting pissed and stoned and getting into fights and getting sacked. The next person to leave here will be Tariq, which will *really* screw our figures.'

'This is *not* very helpful,' repeats Margaret. 'I'm going to have to arrange a course for you, Winston. You definitely need to educate yourself.'

There's a bit more to-ing and fro-ing before Margaret announces something final about liaising with the community and makes a note on some paper.

Then she looks up.

'Actually, thinking about Tariq,' she says, hopefully. 'I've not spoken to him for a while. Is his English…?'

She's just itching to get Tariq an interpreter: according to the QAF, 'where necessary, service users [should be] able to communicate in forms other than English', which means providing a translation service if they don't speak the lingo.

'His English is better than ours,' says Brendan.

Margaret sighs.

I sigh, too: never mind translators, how about teaching foreign service users the official language of the country they're living in? *That* I'd sign up for. After all, it would probably help them a bit in applying for jobs or training. But nowhere in the QAF does it suggest that we should even help people to grasp the rudiments of English, because – according to the worldview of the mindlessly politically-correct zealots who formulate these regulations – this would be tantamount to discrimination.

'I'm going to put down in my notes that we need to mindshower this topic at a later date,' says Margaret, at last. 'In the meantime, can we all just be aware that this project is not fit-for-purpose if we're not serving a diverse range of people?'

She moves on to a couple of boxes of new leaflets.

'These have arrived,' she says, 'and I think they're rather good. Can we ensure that residents are made aware?'

I take one of them – it's a religious propaganda sheet – and find, not very much to my surprise, that it's hardly any different from the old ones. Something must have justified the cost of designing, printing and sending it out, but I'm not sure what.

Like the last lot, it gives addresses and directions to our nearest church, mosque, temple or synagogue, and outlines the essential tenets of dozens of religions – from Anglicanism to Zoroastrianism, basically. It *doesn't* mention that most of these deluded (my opinion) people have spent the last thousand or so years knocking the shite out of each other, or – somewhat ironically – that many of these faiths don't value diversity in quite the same way our own organisation does. I've had a quick read through the various holy books, but haven't been able to locate their 'valuing diversity' sections; I *have* come across some disturbing approaches towards homosexuals, non-believers and women.

It's all pointless, anyway. We have no Zoroastrians in the building, we never have had to the best of my knowledge and we are never likely to. In fact, 99% of our residents are utterly uninterested in religion of any kind. But as the old Welsh proverb says, Failures are but the pillars of success: we can incorporate all of this into 'key work sessions' and develop 'action plans' to document in the relevant 'support plans'. This is unlikely to result in any Damascene conversions, but it will help us to demonstrate compliance with the diversity QAF, and will also give the bureaucrats something extra to read when they come out to carry out an inspection.

In the other box there's a variety of new posters – again, not discernibly different from the previous ones – to be put up in the reception area and common rooms. Most have headers like 'How to Complain' and 'What you can expect from our Service' (naturally, there isn't one saying 'What the Project expects of Residents'). One welcomes resident involvement and input under the heading, 'All ideas are worthy'.*

They all contain illustrations of individuals from several ethnic groups, and somebody in a wheelchair, and all of these people are smiling broadly and look well-pleased with their lot. This is a typical and wilful deception, the suggestion that if you put up posters showing lots of happy and diverse people, it means that people *are* happy and diverse. The truth is that – taking the photo illustrations to their logical conclusions – the people they represent will be sharing accommodation with at least some members of the feral underclass who will be thoroughly vile to them and will generally make their lives hell while the staff do sweet FA about it. Respect for others, consideration for the weak and vulnerable and concepts of political correctness, or even basic good manners, are entirely alien to these people, and kids in wheelchairs are just fair game.

I briefly try to lighten things up.

'Hey, Margaret,' I say. 'Talking of diversity, I've noticed that there are no obviously Celtic-looking people on any of our posters – there's no pale-faced, freckly, ginger folk, to put it bluntly – and I have to say I'm minded to find this deeply offensive. I'm thinking I should forward a complaint to the Diversity Officer up at head office, asking

---

* This is not me overdoing the Orwellisms, this is very close to the actual title.

them to make up a new poster featuring a youth dressed from tip to toe in emerald green and wearing a shamrock. If they refuse, I shall draw the obvious conclusion that my own ethnicity is not being valued by the organisation.'

There's a brief pause, and a look of horror momentarily steals across her face. Then she relaxes. 'You're joking, aren't you Winston?' she says.

'I'm not *really* offended, if that's what you mean,' I say. 'But it's all rubbish, isn't it?'

She looks at me. 'I don't know what you mean,' she says. 'This is really important. It's vital that...'

But I don't listen to the rest of it. I've got bins to clean and debts to chase.

'During times of universal deceit,' I say, getting up to leave, 'telling the truth becomes a revolutionary act.'

'Don't try to make yourself look clever by quoting Shakespeare,' she says as I leave the room.

As I walk out, I hear her saying, 'That *is* Shakespeare, isn't it?'

I HAVE BEEN IDENTIFIED AS
REQUIRING RE-EDUCATION

NOW that I've moved from agency worker to being a direct employee of Oceania Housing Association – and especially given my performance in the diversity meeting – I have been identified as requiring re-education, and have been sent down to London for a 'Welcome Day' tutorial for new recruits.

In the morning, we will all be properly indoctrinated as to how wonderful and effective an organisation OHA is. In the afternoon, there's a 'workshop' on the mystical art of getting clients more involved in the running of the service.

This second part is necessary because Supporting People has recently failed us on the 'client involvement' section of our QAF review. As I hope I've made clear, I have absolutely no idea why we would want to get clients more involved in running the service: I think it would be better to start by seeing if we can get them more involved in the running of their own *lives*. But that's all far above my pay grade, and anyway there are worse ways to spend a morning than three hours in an air-conditioned Virgin train carriage listening to Bessie Banks, Jan Jones and Bileo on my MP3 player.

As I watch the countryside flash by, slightly to the alarm of the middle-aged lady sitting opposite I chuckle loudly to myself. I'm recalling the suggestion made by Posy, one of the two night workers, yesterday evening when I told her where I was going, and why.

'Being as the government are so obsessed with client involvement,' she'd said, 'why don't we just hand over the keys to the complex to Perry and Bianca and let them get on with it? After everyone murders each other and burns the place down, we can come back in and board it up.'

Sounds good to me. It would save the country a good few grand, and show a lot of these places up for what they are.

I get to London, take a deep lungful of King's Cross smog and head off to the conference, which is being held in a hotel a mile or so from the station.

I've been to plenty of similar seminars before, but this is my first Welcome Day. It's being attended by lots of other keyworkers from other Oceania projects throughout the country; judging by the sheer number of new staff here – I can't remember seeing so many Che Guevara t-shirts, dangly earrings and earnest expressions in one place since Fresher's Week at university – it seems there is a very high turnover on the frontline. I wonder why?

Despite the ironically undiverse appearance, they are a varied bunch. Some are making their first foray into the sector; others, like me, have been working through an agency with the organisation for some time, and have recently come on board officially. Finally, there are a few middle-aged folks who have worked in other jobs and who now want 'to do something meaningful' or 'put something back'. I'm no prophet, but I have a vision of them in six months' time; a few will have come to believe that they are actually helping teenagers by bribing them with money and takeaway food to learn how to traverse the welfare system and put a condom on, but most will be craving the familiar tedium of old. As I think this, I cannot suppress the uncharitable thought that it would be quicker, cheaper and more effective to deal with their charges by withdrawing their benefits and neutering them. Such thoughts sustain me through my work. We all need hope.

I pick up a polystyrene cup of weak coffee and gravitate towards a few of the older hands. Several have been working in various positions in this sector for years, and wear resigned looks. One of them tells me he is 'trying not to think about how pointless my working life is'.

'I'd love it if we were actually helping kids who actually needed helping,' says another. 'But this is all bullshit.'

Several admit that they are already hoping to jump ship at some stage.

This isn't unusual: in fact, just about the only thing I like about these workshops is that you get to hear other people's experiences of working in supported housing, and that these confirm that I'm not just some jaded, prematurely-aged cynic.

We get called into a conference room and the 'Facilitator' of the Welcome Day makes herself known and starts talking about the various values of the organisation. She talks a lot about these values, in fact, and I regret to say I cannot reproduce much of it here. I have tuned out: I cannot listen to this stuff for more than about 30 seconds at a time without risking an aneurism. However, I remain 'in the room' for long enough to report that she refers repeatedly to our residents as 'customers'.

'We need to ensure that we are helping to deliver an effective customer service to them,' she intones, gravely.

The Cambridge University online dictionary defines a 'customer' as: *a person who buys goods or a service*. It does not define a customer as: *an unemployed, dope-smoking, idle, work-dodging person who has goods or a service bought for him or her by someone else, and then has the cheek to moan endlessly about it into the bargain*.

Thus, I generally refuse to recognise the word in the context of our project.

I make two exceptions.

The first is that minority of our residents who work. They tend to be in low-paid jobs; often, after a full 40-hour week, they will end up only £50 or £60 a week better off than those who sit around on the best package of benefits, getting stoned, sleeping until the afternoon and playing video games. These working few pay rent, to the level that they can afford, with their own money. *That's* a customer.

The second exception is the taxpayer; they are also our customers, and if they knew how we were spending their wedge I think they would be asking for a refund.

At around 11am, I'm asked to deliver a 'group presentation' on how I work to ensure that our project reflects one of the organisation's key values, that of 'Openness' to our 'customers', statutory agencies and staff.

I stand there talking a lot about client involvement, client consultation meetings and all the other management manure I am actually thoroughly opposed to. I talk about it in as an objective manner as possible, trying to make clear – without saying as much – that I don't personally advocate any of this crap. I still feel like a complete phoney. There is a knot in my stomach from concealing and censoring my beliefs on the work we're involved in. I feel that I will be unable to hold this in all day; at some point, I'm bound to vent.

As the morning progresses, and the ice breaks, many of us begin to tell the truth about the services we provide.

There are staff from projects that deal solely with young offenders, or adult offenders and drug addicts. There are staff from projects like our own, which accommodate a variety of residents from basically responsible young adults who just need cheap accommodation for a while through to young offenders, druggies and thugs.

A common theme emerges, to my slight surprise: most speakers say that the people they keywork do not want the support. They just want to be housed by the State and in many cases stay on benefits or look for work when it suits them to do so.

One woman tells the Facilitator, 'It's a battle to get them to turn up to keywork meetings in the first place, and then when they do they show little or no interest in any of it. Can we get them to formulate their own action plans? No. We end up doing it for them so as to ensure we have something to show the man with the wallet from Supporting People.'

Lots of people are nodding in agreement, myself amongst them.

The Facilitator isn't quite so sure. 'The fact that our clients don't wish to engage in support to improve their lives and become responsible and productive members of society just proves that they need that support,' she says. 'We need to continue to try to deliver it to them.'

I love the circular – and empire-supporting – nature of this logic: If they want support, great, we'll deliver it. If they don't want support, we just need to offer them more support. I can see why it is attractive if your livelihood depends on the whole snowball rolling ever onward.

'What if the government decided that all vegans must eat dairy products?' says a young guy with red hair. 'And despite protestations from the vegans they just kept delivering dairy produce to their door, day in, day out, at great expense to the taxpayer?'

'Well, with respect that's a pretty ludicrous analogy,' says the Facilitator.

'But that's exactly what we're doing,' protests the guy. 'Trying to get vegans to eat cheese.'

We break for lunch. I'm only a veggie, not a vegan, so I grab a cheese sandwich and sit down in the meeting room. The table I'm at is full of newbies discussing the country's social problems. In particular, they're talking about how poverty and disadvantage are leading factors in crime, drug addiction, violence and other forms of anti-social behaviour. Several of my colleagues suggest that the impoverished backgrounds of many of our residents mean they are literally unable to live functional lives. I decide to speak up.

'If you ask me,' I say (they aren't), 'the problem isn't an abundance of poverty, it's a lack of it. If all you really want in life is a roof over your head, enough money to buy some food, a bag of weed and a bottle of vodka, and plenty of free time to watch the telly and play video games, it's all there for you, isn't it?'

'I don't think you really get it,' says a girl with half a dozen facial piercings. 'We're talking about real poverty, here.'

'How do you square that with the fact that half of the people who walk through our door can barely fit through it?' I say. 'The really poor, in Africa and India, don't tend to be morbidly obese. By any international standard, the teenagers at our place are wealthy. It's the fact that they are comfortable, and have nothing to motivate them, that's the problem. We need to go back to the days of gruel and the workhouse.'

Obviously, I'm being facetious, but shocked looks and gasps of disgust fill the room.

'Christ, I'm kidding,' I say hastily. (I don't want to be signed up for any more intensive re-education). 'I'm not advocating a return to Dickensian poverty. But how anyone can be deluded enough to believe that a person living in a clean, heated room with an en suite bathroom, access to a kitchen, all his bills paid and with endless leisure time is poor, or disadvantaged, is beyond me. They don't have lives *we* might want, sure, but they've the perfect springboard to get better lives if they'll only take the opportunities that are there for them.'

Everyone else gets up and leaves. At the table next to me, a woman in her 40s says, 'You're damn right.'

*****

In the afternoon, we have the get-together to discuss the ever-thorny issue of client involvement. As we're sitting there waiting for it to start, a Welsh guy behind me says, 'This stuff is such a load of nonsense. Most of the young people we work with won't even come to their keywork meetings, never mind get involved in "delivering and influencing the service". It's all just box-ticking.'

A woman of African origin shares his view. 'You're right,' she says. 'Client involvement is all well and good, but it's a full time job for me to ensure that all the people I keywork are maintaining the benefits they are entitled to. Most of them assume very little responsibility for this which is crazy. If people in Somalia saw this they would not know whether to laugh or cry. There, if do not work you starve.'

In fact, all around me are disgruntled keyworkers from various projects expressing their frustration at trying and failing to get their residents to engage with them.

'They don't want any support, they just want to be left alone,' says a guy who works somewhere down south.

'Yeah,' says a Geordie woman. 'Most of our residents just want somewhere cheap to live.'

Into this fog of cynicism blows a breath of fresh air in black jeans and John Lennon specs. 'Hi, everybody,' he says. 'My name's Don, and I'm the Client Involvement Officer at the Donald DeFreeze Project across town.'

He's in his 30s, with a ponytail. He seems an affable chap, but I don't trust him one bit. He grins too much and he's too damned upbeat. But then, why wouldn't he be? Oceania recently advertised for a Client Involvement Officer at between £31,000 and £34,000 per annum, with regular working hours and weekends off. I know £34k a year isn't that much, but it looks pretty good against a keyworker's salary of between £18,700 and £21,000 – especially when we work late evenings, waking nights (where you're on duty and awake all night, maybe standing in for a night worker who's sick or on holiday), sleep-ins (where you as a responsible adult stay on the premises all night, but are at least allowed to get some kip – in theory*), and lone working at weekends, with plenty of verbal abuse and threats thrown in for good measure.

---

*I dread sleep-ins. You get woken several times during the night by anti-social residents, and when you ask them to be quiet and request that unauthorised guests leave, they tell you to 'fuck off'. There's nothing you can do about. In the morning, those young people *not* involved in the disturbances complain about being kept awake until the early hours and demand that something is done. You write a warning letter, which is ignored. After three of these, you serve the perpetrators with notice of eviction. They then appeal to the area manager, who almost always overrules you. It can easily take months to kick out these troublemakers, because of the need to respect their 'rights'. For some reason, we never seem to give much of a toss about the rights of those youngsters whose lives they are making hell.

'I do recognise,' says Don, with a reassuring grin, 'that it isn't always an easy task to get clients involved, but half the battle is remaining positive.'

My battle is more with stopping myself from telling you that you have a silly fucking job, Don, I think. *A clown would have more dignity.*

He continues with more nonsense. 'In fact, when interviewed for this job I informed the panel that I actually expected to be sitting on my own in a room a lot of the time at client involvement meetings.'

At least he was honest at the interview, but it's hard to imagine a shop worker getting hired after predicting he'd spend next to no time with his customers, and that his job was therefore essentially redundant. Luckily, Don is able to turn everyday tasks into 'Client Involvement Exercises', with or without the actual involvement of clients, and this helps him tick the right boxes to ensure that he and those above him receive nice fat pay cheques every month. The fact that there is actually no need to take money from the public purse to fund a Don, or any other Client Involvement Officer, seems not to be relevant. He explains how this works.

'If you think about it, client involvement doesn't have to mean an event that takes a whole lot of planning or organisation,' he says, gesticulating wildly and flashing a slightly messianic smile at us. 'If you organise a DVD night for a few residents and get them to help you, that could easily work. It's all about being able to say that the clients have organised a social activity for the service. It's basically about empowering them.'

At which point I almost fall off my chair. They watch DVDs every bloody night in our project, for God's sake. They don't need to develop an action plan for it, and plaster the building with posters advertising the event to all and sundry.

Don asks for suggestions. Someone puts up his hand and talks about the 'Cook and Eat' nights they have at his place. I listen intently: apparently, these involve a keyworker cooking a meal with some residents and then watching them eat it. It's genius. I'm tempted to suggest 'Skinning up with your mates afternoons' – that would definitely get a high turn out (excuse the pun). But I think better of it, and look at my watch.

Only another hour or so of this left, and then I'll be back off to King's Cross.

LAURA IS STARTING
TO ENGAGE WITH US

WE'RE EVICTING TWO people today, which makes it a good day in my book.

The first is Laura Miller – the single mum who was first evicted last year, went to Cornwall, lost her council flat and then was unaccountably allowed back here.

Despite the assistance of Margaret and a very simple support plan, she ran up a whole new set of arrears.

It started almost as soon as she moved in. Despite her assurances that this time, things would be different, she quickly began refusing to pay all of her rent – nominal amounts were handed over sporadically – despite having enough money to get herself dolled up most nights so that she could hit the town with her mates.

She was working full time at first, but she left her job at the old people's home after a couple of months. When I asked her why, she said it was because she had to deal with dead people. Personally, it's the living that I have trouble with; anyway, I don't know what she expected to happen to people in their 80s and 90s – perhaps a real-life version of *Cocoon*?

Even if you leave your job voluntarily, you may still – wrongly, to my mind – be entitled to full housing benefit, if you're in receipt of jobseeker's allowance.*

But even with Margaret acting as a personal assistant, Laura couldn't manage to claim this benefit successfully (perhaps because she avoided meeting up with Margaret in order to ensure that she set herself 'the goal' and carried out 'the steps' necessary).

---

* I say 'wrongly', because it seems to me that if you walk out of a job to go on the dole then you have put yourself out of work and you ought to deal with the consequences yourself. I have recent personal experience of this. I left a job a couple of months before the contract ended because I was unhappy with the ethics of the business I was working for, and when I signed on I was asked what had happened to that job. I replied that it had 'ended'. No further questions were asked, and I was given JSA immediately. I feel slightly guilty about this, but in my defence I was a) actually seeking a job and b) intending, as I duly did, to find a new one very quickly.

A week or two back, as her arrears started to rise towards the £1,000 mark, Margaret tried to assuage the concerns of Martin the manager and the rest of the staff.

'I've finally talked to Laura,' she said, 'and she has agreed to meet me and discuss her rent situation. So at least she is starting to engage with us, which is some good news.'

I hear this sort of stuff all the time: how is it 'good news' that someone who owes us a stack of cash has agreed to have a conversation about it at a later date? The trouble is, we have such low expectations of people in the supported housing sector that we praise them for just about anything. Is it any wonder that we have the problems we do?

Anyway, whatever kind of engagement Laura agreed upon, it didn't lead to her sorting out her housing benefit claim and paying her dues. As a result, once again she has been kicked out of the Project for rent arrears and has gone back to live at her mother's again. Presumably this was an option that was always available. I think she took us for mugs.

Today's second evictee is Barry Jameson, and I can't say I'm sorry to see him go.

Although he's only 17 years old, he's a violent and unpleasant thug who has been abusing staff and other residents since he moved in. The final straw came when he assaulted his girlfriend, also a resident. They were both drunk and arguing, and she spat in his face and slapped him. By way of retaliation, he broke her arm.

If I were a betting man, I'd predict that they will be back together within the month, and that she will go on to have several children by him, in between visits to A&E.

For now, though, she is co-operating with the police; he has been arrested for this offence and will be in court again soon. (I doubt much will happen to him. He's never out of court, yet he's always on the streets and up to something.)

We've just watched him walk away, spitting and cursing, and now Sally and I are walking up to his room to prepare it for the next resident. What greets us there is disgusting, if not particularly surprising. It seems that Barry has vandalised the place as a means of expressing his inchoate anger at our intolerance of his lifestyle choices. He has carved human fertility symbols (a polite euphemism for large, naïve art penises) into the plaster on the walls. He has pulled apart the intercom system (which allows us and outside visitors to buzz residents in their rooms) and smeared raspberry jam into the wiring. He has trodden food into the carpets and also spilled bleach on them; they will need replacing. I'm no plasterer or carpet fitter or sparky, but it looks to me like there's a couple of grands'-worth of damage here.

'I'll go and call the cops, Sal,' I say. 'Do you want to make a start on clearing up?'

She looks at me. 'Thanks,' she says.

Back downstairs in the office, I ring one of our local officers.

'Hi, PC Jones?' I say. 'It's Winston Smith here, down at the Emmanuel Goldstein Project?'

'Hi Winston,' he says. 'How's it going?'

He knows us well – he's always at the Project for one reason and another.

'Alright, thanks,' I say. 'Listen, I'm calling to report criminal damage done to a room here by Barry Jameson.'

I run him through the details. It takes quite a while.

'He's a nasty little bastard, that Jameson,' says PC Jones, when I finally finish. 'But I can't see this one going anywhere, I'm afraid.'

'You can't?' I say.

'Nah,' he says. 'Did anyone see him do it? On what day did the damage occur? Were there other people in and out of his room during that day? Look, Winston knowing him and the sort he is, he probably did do it, but without conclusive evidence I can't arrest and charge him for the damage.'

'Well, we don't have any witnesses,' I say. 'We only discovered the damage after he left, and there were always lots of people in and out of his room. But he wouldn't have stayed in there with the room in that state if someone else had done it – he'd have been straight down to complain to us. Given that he had a motive, it was obviously him.'

'Yeah, *you* know that and *I* know that,' says the policeman, 'but that still isn't enough evidence to charge him. The Crown Prosecution Service would laugh at me. All he's got to say is he left his room unlocked, or a window open, and someone sneaked in. There's not a lot to go on here, I'm afraid.'

I put the phone down, disappointed but not all that surprised.

'How's it going, Winston?' says a voice behind me.

It belongs to Gene, the tutor.

'Don't ask, Gene,' I say. 'By the way, you can cross Barry Jameson off your Way Forward list.'

'Gone?' says Gene.

'Broke his girlfriend's arm and been evicted,' I say.

'Nasty,' says Gene, before disappearing.

Gene runs a series of in-house programmes aimed at 'supporting' our residents, and one of them is the 'Way Forward Award'. This is a scheme under which they get allocated points for getting a job, or enrolling on a course, or attending various other in-house workshops and training sessions, or participating in other activities.

When a resident reaches 100 points, he or she receives £20; at 200 points, a second payment of £40 is dished out. Getting a full-time job, or starting a full-time college course is worth 40 points, with the part-time equivalents of each worth 25 points. Just for *applying* for a job, or producing a CV – which you might think are the very least they ought to be doing, anyway – earns 10 points. A further 10 points are awarded each time they turn up to the various workshops or seminars run by Gene or a keyworker.

You might be wondering why we have to reward unemployed teenagers for trying to find employment but if so you haven't been paying attention up to now, and you're certainly not involved in youth work.

It doesn't just stop at points, either. Although those residents not in work or education are (technically) compelled by the conditions of their licence to attend Gene's little gatherings, they refuse unless we offer them additional bribes. These add-ons usually comprise things like take-away pizzas, a wide selection of soft drinks and lots of confectionary. The rationale behind the additional bribes – I'm speculating, as none of this is officially stated or admitted – is that the Project needs to be able to demonstrate the provision of a certain level of support to our government regulators at Supporting People. If residents fail to turn up and 'access' our support, the very existence of the service itself would come in to question. Funding could be withdrawn and people might lose their jobs.

It might not make me want to pull out my own eyeballs and eat them if the 'training' was all worthwhile. But plenty of it is utterly absurd.

Not long ago, we ran a two-hour session entitled 'Benefits', where an expert on scrounging off the State came in to instruct our clients on any additional payments that they might be entitled to. This expert is called a 'Benefits Officer'; in this little vignette, assuming you're a taxpayer, you are paying him to turn up, and you are *also* paying to bribe our residents to turn up, all so that they can be better educated in the ways of sponging from you (not forgetting, of course, that the information this guy offers is quite readily available to them anyway, if only they could be bothered to look for it).

Gene's presence is replaced by that of Bianca the Boozer.

For the past few weeks, Bianca has been keeping her head down a bit. I wish this was because she's sulking at my appointment, but it's actually because of Martin's bizarre decision to give her a DVD player and computer.

You won't be surprised to hear that I was dead against this – not least because I can't afford either myself – but it was justified as being part of our requirement to help and support her in to independent living. I tried to point out that one of the key indicators of independent living was that you buy your own consumer durables, and moreover that Bianca's refusal to turn up to any Keywork sessions, or take steps to find work, or join a course, or enrol in a training programme, mitigated against her being given stuff, but apparently I was 'out of step' with the thinking.

One beneficial side-effect of all this, though, is that Bianca now spends a lot more time in her room, rather than coming down to sit in the office to demand the staff's attention, or lounging about getting drunk and abusing people. These days, we only really see her as she passes by on her way out to the off licence to get some cans that she can drink whilst watching a DVD or playing a video game on the computer. I think we call this progress.

Just now, though, even those attractions are insufficient to keep her at bay.

'Hi, Winston,' she says, as I look up. She seems surprisingly sober, though her tongue is stained a deep blue from that vicious aquamarine filth she likes so much. 'How's it going?'

She's often amiable when she wants something, so – suspicion being the companion of mean souls – I am immediately on guard.

'Hi Bianca,' I say. 'You're looking chirpy this morning... I'm alright. Yourself?'

'Yeah, pretty good,' she says. 'Listen, I need to use your phone to ring my mum.'

Ah – here we go.

'Well,' I say, 'the thing is, as you know we're only allowed to let residents use the phone for job interviews [a rarity, sadly] or if you have an enquiry about benefits [an everyday occurrence, though often something done by the staff on behalf of the resident]. We can't let you use it for personal calls.'

Her *mien* changes instantaneously, and she storms into the office, heading for the phone.

'You're a bunch of pricks, you are,' she yells.

I have been called a prick on many occasions, but to be called a *bunch* of pricks is a new low, or high; I am actually impressed by her creative use of invective. She grabs the portable office phone from its cradle and stalks back out of the office, already dialling.

Martin opens his door. 'Everything alright?' he says.

'Phone rage,' I say. 'Don't worry, I'll handle it. I'm just going to grab it back from her. We can't have her walking all over us like this. It sets a bad precedent.'

'Aaahhh,' he says. 'I wouldn't bother. It's best to just leave it, you don't want to escalate the situation.'

Like a lot of project managers I've known, Martin believes in capitulating to aggression and bullying. If, as I try to enforce the clear and well-known rules, Bianca kicks off further, and becomes more aggressive, it will somehow be my fault for having tried to ensure our boundaries are maintained.

I say nothing, but as he goes back into his inner sanctum I reach down and pull the lead from the socket by my desk. When Bianca appears a moment or two later waving the handset and asking what's gone wrong with it, I affect an air of sincere concern crossed with impotent mystification.

* * * * *

I get back from a lunchtime stroll in the park to find a man in a suit at the front door, ringing the buzzer. He is clutching a white envelope.

I walk up the step.

'Can I help?' I say.

'Is there a Mr Kenneth Mulligan living at this address?' he asks, in a rather officious tone.

'I bet you're from the finance company he took that loan from, aren't you?' I say.

I probably shouldn't ask this – or chuckle with glee at the same time. But I can't wait to tell Kenny the good news.

'Under the Data Protection Act, I am unable to inform you of the details of my dealings with Mr Mulligan,' he says.

I touch my nose and wink at him. 'Got you,' I say. Then I open the door. 'In you come. Tell you what, you take a seat there. I'll go and get him for you. If he's up.'

This is only a half-joke. It's gone 2pm, but Kenny often sleeps until this time and later; it's only fair, given that he's often up all night on his Play Station or Xbox.

I don't bother going to Kenny's room, mind. He spends most of his time in Kirsty's, so I knock on her door.

'Kenny, are you in there?' I say.

'Yep,' he says. 'Come in, mate.'

He's sitting on the bed playing a video game. Technically, according to the conditions of his rental agreement, he should be working, studying or seeking to work or study. I look at the screen: unless he is planning to enlist in a US Marine Corps of the distant future, I don't think he's in compliance. Never mind: for once, I'm not too bothered.

'Hi Kenny,' I say. 'There's a man downstairs that wants to have a word with you. I think he's from that finance company that you took the loan from.'

Kenny's eyes remain fixed on the screen, and his thumbs are a blur. This is disappointing: he doesn't seem fazed at all. While simultaneously running through an urban dystopia shooting enemy robot soldiers, he dictates to me how I should deal with the situation.

'Just tell him I'm not in will you, mate,' he barks. 'I don't want to see the bastard.'

Kenny is an untruthful person, and he has no scruples about roping others into to his web of deceit. Indeed, he often seems keen to do so. The other week he wanted me to ring the Jobcentre and complain that they hadn't told him his signing-on date had changed. (They had – he had just forgotten. I declined to make the call, and instead joshed him for failing even to successfully draw the dole.)

'Kenny,' I say, raising my voice to be heard over the on-screen mayhem, 'I'm not lying for you here. Did I not warn you that this would happen if you took out that loan? As part of my job to support you towards independent living, I advise you to go down and deal with the consequences of your actions. *Independently*.'

'Well, tell him what you fucking want then, Win,' shouts Kenny, still bashing away on the control pad and concentrating on his flickering, 2D alternate reality. 'I don't give a fuck and I ain't going down there to see him or anyone else. I'm fucking busy.'

Almost three years of supported housing have done Kenny the world of good. While you and I are out working to pay for his very comfortable accommodation, complete with a butler like me, he's free to sit around on his backside playing games. It's also nice to know that the cavalier attitude to loans and debts exhibited by him and tens of thousands like him will result in higher rates for us if we ever need to borrow money.

I head back down to the reception and walk across to the debt collector.

'Kenny's in,' I say, 'but he is too busy playing video games to come and speak to you.'

'Could you please give him this letter?' says the guy.

'With pleasure,' I say. 'But if it's being paid back you want, I wouldn't get your hopes up.'

THE LEPRECHAUN STRIKES BACK

BACK IN THE OFFICE, I dig out Kenny's file to check his situation with us.

It's been a good month now since I gave him his second official warning for non-payment of rent and warned him to make sure he submitted all the required documentation to the good folks at housing benefit. I wonder if he has?

Call me a cynic, but I don't have a lot of faith in Kenny so I decide to telephone the lady at the council who processes all the claims for our residents.

'Hi Winston,' she says, when I get hold of her and explain why I'm calling. 'Just let me check…' I hear fingers tapping on a keyboard. 'Ah, here we are,' she says. 'Mulligan, Kenneth. No, I'm afraid we haven't had his paperwork in so we've closed the application.'

Later, I see Kenny passing by the office. I spring up from my chair and run to the door to call him in. I decide to give him enough rope to hang himself, metaphorically-speaking.

'So, Kenny,' I say, 'did you manage to get all the documentation you needed in to the housing benefit office?'

'Yeah,' he says. 'Yeah, I got it all in… they said they'll be making a payment next week and that will clear a lot of my arrears as well.'

'That's funny, because I was just talking to them and they don't have anything from you?'

'Oh, man, what?' he says. 'Oh, man, no way. I swear I dropped it in. They must have lost it.'

If he doesn't start telling me the truth, I'll be the one losing it in a minute.

'Kenny, stop the bullshit, I don't believe you. Here's how I see it. You didn't get around to filling in the change of circumstances form as you don't like forms and you just put it out of your head and forgot about it, and you've been too busy enjoying yourself with the cash from the bogus loan you also haven't paid off to bother to deal with the massive rent arrears you have here. You probably thought the nominal payment you made us would keep us off your back for a while.'

He shakes his head. 'Nah, I swear…' he says.

170

'Your rent is due every week, and if you don't pay it every week your debt increases. What is it about this that you don't understand? You know you're on a second warning already.'

'Look, Winston...' he says.

'Look nothing,' I say. 'Knowing you, you probably told yourself you'd do it tomorrow, and tomorrow never came. This is it, Kenny, you've had all your chances with us. You've been chased and asked and warned and had official letters and the upshot is, you've shown yourself to be untrustworthy in sorting out your benefits.' I reach for my note pad. 'I'm giving you 28 days' notice now. You are out of here at the end of the month. However, I will withdraw it under the following conditions. You need to reapply for housing benefit all over again. You can request to be backdated to your original claim date, but you will have to write them a letter explaining why you failed to successfully submit all the documentation they repeatedly asked you for. Don't just say you forgot, either. *If* you get the housing benefit sorted, we'll sit down and do a repayment plan for the portion of arrears that you will have to pay from jobseeker's allowance, or a job if you manage to get one. *If* this is all done and dusted within the notice period, and the council agrees to pay off a large portion of your arrears, and if *you* pay some as well, then I will suspend the notice. I'll also be in touch with the housing benefit office to ensure that you get them everything they need. If you tell me *one* lie, or fail to get them everything they request, I will let the notice run and you *will* be evicted. Do you understand?'

'Yeah, I do,' he admits sheepishly. 'I know I've messed up. I'll sort it out.'

On the upside, at least Kenny is rarely abusive and never violent: I'd have been wary of having a conversation like this on my own with some of our other residents.

On the downside, while he'll happily admit his faults, he seems almost incapable of doing anything to correct them. In a way, it's not really his fault. In all his time living in supported housing he's had a State employee 'supporting' him to access his benefits and look for and maintain work. Along with becoming habituated to other people doing almost everything for him, he is also accustomed to facing no serious consequences for any of his actions or inactions. It's a toxic mix, and it's no good for him at all in the long run. But I think he can see that this is serious, now; a looming eviction – one we're serious about – might just be the spur he needs.

'Look,' I say. 'Come back at seven o'clock and I'll have a new housing benefit application ready for you.'

Keyworkers tend to fill in about 80 per cent of these forms on behalf of the residents, the rationale being that quite a lot of the required information on the form pertains to the Project. As I've said, I think this is wrong: if Kenny wants the free money, he should book an appointment, bring the form (and a pen) and ask for the information he needs. If he can't be arsed, as far as I'm concerned he has made himself intentionally homeless; being sent back to live with his mum would probably be just the kick up the backside he needs.

The trouble is, if we rigidly enforced a rule like this, loads of the residents would just never turn up. We'd spend half our lives either chasing people or kicking them out, and the other half being hassled by management over the rent arrears. Sometimes it's just easier for us if we do most of the writing.

He ambles off to his room, having the good grace to at least look a little shamefaced, and I turn to the two-foot-thick pile of files in front of me.

To my amazement, he comes back inside half an hour to sign the new form.

*****

Next on my agenda is Barry Jameson – the tough guy who likes to break young girls' arms.

He may be gone, but he's not forgotten. He's hanging around the place like a bad smell, and a number of other residents have told me that he has been shouting abuse or threatening them as they pass by him in the street outside.

We've asked them to make statements to the police about this, but they're either afraid to do so or they don't 'do grassing'.

I call PC Jones anyway. He tells me that he cannot arrest Barry simply for being on the grounds of our premises, even if he is barred by us. Trespassing is a civil matter, and needs to be dealt with through the civil courts. If we travel down that road and spend money getting a court order ordering him to keep away, it will take months and I can safely say that he will ignore it. He could *then* be nicked for contempt of court, but what would happen to him as a result? At the most, a fine (which he won't pay) and maybe some community service (which he won't do). And he'll be back hanging around the Project before the ink on the order is dry. The fact is, the only way Barry will stop hanging around is if he gets bored.

'Hopefully,' says PC Jones, 'the next time he threatens someone they'll be prepared to make an allegation. Even better, if he threatened *you* with violence you could report it and *then* we could do something. If it went to court, it could be made a condition that he stay away from the place.'

'Any news on his girlfriend's arm?' I say.

'She's now refusing to co-operate,' he says. 'They're back together. We're looking at taking it on without her involvement but, without a statement and her giving evidence, it's going to be hard.'

It's all more than a little irritating. A violent yob who committed a very nasty assault on a fellow resident and some serious criminal damage on our premises, and is now trespassing daily and threatening people, isn't going to be prosecuted for the assault and can't even be kept away.

I put the phone down, and as I do so I see that, coincidentally, Barry is striding up the path and heading towards the door. I wonder if he's psychic? He buzzes the office. What can he want? He knows we don't want him here and keep telling him he's barred. I go to the door, hoping he threatens me so that I can call the intrepid PC Jones.

'Yes, Barry,' I say. 'I'm sure I don't need to remind you that you're barred. You shouldn't be on the grounds, so can you leave, please?'

He ignores this. 'Do us a favour, will you?' he mutters from underneath his No Fear hood. 'I'm looking for that weasel-faced cunt. You know the one.'

Actually, it's a description that applies to 30% of our residents, but he's right, I do know which particular weasel-faced gentleman he's after: Kenny, a weasel in both appearance and character.

Barry continues. 'He owes me a fucking fiver. If you get him for me, I'll piss off.'

'Why would I do you a favour?' I say. 'I had to spend half the day cleaning up your room after you left. How about *you* do *me* a favour and clear off.'

Barry isn't used to this type of directness from a worker in the social services industry. He also doesn't respond too well to adult authority figures, generally, probably because there aren't many of them around anymore. Needless to say I get a mouthful of abuse. 'Listen, just get me that fucking weasel face bastard will you,' he hisses. 'Or I'm going to lose my fucking temper.'

'No,' I say. 'Clear off, you're barred.'

Somewhat to my surprise, he turns to leave. As he shuffles away up the path towards the grounds exit, he turns and shouts, 'Why don't you just fuck right off to the end of your rainbow, you leprechaun-headed, potato-eating bastard, and find your pot of gold!'

I wave and grin, chuckling to myself as I do so. As insults go, that was actually quite a good one, and at least it displayed a bit of creativity with language. As I close the door, I reflect that it's a pity he didn't threaten me so that could have him arrested. If only there were laws against insults based on inaccurate racial stereotyping!

*****

It's a day or two later, and PC Jones is out again, looking for another resident over a misunderstanding in an electrical goods store.

After establishing that I have no idea where the young rascal is, we start chatting.

'Is Barry still hanging around causing trouble?' he asks.

'Indeed he is,' I say. 'But nothing's changed. None of the young people will talk to the police and he hasn't threatened any of us, so you won't be able to lift him for anything. Actually, he was quite funny the other day… he called me a leprechaun or something and told me to fuck off to the end of my rainbow.'

PC Jones sits up, suddenly alert.

'Hey,' he says, pulling out a pocket notebook. 'We can get him for that. I can lift him and charge him; it's a racially-motivated offence.'

'You've got to be kidding,' I say. 'I mean, I wasn't actually offended by it. You mightn't have noticed, but I'm not really a leprechaun.'

'Let me put it to you like this, Winston,' says PC Jones, intensely. 'If you perceive his outburst to be racially offensive then it is. End of story. If you make a complaint then we can arrest him and have him charged. He will then be unlikely to hang out around here in the future causing the Project trouble, as him making contact with you before any case could be construed as harassment. So let me ask you, do you feel that you were the victim of racial abuse or not?'

'Yes,' I answer. 'I suppose I was.'

I'll do anything to see the back of Barry.

PC Jones asks me some more questions, and then the wheels of justice are set in motion. I get a call later in the evening telling me they have arrested and charged Barry with a racially-motivated offence.

What a result – particularly as it's a condition of his bail that he doesn't come within 50 metres of the Project.

Later, I reflect that the law really is an ass. You can bust a girl's arm and smash up a room, and hang round spitting threats at all and sundry, and the cops can't even move you on, but you make one reference to someone as a character from the land of make-believe and you're in court the next day. It truly is weird.

A day or two later, it gets weirder still. In what must have been a bureaucratic reflex response – i.e. one involving no human independent thought or discretionary input whatsoever – the cops have forwarded the information regarding the case of Barry v The Leprechaun to the council's Racist Incident Team, which in turn has contacted me by letter and is offering me counselling, should I need it.

This actually winds me up far more than Barry's outburst ever could. Why are the council wasting my taxes by offering me counselling for being referred to as a fairy tale character? Can't they use some discretion? I'm all for anti racist initiatives – I abhor racism. But surely the race laws were developed to help vulnerable people from ethnic minority communities who are subjected to actual racist abuse or violence? As a 34-year-old man who was called a leprechaun by a semi-literate feral, I think I'll cope. Apart from anything else, I have a pot of gold to comfort me.

BEN'S CONVERSION TO SATANISM RAISES SEVERAL ETHICAL DILEMMAS

ONE OF OUR newer residents, Ben, is being led up the path of the Project in handcuffs and accompanied by PC Jones and another police officer. A man I recognise as the vice-principal of Lev Bronstein College is also present. Ben is in floods of tears and very distressed. He has a small cut on his head and a bruise near his temple.

Once he's inside the building, the cops click the cuffs off; he struggles free and runs for the stairs to his bedroom.

'Can I ask what's going on?' I say to the vice-principal.

'Ben was involved in an incident several weeks ago at college where he hit a female student,' says the V-P. 'It wasn't entirely his fault. The female student had spent weeks taunting Ben every time she saw him. On the day he lost it, as it were, she had taken to throwing mud at him for some reason. He went slightly berserk and assaulted her. And whatever the provocation, we cannot tolerate physical attacks on other students. So we excluded him.'

This is news to me.

'However, we told him he could return next year and finish the remainder of his course, provided he stays away from the college. He didn't accept this – he just keeps saying he loves the course – and he's been finding it hard to stay away. He turned up today and when he was asked to leave he lost control of himself and started running around the sports pitch screaming, hitting himself over the head with a brick and threatening to kill himself if he wasn't allowed back on his course. We called the police and they kindly came to collect him and bring him here.'

Having worked in a fairly average comprehensive school, I'm actually pretty impressed by Ben's passion for education – even if it's expressed in an unconventional, not to say slightly disturbing, manner. I see plenty of self-harming in the work I do – from people genuinely slashing and scarring their arms to others who are less serious – but none in the pursuit of bettering oneself.

The V-P and the cops leave, and I go up to talk to Ben and check he's OK. I knock on the door.

'It's Winston, Ben. Can I come in?'

I hear a muffled agreement, so open the door and walk inside.

He is attending to his pet hamster, which he adores. His course was in animal care – he loves animals and seems to prefer them to humans, struggling to bond with his peers. His parents split when he was young, and his mother suffers with bipolar disorder which affects her parenting skills. Her propensity for psychological problems has rubbed off on Ben, unfortunately: he behaves at times like a highly disturbed young man. Yet there is something childlike, innocent and endearing in his character; when not having one of his tantrums, or in the grip of a psychotic rage, he is extremely polite and likeable. With the right kind of support, therapy and medication, I'm sure he could do well.

I look at him, stroking the hamster. 'You OK, Ben?'

'I love that course,' he says, anger in his voice. 'Why won't they let me finish it? I'm going back there tomorrow with a baseball bat, and I'm going to get that bloody vice-principal that expelled me and let him have it.'

He looks over the top of my head as he speaks: he finds it very hard to hold eye contact. I don't doubt his capacity to carry out his threat against the teacher.

'Hey, listen Ben,' I say, 'don't be hasty, there. They'll let you back on the course next term. That's… what… three months away? It's not like you'll have long to wait. Besides, your grades weren't that great, were they? Because of your mental health, I mean. This way you can recover a bit, put more into the course next year and maybe get higher grades.'

'No,' he says, shaking his head fervently and staring at the ground. 'I'm going up there tomorrow. I'm going to beg them first, and if that doesn't work I'm going to baseball bat him. I can pass that course, I know I can, and then I can get a job working with animals, which is all I want. Why is my life so shit? I fucking hate it.'

'The thing is, a baseball bat won't solve…' I start, but he interrupts me.

'I keep having all these problems despite asking God to give me what I want. So I've given up on Jesus and all that born-again Christian stuff and started praying to the devil.'

He had turned into a bit of a God-botherer recently, I knew that, but this switch to the dark side is a departure.

'You don't really believe in the devil, do you Ben?' I ask.

He hands me a book: it's some kind of Satanic bible, or manual, or something.

'I don't know if there's a devil,' he says, 'but I'm giving it a go. God wasn't up for helping me much, that's for sure. All the time I spent praying with those bloody happy clappy Christians, and it got me nowhere.'

His conversion to Satanism raises several ethical dilemmas for me (and, arguably, for Ben).

As his keyworker, I'm required to support him in 'accessing and participating in cultural and faith-based activities', should he require it, and I imagine that goes as much for devil worshippers as newly-converted Buddhists. What if he needs a virgin, for sacrificial purposes? Not much hope of finding one of those round here. I could probably get hold of a goat, at a stretch, but that wouldn't sit well with *my* beliefs. I'm a strict vegetarian… professionally I'm supposed to adhere to the prescribed doctrines of non-judgmentalism, moral relativism and respect for diversity, but it would stick in my craw a bit. My personal beliefs versus his need to honour the antichrist: which wins?

Parking all this to one side, I reassert the importance of his staying away from college for the rest of this term in order that he can get back on the course in the autumn. I think from his glazed expression that he's not taking in what I'm saying. Perhaps he's on another plain, communicating with Beelzebub and his demonic support workers. I wonder if they have bureaucracy in hell? What am I thinking; of course they do.

'OK,' I say, 'well, I'll leave you for a bit now, Ben. But if you need anything, you know where I am.'

A couple of hours later, he turns up at the office with several empty packets of paracetamol and psychiatric medication.

'I listened to what you said about the baseball bat,' he says, 'and I've taken an overdose instead. Can you get me to A&E?'

Judging by his swift appearance at the office and his request for medical attention, I assume he doesn't want to die. I escort him to hospital where he is already on a first-name basis with most of the staff (there have been numerous episodes of this type). Although he is clearly a drain on their time and resources, he is at least polite and respectful to the doctors and nurses, unlike so many of the other time-wasters who clog up casualty, demanding their rights through drunken and opiate-induced grunts and howls.

I leave him behind a flimsy nylon curtain with a nurse taking his blood pressure and making notes.

It transpires that Ben has taken only some of the medication he claims to have swallowed, so the next morning he is released back in to the mainstream of society to continue his life of psychological instability, hamsters and spiritual union with Lucifer.

* * * * *

It's a week or so on from Ben's not-really-an-overdose, and we haven't seen hide nor hair of him for the last three days. I telephone his mother to see if he has been around to hers. She is immediately on the defensive.

'No, he definitely isn't here,' she says. 'Why would you say that? He knows he's not welcome to stay overnight. The last time he did, he scared his little brother senseless. He woke up in the middle of the night and found Ben sitting in the living room chanting and trying to conjure up the devil. So no, he's not here and, to be honest, I don't really want him here, other than to say hello and see how he's doing.'

I can't say I blame her. I don't even believe in a devil, as such, but you can't be too careful where the underworld is concerned and I wouldn't want anyone in my home trying to communicate with him. Apart from anything else, there are the practicalities of the whole odd business: if there's one thing I know about Satanists, it's that you need to have firm boundaries with them. Give them an inch and they'll walk all over you, and before you know it your living room has quickly become a temple of evil, awash with burnt offerings and weird symbols.

Next, I ring his Community Mental Health nurse – she knows Ben well – and we have an illuminating conversation.

'Let me just check my notes…' she says. 'Ah, yep. Ben was admitted to the local psychiatric hospital late on Saturday evening, and he was assessed this morning [Monday] and released, having been deemed as in a stable mental condition.'

'Why was he admitted in the first place?'

'The police found him in a distressed state sitting on the wall of the house of his college vice-principal,' she says. 'Apparently he was chanting some kind of curse or spell. It was all causing quite a lot of distress to the neighbours and the vice-principal and his family.'

I silently resolve never to get on Ben's wrong side, just in case there is any truth or power in this Satanic claptrap. He seems to be more than willing to use it to bring unpleasantness to the lives of those who aggrieve him (though I suppose that's at least part of the point of being a Satanist).

'OK, let me get this straight,' I say. 'Despite the fact that in the last week he has been running screaming around a school football pitch hitting himself on the head with a brick, has kind of attempted suicide and has tried to cast Satanic spells on his vice-principal, he is still being deemed sane by psychiatric services?'

'Ben's problems would be seen as having more of an emotional cause than a psychological one,' she says. 'At least, so they might argue.'

'OK,' I say. 'Well, thanks, anyway. At least I know where he's been for the past few days.'

I put the phone down and realise this hasn't answered the crucial question: where is he *now*? Out buying a jackal, perhaps?

As it happens, he shows up a few minutes later – once more, he is being led up the path of the Project by the police. He has been back at the college, this time running frantically around the premises shouting out the name of the vice-principal and challenging him in the name of Satan to come out and face him.

The police release him, he flees to his room, I follow – it's pretty much *déjà vu* all over again.

He's lost his door key, so I find him in the corridor outside, head leaning against the wall, sobbing uncontrollably. He is in a deeply miserable place, poor lad. I open the door, and can't help but notice that, at some stage in the last week, he has smashed the room up pretty badly. Despite this, I feel sorry for him. He is clearly not well, and whether his problems are rooted in a dysfunctional emotional disposition or an overt psychiatric disorder, he surely needs some kind of professional help. The emotional/psychiatric distinction seems to me to be wholly pedantic when faced with someone displaying these genuinely chaotic and destructive tendencies.

There's not much I can do for him, other than reassure him that I'm around if he needs me. So I leave him crying into his Satanic bible, his hamster and his ADHD medication and go to write up in his file how I've 'supported' him.

WE DRILL DOWN INTO
ALL OUR PAPERWORK

I'M ON MY WAY to work and I pass a newsagent's; as I do so, I catch a glimpse of the local paper on the stand outside.

That kid looks like… it *is*, it's a picture of an ex-pupil of mine, from my time working at a local comprehensive. What's he doing splashed across the front page?

I stop, and to my horror I read that the boy – Jimmy Joyce, a 15-year-old – has been murdered.

I buy a copy of the newspaper and read it as I walk slowly down the road. Jimmy was attacked as he slept at a party in a friend's house, the report says. He was stabbed repeatedly in the stomach and head by a 17-year-old who had also attended the same comprehensive.

My stomach is reeling. I liked Jimmy. For a start, he called me 'Sir', which was a rarity. He was also a loveable rascal: though he was persistently disruptive in class, he was never aggressive or terribly offensive. I was a bit like that myself at his age, which is maybe why I was fond of him. Around the time I left, he had started truanting quite seriously, and as I read the story I begin to think about how Jimmy is a victim of a society which is failing adequately and effectively to socialise and educate its young people.

The school, like so many others throughout the country, was unable to do much with Jimmy in terms of instilling discipline or stopping him from bunking off, and so he started to hang out with slightly older and more troubled boys. It was one of these 'friends' who murdered him, for reasons that may never be known.

In my experience – and I'm only in my early 30s – youth violence is on the increase. The figures – particularly for murder and serious assaults – do seem to bear this out, and I think the collapse in adult authority, or even any pretence to it, in some homes, schools and in projects like mine is partly to blame.

I read on. It turns out the youth who carried out the attack should have been tagged. Apparently, a cock-up by the courts led to a failure to issue the correct paperwork to the private security firm that was to have fitted the tag. The article suggests that if Jimmy's killer *had* been tagged he might have been at home where he was supposed to be, and not at the party where he carried out the murder. Going on my own experience of tag-ees – such as Perry – this seems unlikely. If you're the type of person who is prepared to stab a sleeping teenager to death, you are probably not the type of person who's going to worry about observing a curfew. But then I am not a criminal justice professional, and I don't work for the Youth Justice Board, so maybe I'm wrong.

* * * * *

I'm still feeling slightly queasy, and pretty miserable, when I get to the office. I'm just telling Brendan about the tragedy when Stella walks in to the office to hand over some rent.

Normally I'd remind her about the 'knock first' rule, but I haven't got it in me at the moment.

'Cheers, Stella,' I say.

'S'alright,' she says. 'What's up with you? You look like your mum's just died or suffink.'

'It's a lad I used to teach,' I say. 'Only 15. He's just been murdered.'

'Oh, right,' she says. 'That's a bit shit, innit?'

She sniffs, the matter closed for her, and makes to leave.

'Listen Stella,' I say. 'I know we have the odd whinge at you, but I've got to say… you do generally pay your rent and it's refreshing not to have to chase someone for what they owe. So thanks.'

'Yeah,' she says. 'Since I got me new job' – she's now a sous-chef at a local hotel – 'I'm trying to keep it for once. You know how I like cooking and learning new recipes and that, it's not boring. And everyone has to pay rent, so it's no big deal. If I don't pay it I'll eventually have to leave and I've nowhere else to go so I don't want that. There's no point being evicted.'

'That's really sensible,' I say. 'You've really started growing up lately. I wish everyone here thought the way you do. I know you're not on massive wages, either, which makes it doubly good.'

Unfortunately, she shatters my illusions.

'Well,' she says, 'like I said, paying rent's no big deal. I get fed mostly at work, so that saves me money I'd have to spend on food, like.

All I need is enough to go out at the weekends, and anything else that I need I just nick. So it's not like I go without, is it?'

She says all this as if it is perfectly normal; Brendan and I nearly fall out of our seats at her openness.

'Did I hear you right?' says Brendan. 'Did you say you just steal stuff if you need it?'

'Yeah,' she says, looking somewhere between surprised and defiant. 'Course.'

Unable to help himself, Brendan's started giggling, and I join in, sniggering behind my hand; I think it's the shock at how blasé she is.

'Like what?' I say.

'Earrings,' she says, shrugging. 'Lip gloss. This hat. Me blue handbag. Me red handbag. Tights. Vodka. Magazines.'

'Blimey,' I say, half-impressed that she actually reads. But she hasn't finished.

'Nail polish,' she says, now staring into the middle distance. 'Chocolate. I once nicked a stapler, dunno why. Er, perfume. Er…'

'We get the picture,' says Brendan. 'You know you'll end up getting arrested? I mean, joking apart, you can't really do this.'

'Course I can,' says Stella. 'I don't care if I get nicked. Anyway, I mightn't get caught. I'm quite good at it, you just have to look confident. What I normally do is buy one thing and hide a few other bits in my bag. If you pay for something, they never suspect you. If I get caught, I get caught, I'll worry about that then. For now, I just want what I want when I want it.'

She wanders off, and as soon as the coast is clear Martin's door opens.

'Just a quick heads-up,' he says, with a slight twitch. 'I'm leaving.'

He smiles – for the first time this month that I've seen.

'Oh,' says Brendan.

'To where?' I say.

'I'm going back to Joseph K House,' says Martin. 'I'm working out my notice till the end of the month, though.'

Joseph K is Martin's previous project. It's also owned by Oceania; there he'll only have to deal with 10 residents and four members of staff, rather than our 66 residents and nine staff.

I might be wrong – he's not one for sharing his thoughts – but I get the impression that Martin hates the sight of The Emmanuel

Goldstein Project. His body language is the big giveaway; he comes in each morning through the back door of the building, meaning he can make it to his office without having to make contact with staff or residents. I can't say I blame him for this – I sometimes feel like hiding in a cave to get away from all this madness.

He stays in his office for most of the day, keeping the door firmly shut in order to try to tackle the mound of bureaucracy that goes along with his position – and, believe me, there is plenty of it. I regularly hear him muttering away to himself in frustrated-sounding tones.

He rarely deals directly with the residents unless one of them brings a complaint to him. He tends to expedite these as much as he can – like last week, when he overruled an overnight guest ban on Martina (usual story – non-payment of rent and staff abuse). Afterwards, I asked him why. He replied, 'She was going on and on, and I just didn't want to have to listen to her any more.' I sympathised, but this kind of thing makes management look like the good guys while the staff who actually have to deal with the likes of Martina every day end up being seen as the villains. This makes our jobs a lot harder.

'Before I go,' he says, 'I really want to drill down into all our paperwork and make sure everything is absolutely in order. Supporting People are coming in to audit all of our support plans, and I don't want them to fail us on anything. I want everything best practice. I'm working on a gold standard document which I'll circulate later.'

Great – an audit.

How this works is, first, managers from other projects within Oceania Housing Association come and inspect our files to see if they're up to the requirements specified by the government. Then the government sends its own team of file inspectors to have another look.

That's two sets of State-financed bureaucrats examining the same pile of forms, forms which were produced to no discernible benefit to anyone by a third set of bureaucrats (us).

If our files and support plans don't have a certain uniform appearance, so as to satisfy the requirements of government regulators, that is unthinkably bad.

If they do look right, this is good – irrespective of the fact that it's all meaningless. (It does keep a lot of people in work, of course.)

'It's really important, is this,' says Martin, before vanishing back into his own office.

The residents certainly don't view this sort of stuff as being of any importance. If you ask them most will happily admit that they think it's all a load of bollocks. In fact, they complain more than we do about the paperwork and form-filling and counter-signing of everything that goes on in this place. In the majority of cases, they don't know or care what their support plan involves.

The bureaucratic juggernaut pays no attention to any of this, naturally.

Just before lunch, Martin sends round his document to each member of staff. It outlines in painstaking detail the importance of writing up our residents' support plans to very specific standards.

'Please ensure you date, sign and number each new page in a plan – this is essential,' he writes.

It's also 'key' that we remember at each session that residents must sign the page where we detail their progress, or lack of it, since the last session and that we take care to write down the number of hours and minutes we spend discussing each discrete area of support with each resident in each session ('extremely important'). Lots of other stuff is 'vital' or 'critical'.

And so on, and so forth. I won't bore you with any more of this tripe; as I read it, though, I give a sort of twisted cackle as it occurs to me that it is essentially a form telling us how to fill in other forms.

I spend the afternoon re-reading all the bilge I've written in the last few months, and making sure every box is ticked. I hand it all in just before going home time, and spend five minutes chatting with the boss.

'It's all a load of horseshit really, isn't it Martin?' I say, wondering if the façade will crack for just a moment.

'Oh no,' he says. 'Far from it. Our internal audit of the support plans is showing that you've all improved greatly in terms of the standard of recording the work that you do here. We need to keep this up! Supporting People will be here later in the year, and people's jobs depend on those files being maintained to the specified requirements.' He pauses, and then says quickly, 'And, of course, people's accommodation, too.'

I find it revealing that jobs come before homes in his hierarchy of justification for this insane, inane bureaucracy.

'OK,' I say. 'Well, I'll be off.'

Outside, the sun is shining, the birds are chirping and the air smells fresh.

'You say you don't love me no more,' sings George Hughley on my earphones. *'And this I understand... that's why I cry.'*

CHALLENGING PERCEPTIONS VIA THE MEDIUM OF POSTERS

I'M ON THE TRAIN heading to work, and as luck would have it I've bumped into Jo, an ex-manager from the Tom Parsons care home.

Like me, she's had enough of that and is now working in an old peoples' home. As the countryside rattles by, we chat about old times; I wish I could report that we discuss the transformation of dozens of disaffected, damaged and feral teenagers, but sadly, in my experience, that kind of thing is as rare as hen's teeth.

Instead Jo reminisces with me about some of the idiotic dressing downs she received from her superiors for trying to impose standards on the youngsters in the home.

'The girl who really sticks in my mind,' she says, 'is Rachel [the obese, channel-hopping, deodorant-dodging car-seat kicking yobette of earlier]. Despite everything, I really felt she could have been OK. She wasn't stupid, she just needed direction. But they wouldn't let me give it to her. One example – she was getting ready to go to college one morning, but she was very dirty… her t-shirt was completely covered in food stains. She actually *smelled*. You know the kind of negative attention, or even bullying, that could bring from her peers. Anyway, I told her she shouldn't go to college dressed as a homeless person. It might have been a bit blunt, but she needed to hear it. Instead of addressing the issue, she telephoned head office and complained to my manager. And instead of backing me up, he then reprimanded *me*. He said the language I had used could have been viewed as oppressive, or words to that effect.'

'Sounds about right,' I say.

'Then there was the time she smashed up the widescreen TV in the lounge,' says Jo. 'She was having a tantrum because she couldn't get her way over something. I told her that, as a consequence, I would not replace the TV for a month. Once again she phoned head office and complained, and they telephoned me and ordered me to replace the TV immediately as it was Rachel's right to have one. This is even though she had one in her bedroom as well. It was then that I decided I had to get out. Like you used to say to me, Winston, how does that system help Rachel? It's mad, literally mad.'

Jo gets off at the next stop, and the train pulls away. A few minutes later, I see a ticket checker further down the carriage ask four youths for their tickets.

They respond by loudly calling him a 'beardy cunt'. Before long, the train pulls in to a station where several other ticket checkers join the first. They, too, are given nicknames which conflate an aspect of their physical appearance with that unpleasant swear word. It takes several minutes of persuasion for the young men to get them off the train, but in the end they manage it.

As we pull away from the platform, the quartet are making various threats to the ticket collectors; one of them moons us, and a couple of the others run up the our carriage and punch the windows.

I grin at one of them and wave, hoping he will get my message, which is, 'Ha, ha, I'm on the train and you're stuck out there in the rain with your scumbag mates.'

Childish, I accept.

It gets me thinking a little bit about the concept of scumbags. I wonder if they *know* that they are scumbags? Do they ever look at themselves in the mirror and think, 'Jesus, I'm a terrible waste of space… I must sort myself out.'

Actually, I know that this happens: I'm a bit of a reformed character myself, and I've met a few others in my time. I wonder if their transformation to decent people was a gradual process, like mine, or the result of an epiphany?

Partly, I know, it's just youth. In my experience of being a public transport commuter who travels days, nights and weekends to and from work, I've seen a lot of trouble on buses and trains but I have yet to see a man in his 40s or a little old lady refuse to show their tickets and start shouting abuse and threats. It's always people in their teens and 20s.

That said, not *all* people in their teens and 20s behave in this way – in fact, the vast majority don't. So how to tell who will? Well, maybe it's a cliché but those who do almost always seem to wear a uniform: scruffy tracksuit bottoms, trainers, hooded tops and a truculent and aggressive facial expression.

Funnily enough, and God knows why, I have with me a copy of the latest edition of *Children and Young People Now* ('the only dedicated weekly title for professionals working with children, young people and their families' which 'circulates to 18,000 key decision makers, reflecting multi-agency working across the public, private, and voluntary sectors'). With 40 minutes until my destination, I open it. I read that Suffolk Police believe that people like me – that is, people who believe you can, to a large extent, judge by appearances, otherwise known as 'normal people' – are mistaken. So concerned are they about this that they have recently started a public awareness campaign challenging prejudices towards hoodie-wearing youths. *CYPN* carries an important article about it.

> *A poster campaign encouraging adults not to judge young people in hoodies has been launched by Suffolk Police,* it informs readers. *The 'What are you looking at' poster was put up across the Waveney and Suffolk coastal district last week and depicts two men, one in a hooded top, and the other in a police uniform. But on closer examination it is the same person wearing different clothing. The poster suggests, 'Before you judge look a little closer.'*

Here's a public service announcement in the interests of you keeping your teeth intact: if you see a young male in a hooded top and tracksuit bottoms who looks like he wants trouble, whatever Suffolk Police say do NOT approach him for a 'closer look'. Walk the other way. Likewise, if you get on a train late at night, and in one carriage there are several youths with hooded tops drinking and blaring music from their mobiles with little regard for the wishes of those around them, I would advise you to judge them solely by their appearance and move to another carriage. At the very least you will save yourself a mouthful of abuse and some random noise; at best, some unwanted pain.

On the other hand, ironically, I would *not* judge a policeman in Suffolk by his appearance. To the unwary eye, he will look like a stern upholder of the law. Of course, this would be a mistaken impression: he is a social worker in blue.

The magazine drones on.

> *It is the latest initiative in Suffolk Police's 'Let's Get A Life' campaign, which aims to stem antisocial behaviour by encouraging interaction between all sections of the community to break down their stereotypical views of each other.*

The campaign is characterised by a skeleton, Mr Green, to reinforce the message that although people look and sound different on the outside, underneath they are all the same.

People are all the same? Is it possible that the person who wrote this shite actually believes it? Can he or she not think of a few significant differences beyond the mere external between Mother Teresa, say, and Dennis Nielsen – or between the yobs above and the ticket collector they abused?

Detective Sergeant Daye Goodard, the lead officer for the campaign, said the hooded top is often associated with young people deemed to be up to no good, but the poster aims to challenge perceptions.

'Young people have to think about how they're impacting on everyone else,' she said. 'But older people and those affected by the image of a hoodie need to think about the way they are tarring everyone with the same brush. A person wearing a hoodie isn't necessarily bad.'

Do we really need Det Sgt Goddard to tell us this? How much has this cost? I thought we were short of public funds just now? When the word 'Police' comes to mind, do you think of a group of people who exist primarily to challenge stereotypes and dispense fashion advice, or do you think they are a group of people who exist primarily to fight crime?

I work with young people, and I'm the first to say that the majority of young people in hooded tops that I've encountered are fine – a few might be a bit of a low-level nuisance, like most teenagers throughout time, including me – but there are those young people who really do blight communities up and down the country. Detective Sergeants earn £40,000 a year. Last time I checked, judging people wasn't a crime but abusing, stabbing and stealing from people was. Maybe Ms Goddard should look in that direction?

The train judders to a halt, and I get out for the short walk to the Project. The damp grey skies reflect my mood, for once.

*****

Barry the arm-breaking Leprechaun obsessive will almost certainly never be allowed back to the Project (though I wouldn't bet my life on it), but, as we saw with Laura Miller, being evicted does not necessarily mean you're barred for life. It may be that you can apply to return at some time in the future, and depending on the reasons for your eviction you can be back in within a few months.

At today's staff meeting, Margaret is pushing for Frank, evicted only 12 weeks ago, to be allowed to return.

I have to say, I like Frank. He's a nice lad who doesn't have a malicious bone in his body and has never been abusive to the staff or anyone else. That said, he had a serious drug problem that he wouldn't address and he used drugs daily on the premises.

He originally came to live with us a few months after coming off heroin. Unfortunately, part of his self-administered kick-the-smack routine involved smoking heroic amounts of skunk weed all day, and washing the THC down with industrial quantities of alcohol.

Granted, this was the lesser of two evils, but we have a supposed zero tolerance policy to any kind of drug use within the Project. It's not always easy to police this problem, as we only have two or three members of frontline staff on any shift and over 50 bedsits in the complex. But we do regular building patrols, and if we smell cannabis emanating from a person's room we take it seriously. We give one warning if a resident is caught using drugs on the premises, and the second time it's marching orders.

Frank had his first warning, but you didn't need to be an ex-dope head like me to see he was still at it. Skunk continued to waft out of his room, and every time you saw him he was completely wasted. He would often come to the office in the morning to collect his post with his hoodie unzipped, exposing his bare chest, and with puffy, slanty eyes from his morning super-strength joint; you could smell it on his breath. He would then stagger off to work as a trainee mechanic.

Credit where it is due, he did manage to hold down a job, and a fairly tough one at that, and partly because of this and partly because he was a decent lad I didn't want to see him evicted. So I took him aside one Saturday morning and gave him another read-through of my unofficial drug chat, about smoking in the park if he had to smoke.

Even when caught red-handed – or red-eyed – many of our chemically-enhanced residents will deny everything, thus sparking off an interminable series of meetings and appeals. Frank was no different, at first.

'Come on, Frank,' I said, when he claimed he wasn't using the stuff. 'That's just not true. I constantly smell skunk coming out of your room, and that's all the evidence we need. Now, from deep personal experience I am advising you against smoking this shit full stop, because it'll rot your brain, particularly the amount you smoke and the strength of the stuff. I mean, it's only 10.30 in the morning, and you're already stoned. But if you're daft enough to want to mess your head up smoking dope at every available opportunity, that's your own business as long as it's off the premises. Here, it's a different matter. You know the rules – they're not a secret. If you're caught in here one more time you'll be out. We're funded and regulated by the government and we have to offer a service that is compliant with the law of the land. Plus a lot of the other residents are very opposed to the use of drugs on the premises. So we will not stand idly by and let a drug culture take root in here.'

There were a couple of fibs in the last couple of sentences there: our drug culture is already thriving, and most of the residents are only opposed to drugs in the sense that they are opposed to not having any. But I wanted to sound tough and like we're the ones in charge.

'Point taken, fella,' said Frank. 'I promise you I'll go out from now on.'

'I'd prefer it for your sake if you stopped altogether,' I said. 'But I don't want you to end up homeless so knock it on the head in here, eh?'

A week or so later, Martin was passing by Frank's room around lunchtime and smelt a strong whiff of cannabis. An hour later he confronted him about it, and he admitted he was still using drugs on the premises. He gave him his 28 days' notice there and then.

Spin forward three months, and at today's staff meeting Margaret is championing Frank's case to return to the Project. He's been turning up regularly, appealing to her tendency to ignore rules and boundaries and consequences – the very things he needs to come up against if he's ever going to learn to function, long-term, in the real world.

'He's been back living with his dad and his step mum since leaving here,' says Margaret. 'He says there's a lot of tension in the home with the step mum. He's still smoking skunk, and she doesn't like him living there because he smokes it at home. So, because of this tension, he's had to crash a few nights a week with some old friends, and occasionally at the hotel where he works. He says the friends are still using heroin and that if he is around them too often he may be tempted to use heroin again. So can he come back here, where he says he'll be less at risk?'

It's funny, but if a police officer – for instance – 'says' something, the default position of many in my industry is to disbelieve him or her, and look for the hidden agenda. If a lad who can't stray more than 10ft from a joint 'says' something, it's accepted as though it were gospel truth.

'I might be missing something,' says Brendan, 'but why doesn't he just stop using skunk in the family home? Then there wouldn't be any tension, and he wouldn't have to crash with his heroin-using friends. Of course, if he really *has* to stop with them, he could try just not taking their smack.'

'I think we need to look at the bigger picture here,' says Margaret. 'We should be judging each young person individually. First, he's paid off the few hundred pounds in rent arrears he left here owing. Second, he isn't on hard drugs any more, and that's positive. He's also still working, which is another plus sign. I think we should give him another chance.'

'It's got nothing to do with this mythical bigger picture and all these supposed positives,' I say. 'And we can't judge everyone as an individual, either – we have to be objective and fair and apply the rules equally to everyone. The only reason he's paid off his arrears is that you informed him that his application wouldn't even be considered unless he did that. The fact is he should never have got into arrears in the first place – he's got a full-time job, hasn't he? I like Frank, he's not a bad lad, but he consistently broke our rules, his eviction was entirely justified and we know from his own account that he is still smoking, and still doing it in a place where he shouldn't. We have a long list of young people waiting to come here, many of whom are likely to be a lot less trouble than Frank, and who have a serious need of accommodation. Letting him back robs them of their opportunity for a roof over their heads.'

Brendan is similarly sceptical. 'When Frank was here it wasn't just his own drug use that was problematic, it was the fact that he used to bring his mates round here to use drugs with him. How do we know that won't start up again? And how are we to know it's just cannabis he's using?'

'Well, he says he's only using cannabis, and he's only using that because he feels it keeps him off the heroin. He says he's learned his lesson and won't do it in the building again. He says he's cut down anyway.'

'He says, he says, he says… he said all this to my face several times while he was still here,' says Brendan. 'And look what happened. Personally, I'm with Winston – nice lad and all that, but he had his chance with us and he messed it up, so I don't want him back. Why doesn't he just go and rent a bedsit or a room in a shared house? He's got a regular income.'

It's my turn to back Brendan up.

'Margaret, Frank's not a social smoker who has a joint on a Friday night to unwind,' I say. 'He's psychologically dependent on the stuff to function on a daily basis. I know what that's like, I've been there myself. He's an addict, basically, and addicts are notorious liars when it comes to disclosing the details of their drug use. He just cannot be trusted to be honest with us – for all we know, he could be back on the smack. And on the issue of him renting, I also agree with Brendan. We're supposed to promote people towards independence. Well, he *is* independent. There's nothing to stop him renting a room in a shared house or flat, so why are we even considering him returning? To be honest, I don't know why he'd even want to.'

Margaret shoots an angry look at me. 'You're being unfair and judgmental,' she says. 'You just can't generalise about people like that.'

'With all due respect, Margaret, it's long-established that part of the basic psychology of people with addictions is lying. It's a part of their defence mechanism. They lie to themselves and to others. I've worked with lots of drug users at other posts and I've also had personal experience of dealing with addiction, and in my experience *all* active addicts are liars. Any expert working with them will tell you the same thing. It's not that they're bad people at heart, it's just the way it is. The other thing is, forget Frank, what about the other residents? Don't you remember how some of them used to be scared of his friends when they came round? Why are their concerns not being given precedence over an ex-resident who broke the rules, got caught and is now dealing with the consequences?'

Margaret isn't convinced; her heart is still bleeding for Frank. 'I still think he deserves another chance.'

'I don't,' says Brendan. 'It sends out the message that our rules, of which there are only a few anyway, can be broken and there are almost no serious consequences.'

Despite putting forward what I think is a pretty powerful set of arguments against re-admitting Frank, Brendan and I are in the minority. Martin and the other project workers agree to give him another chance. The meeting ends, and Margaret runs off to telephone him to give him the good news: he will be allowed back within a month.

As I watch her go, Brendan and I raise our eyebrows. I think I know what he is thinking, and it's probably the same thing I'm thinking: I guarantee that we'll end up dealing with the same problems all over again.

FRANK'S NOT THE PLANNING TYPE

IT'S THE DAY AFTER Frank's readmission was agreed, and I've just arrived at work.

I pick up the daily logbook to see if Nigel the night worker has noted any incidents or issues arising of import since yesterday. I see that Sharn was carted off to hospital again, and that the police have been around looking for Perry. But somewhat to my surprise – given that he hasn't even come back yet – I see that Frank has the starring role in the log entry:

> *Frank arrived on the premises with Stella just before midnight, he was very out of it and swaying back and forth, generally being loud and a nuisance. His eyes were rolling and he appeared to me to be under the influence of more than just alcohol, in fact I'm not sure if he even smelled of alcohol. I can't remember. Anyway, he was well out of it on something or other. Stella had to help him to her room as he was barely able to walk. I was concerned for his welfare so decided not to throw him out. Stella later went out again and left him alone. About five in the morning, he came down to get a can of coke from the machine. He was much more coherent at this stage but still a bit out of it. He alluded to having taken hard drugs but didn't specify what. I asked him if he'd done anything stupid and he said he had taken something he shouldn't have. Not sure if this was pills or heroin or something else and he wouldn't say.*

I can't say I'm shocked, exactly, but I'm surprised he's showed his hand this early. Just then, Margaret comes in. She hangs up her coat and then walks over to the logbook. I watch her face as she reads it: she looks disappointed. Margaret is basically a good person, and I don't want to make her feel bad, so I make myself scarce. But I can't help but feel a tiny bit vindicated.

Later, I walk into the office to hear Martin the project manager explaining that in light of this episode the new offer to Frank will be rescinded. 'Do you mind ringing him to let him know, Margaret?' says the manager.

She agrees, and picks up the phone. After a moment or two, Frank answers. Margaret explains the situation, and then invites him in to the Project to discuss it.

Why is she doing this? I think. *He is no longer our concern. We are not here to support failed applicants.* But Margaret is on a quest to save the world: she's always rescuing people from the consequences of their own negative behaviour. This is fine, to a point: children and teenagers need guiding. But there comes a point at which protecting people from the adverse effects of their actions is not helping them. It's often actually ruining their lives, because there usually comes a point when things go badly bent and we *can't* help.

Around midday, Frank arrives for his chat with Margaret. He brings with him a large dose of self-pity.

'I don't know what I've done wrong,' he says. 'I mean, bad stuff just keeps happening to me.'

This goes on, pretty much untrammelled, for a good half hour. Margaret is swelling with compassion to the point she might burst: she's feeling sorrier for him than he is himself. I can't listen to much more.

'Everything was going so well and then it all got messed up,' he says. 'I was just about to get back in here and my job is going well. I've just got really bad luck.'

That's it. I interject.

'Frank,' I say, 'there is no such thing as "bad luck", and bad things don't just *happen* to you. Things don't "get messed up", *you* mess them up. You need to take some responsibility for the fact that your housing situation is chaotic. Your own drug and alcohol abuse is causing problems in your life, and until you address those issues you will continue to have these problems. Your dad doesn't want you in the house because you take drugs, you've been evicted from here because you take drugs and you've blown your chance to return because you take drugs.'

'We can arrange some drugs counselling for you if you like?' offers Margaret.

She shouldn't be doing this; Frank is no longer one of our residents. Technically, he shouldn't even be here, having this conversation.

'Yeah, that would be great,' he says.

'Frank,' I say, 'can I just ask you something? Do *you* think you have a drug problem? Do you actually *want* to stop?'

'I like smoking weed,' he says, 'and it calms me down. I get bad anxiety and the only other thing which works is heroin, which I don't want to take any more. I reckon I could stop if I wanted to, but I don't really want to stop, to be honest.'

'Fine, no problem. I admire your honesty. But it's a waste of time talking about going to a drug counsellor unless you want to change. I know about that stuff because I've been through it, and, believe me, you'd just be wasting your own time and his. I reckon you might be just playing along with the idea because you think it will help you get back in here.'

He shoots me an incredulous look, as if I've just read his mind, and laughs nervously.

'I think you need to know that there is no chance of you getting back in here, *ever*,' I say. 'The manager has confirmed that this morning. I'm sorry, but it's not going to happen.'

'Well, that's me totally fucked,' he says, his head sinking. 'I've got no other options. I can't keep crashing at my mates' house or dossing in the hotel. And my dad doesn't really want me there, either.'

'Look, Frank,' I say, 'you're a great lad, I really mean that. I've enjoyed having you around the place and I was sorry when you went. Try to look at this as the positive spur you need to shake yourself up, maybe wean yourself off the weed and get your life together. You've got a job… You earn, what, a grand a month after tax?'

'Twelve hundred quid,' he says.

'So you don't *have* to go back to live with the smackheads or row with your dad and step mum… you can rent a room in a shared house for £60 quid a week, easy. You could actually become properly independent, and take control of your life.'

'I don't trust other people and I don't like dealing with strangers,' he says.

'OK, then,' I say. 'Rent yourself a bedsit or a small one bed flat – the rents for places like that are reasonable on the south side of town, you could do that no problem. All you need is a month's rent up front and a month's rent as deposit. How much money do you have in the bank right now?'

'I've got four hundred quid in it until pay day next week.'

'Right, so you're sorted then. You can easily sort a small loan to cover the deposit and a month's rent and pay it back next week.'

'Yeah, but I don't like dealing with bank staff,' he says. 'I've told you, I don't like dealing with strangers. I'm not good with people I don't know, I find it hard to talk to them.'

'I think Frank might have low self-esteem,' says Margaret.

I ignore this well-intentioned but nonsensical drivel, and offer an alternative take.

'Frank, here's a thought. The reason you don't like dealing with people you don't know is that when you're mashed out of your head new situations make you paranoid. Would I be right?'

'Yeah,' Frank admits, with a slightly ashamed grin.

'Like I say, I've been in your position myself, or close to it, when I was your age,' I say. 'I know all about the paranoia, it's understandable if you spend half your life stoned. If you can stay off the dope and let your head clear for a few days, you'll be fine, trust me. And by the by, I'm living proof that you can get yourself straight and hold down a job. Even if it's a crap one. So look, can we at least talk about you planning to rent a place?'

'I'm not the planning type,' he says.

'Well, you'd better learn to be, because like you said your current living arrangements are no good. So here's a plan, Frank. Stop smoking weed in the mornings, or preferably altogether, and then dealing with people during the day and making plans will be a lot easier. I guarantee it will work.'

He looks at me, and gives it one last shot. 'But it's easier here, isn't it?' he says. 'You have a keyworker to help remind you about stuff like the rent and that, and you don't have to deal with setting up direct debits to pay bills and stuff because it's all covered in the rent payment.'

'You were supposed to learn to deal with responsibilities like that when you lived here,' I say. 'Anyway, those are your options – a shared house or a flat. It would be a piece of cake for you. Look, I've other work to get on with. I'd just like to say one thing to you, that although you think that drugs cause you no trouble, all the problems in your life come directly from ganja. Anyway, good luck whatever you do and I really hope things work out for you.'

I shake his hand and head off on a patrol of the building, nose alert to the wafting herb. I could read Frank like a book because I was very like him at his age. I was a heavy pot smoker who had withdrawn from the world and was spiralling in to the even darker world of alcohol dependency. Luckily, I saw the abyss and drew back in time. It caused me a lot of problems and the only way I overcame it was when I really wanted to. What made me want to was the negative consequences which were piling up in front of me: I needed to confront them, which is why I'm so opposed to Margaret trying to save Frank from his self-created situation. His previous six-month tenancy at the Project had achieved the exact opposite of our ostensible aim as a provider of supported housing – we had created dependence as we were supposed to be trying to encourage independence. The very fact that he viewed the place as somewhere he could avoid taking responsibility for himself is an indictment of supported housing, as it currently exists, for young people like himself.

ONE DAMNED SPLIFF AFTER ANOTHER

SOMETIMES IT'S JUST one damned spliff after another.

It's around 11am on the following Tuesday, and I'm having a desultory walk round the Project when I catch Lee and his brother David smoking cannabis in the building.

I'm just wandering up the corridor when the old nose starts twitching – a bit like in the Bisto ads. I follow the unmistakeable whiff of high-THC skunkweed to Lee's room, knock on the door and he opens it.

'Oh,' he says looking from me to the huge spliff in his left hand, and back to me again. 'We should have asked who it was.'

Definitely not the cleverest of drug users.

'OK, lads,' I say. 'You know the score.'

As it's the first time Lee has been nabbed, he's only getting a warning. But it's David's second time, and unfortunately for him that means 28 days' notice. I won't be sorry to see him go: they're both nuisances.

'You'll get written confirmation of it in the morning,' I say. 'You've made your bed, David' – I'm speaking metaphorically here, obviously – 'so you're going to have to lie in it.'

There's a bit more chat, including lots of denial, and then I walk back down to the office to begin the necessary paperwork.

A couple of hours later, I'm sitting going through some totally pointless action plans – in a witty departure, I've started calling them 'inaction plans' – when Lee barges into the office. It looks as though he is taking the news of his brother's imminent eviction badly. In fact, it soon becomes clear that he believes his brother and himself to be the victims of a miscarriage of justice, along the lines of the Birmingham Six, say, or the Guildford Four. The Eejit Two, perhaps.

'I can't believe I've got a warning and my brother's getting evicted for this,' he says, jabbing his finger at me. 'That was cannabis incense sticks. I never do drugs.'

'You're going to have to do better than that, Lee,' I say. 'I've already heard that excuse – Krystal [David's girlfriend] came down here and concocted it. I told her then it was a frankly rubbish excuse and she said, and I quote, "Yeah, fair enough." I think your memory might be a bit muddled, perhaps because you spend your life smoking spliffs the size of Cuban cigars. When I caught you, the first thing you said was it was just a rolly. I pointed out to you that most people don't roll cigarettes as big as carrots. I also pointed out to you that I am well aware of what cannabis smells like. You said nothing about joss sticks or whatever at the time, because you knew you were bang-to-rights. Anyway, answer me this: what kind of dummy would you be to burn a substance that you claim smells identical to cannabis, knowing that this would affect your own tenancy and get your brother evicted? I mean, if you're going to have the smell of dope in your room, you might as well get stoned.'

It's a comprehensive demolition of his position if I say so myself, and I think Lee knows it, too.

'But neither of us do drugs,' he protests, feebly. 'This is so unfair.'

'Come off it, Lee,' I say. 'It's not just weed, either. Every time I see you, you're both gurning away with pupils the size of saucers. Incense sticks don't cause those symptoms, as far as I know… acid, mushrooms and E do, though.'

'I don't know what you're talking about,' says Lee. But he walks away.

* * * * *

I'm back on a late afternoon shift the following day, and I wonder how the Doobie brothers are getting along. Brendan has been on earlies; I see from the log book that he has issued David with his notice. But I read on and see that Lee has also been given notice to leave. Not for being caught with drugs again, but for something much more serious.

Gene sees me reading the book as he heads out of the building. 'You should have been here, Winston,' he says. 'Lee was so pissed off about his brother's notice that he walked down into the computer room and smashed up one of the brand new monitors. I only bought the bloody thing two weeks ago. He then tipped a pot of blue paint in to the wreckage. It's all on the CCTV camera, so you can watch it back if you like. He got arrested, and Martin gave him his notice for it there and then, but he's already drafting his appeal to the area manager.'

'Of course he is,' I say. 'It's all a conspiracy against him, isn't it? Surely he's gone, though? I mean, if we have it on camera? How can he win an appeal?'

'One would hope so,' says Gene. 'What I don't understand is why we don't just throw the young rascal out straight away. There's a clause in the licence agreement related to serious disturbance and aggressive behaviour. This must fall under that?'

We'll see.

* * * * *

Lee's appeal has been held in abeyance pending the outcome of an appearance in court on a charge of criminal damage. That went against him: yesterday he was fined £150, ordered to pay £150 in compensation to the Project and given 30 hours' community service for the vandalism. You might think he'd now accept the inevitable and go, but Lee's not that daft. He knows he still has a roll of the dice left, and today Tessa, the area business manager, has come in to watch him roll it at his appeal.

Despite the CCTV evidence – which I've watched, it's clear and damning – experience leads me to have doubts as to how this will go.

There are four of us in the room: Tessa, Lee, me (I'm his keyworker) and his social worker, Jim (Lee has recently left care, and the Leaving Care Team still work with him to a degree; it's their statutory duty to do so until he is 21).

I start by handing Tessa a report detailing all of Lee's anti-social behaviour over the months, including his recent drug warning and the subsequent vandalism of the computer monitor.

There has been a catalogue of incidents, and he has had several verbal warnings from myself, Brendan and Abigail, the part-timer – all of which should really have been delivered formally instead. All were for being unpleasant and abusive whilst drunk; the first actually came on his first day at the Project, when he was so pissed that he collapsed at reception and had to be taken to hospital in an ambulance. Several others were given for being drunk and having noisy, late-night fights and arguments with his brother, David. (We have an oft-flouted rule – or 'policy' – that there should be no noise after 11pm, so that those residents who work or go to college can get some sleep.)

Finally, I read through the incident reports for the drug use and the vandalism, stressing that we have clear video footage of the latter incident.

Tessa looks at Lee. 'Have you any comment to make, Lee?' she says.

Drugs-wise, he is still indignantly sticking to his ludicrous joss stick story. 'It's not fair,' he says. 'I was, like, really angry at David being kicked out, because we don't do drugs, we was just burning these incense things which have a bit of a cannabis smell.'

I interject. 'Lee, it has already been pointed out to you that this story has some glaring inconsistencies and holes in it, and therefore isn't a credible excuse. By sticking to it you are proving yourself to be untrustworthy.'

'We don't buy the incense stick story, Lee,' says Tessa. 'What about the computer?'

Lee looks at the ground in silence. Then his social worker, Jim, speaks up. 'Clearly, Lee has done wrong in relation to the computer monitor, and he acknowledges this,' he says. 'But he's a 16-year-old lad who has had a very troublesome and chaotic family background, and he has never gained the tools to deal with his anger.'

The 'tools to deal with his anger'. I sigh. This bullshit makes me tired.

'Lots of people in here have had problematic childhoods and don't commit vandalism,' I say. 'You know Abigail, one of our keyworkers, and I know that you know that she had a really troubled upbringing, too. Would that give her licence to go in to a resident's room and wreck it when they annoy her? Would it excuse her if she whacked Lee in the head for smashing up our monitor? How come some people can use their tough backgrounds as excuses, and others can't?'

'He's seen that he has done wrong,' says Jim, 'and he'll be paying the money back to the Project as mandated by the court. Surely this is enough punishment? At the end of the day, we all want to help Lee and making him homeless will not help.'

Tessa says nothing, so I leap in.

'With all due respect, Jim, I get fed up with all these excuses,' I say. 'We have a lot of residents in here with similar backgrounds. They don't smash the place up. In fact, our most exemplary resident, Catriona, has an almost identical background to Lee.'

I'm not saying it wouldn't be problematic for Lee to become homeless* – it would. But he needs to face the consequences of his actions, and the fact is it wouldn't be *us* making Lee homeless, it would be him. All this talk just feeds Lee's perception of himself as a helpless victim.

Not very much to my surprise, though, Tessa is softening. After some stern words that mean very little, she informs Lee that his eviction will be revoked if he signs up to an acceptable behaviour contract (ABC). She asks me to draw up an agreement consisting of a list of conditions, which he will agree to abide by.

ABCs get dished out like confetti in these places, and in my experience they are next to useless. I can think of only one case in which an ABC led to any change, and even then it was quite limited. This might be because to get an ABC you will already have been issued countless verbal warnings, several formal written ones and possibly an eviction notice. What are the odds that by simply writing down what you should and shouldn't do on a new piece of paper, and getting you to sign it, your entrenched behaviour will change?

If Lee breaks the new agreement then he will once again be given notice. At least that's what the words on the page will say. But the reality is that he will break it flagrantly and repeatedly, and nothing will flow from this at all.

It winds me up; nothing *means* anything round here, even if it's written down in black and white. The ink just isn't worth the paper.

* * * * *

Within a week of Lee signing his acceptable behaviour contract he has already broken it by behaving unacceptably, as wearily predicted.

The notice which was earlier revoked has now been reinstated, and the lunatic merry-go-round whirls ever on.

Part of the ridiculous ABC was an agreement that he would abide by all the house policies. One of these is about late-night noise and disturbance, specifically the lack thereof. Despite pledging that those

---

* As a care-leaver, of course, pretty much *whatever* Lee does he won't *actually* be made homeless in any real sense of the word – the local authority will have to find him a bedsit until he's 21.

days were gone, no sooner had he settled back in than he was inviting all of his mates round for a party. I wasn't in the building, but I'm told it involved loud music, lots of laughter and shouting and – if I know Lee and his pals – copious quantities of beer, blue WKD and marijuana. Despite several complaints by fellow residents who had to be up for work or school in the morning, and a number of requests by the night worker to wrap things up and go to bed, the shindig carried on until 4am.

After – to his apparent shock and outrage – having his notice re-instated, Lee obviously got straight on the blower to his social worker, Jim. Another injustice had been perpetrated, after all!

I'm sitting at the desk in the office, staring out of the grimy window at the dirty shop fronts and littered pavements of the road which runs past the Project, when the phone goes.

'Emmanuel Goldstein Project,' I say. 'Winston speaking, how may I help you?'

'Hi Winston,' says a voice. 'It's Jim here from the Leaving Care Team? Listen, Lee has just informed me that he has received notice again. Is this true?'

There's a note of incredulity – perhaps seasoned with a little contempt – in his tone.

'Yeah, Jim,' I say. 'I'm afraid it is.'

'Well… I mean… how has this happened?' splutters Jim. 'I thought we had an agreement?'

'Yeah, so did *we* Jim,' I say, laughing. 'But you know what a rascal he can be. He signed that acceptable behaviour contract but then, to my complete surprise, he found himself unable to abide by it. What a shocker, eh?'

'What did he do?' says Jim.

I explain what happened.

'Oh, come on!' he says, when I finish. 'Oh, come *on*! You can't really be willing to make someone homeless for making a bit of noise? I mean, he's a young lad, after all. That's the way young people are – they're a bit noisy at times and they can go a bit wild, we know that.'

'With respect, Jim,' I say, 'you're talking rubbish. We got a lot of complaints from other residents of his age – are you going to tell *them* that this is "just the way young people are"? Because I think you'd get told to fuck off, if you'll excuse my language. What are we supposed to say to Catriona? She lives a couple of doors down the corridor from Lee and she couldn't get to sleep because of the noise he was making. He might have nothing much planned beyond maybe getting stoned the next day, but she had college – are we supposed to prioritise his love of lager over her need for an education?'

'I repeat,' says Jim, 'he's just a young lad.'

'And she's just a young girl,' I say. 'I don't think you're listening to me, Jim. Tell you what, how about inviting Lee and a dozen of his mates round to yours so they can have an all-nighter in your spare room tonight? Then you can ring me back tomorrow and see if you still think this is all terribly unfair?'

There's a silence. I bet a pound to a pinch of snuff Jim lives in a relatively nice neighbourhood; I bet he sleeps pretty soundly at night, too. He won't be taking me up on my offer.

'Right,' he says, 'I'm sorry Winston, but I want to talk to the manager. I don't agree with this decision.'

I arrange for Jim to talk to Martin. I don't know what he says, but whatever it is he gets his way because – to my utter astonishment – Lee's reinstated eviction order is revoked again.

Perhaps he used the tactic used by the Government's youth advice agency Connexions when they force us to accept residents they've referred but whom we deem to be too high a risk to reside with us. This is to threaten to complain to Supporting People at the Department of Communities and Local Government. We can be relied upon to fold when that gauntlet is thrown down. Too many evictions or rejections means the figures don't look good, and that makes the horses restless; we can't have that, because our salaries depend on the Supporting People grant. Measured in this balance, Catriona's sleep (and her future) is the merest speck of dust. (Of course, it's but a coincidence that the people at the top of our Housing Association live even further away from Lee – from *all* the Lees, in fact – than Jim does.)

I see Lee walking through reception later, and he smirks at me. I ignore him. In a way, I don't blame him for smirking: he has won, if 'winning' means learning that you don't have to account for your actions, when one day you will.

* * * * *

As a footnote to all of this, a few days later I find Catriona sitting in the common lounge. She's on her own, so it's a good time to see how she is.

As I've said, despite an appalling childhood, Catriona is a great kid – she's doing her best and will end up making something of herself. I like chatting to her when I get a sec.

'Hi, Catriona,' I say. 'How's tricks? Only, I've noticed on the signing-in-and-out sheet [every time a resident comes in or leaves, they are supposed to sign in order that we know who's in the place in case of fire; of course, most of the time they don't bother] that you're not staying here more than two or three nights a week, sometimes even less. Can I ask why?'

'Well, it's because it's really noisy here at night sometimes,' she says. 'I need my sleep for college and work. I stay round at my ex-boyfriend's mum's place. She's like a mum to me, we're good friends, so it's not too bad.'

'Why don't you complain to the night project worker,' I say. 'This is your home, you know. You live here and you shouldn't be put out of it by inconsiderate neighbours.'

'I do complain to them sometimes, and they get them to quieten down for a bit, but then I find I'm lying there on edge, waiting for it to start up again. You can't really trust that you'll get a good night's sleep, and I'm sick of going to work and college exhausted. At least if I stay away that means I get a few good nights' sleep a week.'

This is the kind of thing which infuriates me. We're supposed to be helping young people move to independent living and develop as functioning, responsible adults. Here we have a young woman who is trying to do just that. We never have any problems with her. And yet a selfish drunken, druggie moron like Lee is being allowed to ruin her life. If you think that's putting it too strongly, imagine if *you* had to go and stop with your ex's mum three or four nights a week, just to get some kip.

It is, literally, a scandal – made worse by the fact that the Leaving Care Team, who have responsibility for both Lee and Catriona, are siding with him against her.

Why is Jim not ringing up demanding that we respect her right to live in a quiet and peaceful environment? I honestly do not know the answer to this question.

NON-JOBSEEKING JOBSEEKERS

KRYSTAL HAS COME INTO the office. She is crying, and complaining that she has not received her jobseeker's allowance.

Despite the fact that it is 1pm on Tuesday, she is also barefoot and wearing pyjamas. This is not unusual; many residents walk around in their nightclothes. I challenge it, but some colleagues don't seem to mind.

Krystal is 16 and has been living with us now for four months. Her parents helped her move in after writing the estrangement letter which allowed them to dump her on the State. They visit regularly and take her on outings; it's a pity they won't take her back, as she could do with some parental guidance. Mind you, perhaps they would be the wrong parents to offer it.

She bonded quickly and very well with the other residents. In fact, she bonded so well with David – druggie brother of the computer-smashing Lee – that before he was evicted he impregnated her. One of my colleagues asked her why they didn't use some of the condoms which are freely available to residents.

'David doesn't like them,' she said.

Luckily, I suppose, she had a miscarriage a few weeks into the pregnancy. It was her second in a year: she had the first at 15. A boy her age was the father.

Once I've calmed her down and got her to wipe away the tears, I say, 'OK, let's think about this logically. Obviously, they have suspended your payment for some reason. Do you have any idea why this might be, maybe?'

She sniffs and drags her High School Musical pyjama sleeve across her nose. 'I did miss signing-on yesterday,' she says, 'but that was because it was at 9.45 in the morning.'

To be fair that's like 3am for many of our residents: the Jobcentre can be so insensitive to the needs of our vulnerable and socially-excluded young people. (Actually, in all seriousness, I think they'd do better business if they opened all night.)

'I did ring them up after I got up,' she says. 'I said it was too early for me, and they said they'd change it to half twelve from now on. But maybe that's why they cut me off?'

Brendan has walked in and is leaning in the doorway. He looks at me and shakes his head, chuckling.

'What do you mean, it's too early?' he says. 'A lot of people are at work by 8am you know, Krystal. When you're on jobseeker's allowance, the clue's in the title. How can you be seeking a job if you can't get out of the house before midday?'

'Well, it's too early for *me*,' she says, shrugging her shoulders defiantly.

'Look, Krystal,' I say. 'Let me give the Jobcentre a call and see if I can find out what's going on.'

I know I ought to put the ball in her court, but I'd like to find out if she's telling the truth about them changing her signing-on time so she could have a lie-in.

I pick up the phone and ring through.

'Hi, it's Winston from Emmanuel Goldstein,' I say. 'I'm ringing in relation to Krystal Johnson's claim. I'm just wondering why her payment has been suspended?'

'Bear with me a sec, Winston,' says the lady dealing with the case. 'I'll just check the file… Ah, yep, I thought so. She was supposed to bring in some documentation a while ago. It's to do with a part-time college course she's attending up at Lev Bronstein? But she failed to do that, so we have suspended her claim until she provides us with the documentation.'

'Nothing to do with missing signing on last Monday?' I say.

'No,' she says. 'In fact, that was too early for her so we've changed it to Monday afternoons from now on.'

This aspect of it surprises me. 'Surely she should be up looking for a job?' I ask.

'Well, we have to be responsive to their needs,' she responds. Maybe she doesn't see that she and her colleagues are part of the problem; indulging Krystal's laziness can't help.

I put the phone down and explain the situation to Krystal. Further tears. More to get rid of her than anything, I tell her I'll help her fill out the form later.

When she's gone, Brendan says, 'At least she's *at* college.'

* * * * *

211

The following week, though, I discover that the college course isn't exactly going swimmingly.

A month or so ago, Gene the tutor, with help from Abigail, arranged for Krystal, Martina, Kelly and Kirsty to undertake a part-time course, one day a week, something business-related – I can't recall its exact title (and a fair number of its students would probably struggle, too).

Today, I see them hanging around the Project at 11am-ish.

'Hey, ladies,' I say. 'Shouldn't you be at college this morning?'

'We don't go any more,' says Martina. 'Abigail knows all about it.'

The four of them slouch out of the front door before I can ask why.

Neither Gene nor Abi work on Thursdays, so I call the college. I explain who I am and why I'm calling, and the secretary puts me through to the staff room. As luck would have it, the lecturer is on a free period, so I get hold of her.

'Miss Jenkins?' I say. 'It's Winston Smith here, from the Emmanuel Goldstein Project. I just wondered if I could…'

'You're calling about Krystal, Martina, Kelly and Kirsty, I imagine?' she says. 'I've been through this with your colleague, Brendan Blair.'

'He's not here at the moment,' I say. 'Could you just…'

'Unfortunately, we had to ask them to leave the course,' she says. 'Their behaviour was inappropriate.'

'Inappropriate how?' I ask.

'They took a dislike to another group of girls on the course,' she says. 'I never found out why. It started with funny looks, but once it escalated to abuse and threats during lessons… well, we couldn't accept that. I couldn't teach the rest of the class in that atmosphere.'

'That's a shame,' I say. 'I was hoping to see them on the next series of *The Apprentice*.'

'You still might,' says the lecturer. 'I've agreed to split the course in two and I'll be delivering the lessons to them at your project.'

'You will?'

'Yes,' she says, sounding surprised that *I'm* surprised. 'I'll be drawing up some lessons for them, I'll drop them round on Fridays so they can get on with coursework and reading and so on. Then I'll come in on Wednesdays for a couple of hours to teach them face-to-face.'

Another example – as if more were needed – of bad behaviour being rewarded by society bending over backwards to help those who spit in its face (the sort of metaphor a contortionist would be proud of).

'I'm in tomorrow morning, actually,' she says. 'They should be working their way through some basic economics material as we speak.'

I can't work out if this woman is deluded or just naïve.

'Blimey,' I say. 'Isn't this all a bit time-consuming and expensive?'

'I suppose so,' she says, 'but I think the four girls will appreciate it.'

Don't hold out too much hope of that, I think. But I say, 'Great. Best of luck, then. See you around.'

And the conversation ends.

* * * * *

It's six weeks later, and Miss Jenkins, eternal optimist and business studies lecturer to the frankly unlecturable, is sitting in reception.

She looks forlorn, and keeps glancing at her watch.

'They'll be down in a minute,' I say. 'Olive's just gone up again.'

This is the sixth Wednesday on which she has turned up to pass on her insights and expertise in the arcane world of commerce, and it's the sixth Wednesday she has been kept waiting by some or all of her pupils.

To be fair, on a couple of occasions I have seen one or two of them get up on their own initiative. However, this is the exception rather than the rule, and I've never seen all four of them together.

Instead, what happens is, she arrives at 9am, finds the place like the *Marie Celeste*, student-wise, and waits while one of the keyworkers goes and rouses them from their slumber. This can take some time.

This morning turns out to be a particularly bad one.

Miss Jenkins has made her way to the study room (I use the word 'study' very loosely) by the time three of the four surface. It's 15 minutes since Olive first knocked them up, and 20 minutes or more after their course was supposed to start. All look groggy and grumpy, and two are still in pyjamas and dressing gowns.

213

'Hello,' says Miss Jenkins, brightly. She doesn't challenge them about being late and wearing nightclothes. I can't believe it. The door shuts and the study begins. After half an hour, the three girls re-emerge for a cigarette and can of Coke each. There is still no sign of the fourth, Martina, and indeed she never shows up.

Miss Jenkins leaves at 11am: she shoots a thin smile at the staff as she heads out of the door. Personally, I think she has the patience of a saint: she gets about half of the planned lesson time with whoever can be arsed to be there, and I would imagine that she struggles to impart anything of value to any of them. They rarely thank her for making the effort to come out and teach them. I don't think she'll carry on with this forever; I'd certainly find it dispiriting.

As she goes, I think about my own future and a shiver runs down my spine. I'm 34, and I have made my home in a country with an ageing population. I have no pension – it's hard to pay one out of my salary – and the great Ponzi scheme that is the British State system depends on funds paid out by young people in work. I don't know about you, but having seen first-hand the rigorous educational standards in the post-compulsory sector, I suspect I'll be working well in to my 80s.

HAPPINESS TEMPERED BY REALITY

IT'S A GREY MONDAY morning in early November and so far it's a pretty average sort of day: Satanic Ben has been arrested again, Bianca has just announced she's pregnant – she's being coy as to the identity of the father – and Barry Jameson has just been on the phone threatening to come round and 'do' Kenny.

Martin left on Friday – we didn't bother with a leaving do, it's not that sort of place – and the new manager, Nicola, is just getting her feet under the desk.

I haven't said more than Hello to her yet, but she seems decent enough. No doubt later today or tomorrow we'll get the big talk about how 'vital' and 'crucial' it is that we stay on top of our support plans. Anyway, she's just about to encounter Martina.

Remember Martina? She was the foul-mouthed 17-year-old chosen to help interview applicants for the position of keyworker at the Project, despite the fact that she is one of our worst-behaved residents and refuses to pay the paltry share of her rent that housing benefit doesn't cover (social services pay most if it, because she is an under-18 care leaver).

Today is a happy day: after spending months directing verbal abuse and aggression at all and sundry, she has finally been issued with 28 days' notice to vacate her room.

Martin approved it at about two minutes to 5pm on Friday, his last act before leaving the Project. I'm not sure whether this was because he wanted us to remember him fondly, or because he didn't have the stomach for the fight and, thus, waited until the last minute. I think it was the latter: let someone else deal with the appeals.

In the slightly topsy-turvy world of supported housing, as you'll now be aware, receiving an eviction notice doesn't actually mean you will be evicted. This is because one of your many rights as a resident is the right to a seemingly endless series of follow-up hearings, meetings and conferences at which you will plead your case.

True, if you commit acts of violence against either staff or other residents – or make credible threats to do so – you will usually be removed immediately. Anything else, though, and you can spend weeks or often months in the appeals process. During this time, you can continue to abuse staff and intimidate and inconvenience the decent residents.

So Martina's 28 days' notice does not mean she will be gone within 28 days, or soon after it, or at all. So my happiness at the long overdue news is tempered by reality.

How did she come to find herself facing eviction? It all started about four months ago, when she decided she wasn't going to pay that £7.50 slice of the rent out of her jobseeker's allowance.

'The thing is, you need to budget and set aside money for the rent,' I said to her at the time. 'This place is all about moving you towards independence. It's the entire *raison d'être* of the Project. This is just a friendly reminder, but if it gets to the formal stage you'll lose the right to have your boyfriend stay overnight.'

She exploded at this, claiming that it was 'unfair' that she should be expected to pay anything.

'All I get is £46.85 a week JSA,' she said. 'How am I supposed to live off that?'

'Look,' I said. 'Most of your rent is being paid by social services. That JSA is basically designed to keep body and soul together, not to give you the life of Riley. If you want more money, you need to get a job.'

She told me I was rude, and stormed out of the office.

There have been many conversations along similar lines since then – Brendan, her keyworker, has also raised the matter with her, as have other members of staff – but Martina has continued to ignore her rent and during the interim her arrears have grown to a significant level.

By the way, you shouldn't cry too many tears for her. It's worth making the point that, despite her supposed lack of funds, Martina is never short of a six-pack of Breaker lager, usually smuggled in for her by older residents or visitors. And other goodies, for that matter: the other day, she waltzed in to the office to show Olive the receptionist a bagful of clothes she'd just bought.

'That's nice, Martina,' I said. 'But it's not like you were in rags before, is it? Would it not be more in your interests to ensure your rent is paid? Instead of spending money on beer and clothes?'

'I needed to buy some treats for myself,' she said. 'I've been feeling down.'

The long and short of it is that she started to receive formal warnings. Once you're in that 'formal warning' stage, you lose the privilege of being allowed to have overnight guests. When this restriction was invoked, she exploded again, suggesting this was thoroughly unjust and communicating this feeling by barrages of screaming and swearing. (It was while she was in the formal warning stage, by the way, that she was picked to interview potential staff for the Project; I got the job nearly six months ago, so you can see how long it has all dragged on for.)

Anyway, her notice letter was delivered this morning. She has read and inwardly digested it, and is now marching towards the office, where I am on the phone. I can see her coming through the plate glass window that forms most of the wall: she looks to have a determined air about her. She storms in without knocking (naturally) and stands in front of me, waving a letter of appeal.

'Right,' she says, 'I'm not fucking having this shit about eviction, so I've...'

'I'm sorry, Joe,' I say to the resident I'm talking to on the phone. 'Can you hold on a sec please? Martina, I'm on a confidential call, here. Can you wait outside until I finish it, please? Five minutes, that's all.'

'You're an arrogant wanker,' she says. Then she turns on her heel and marches into the manager's office.

Nicola ignores her uninvited entry and takes the appeal notice from her. I go back to my call with Joe – a decent young lad who wants some help with an issue he's having at work – and try not to listen to the racket emanating from the manager's office.

* * * * *

I'm still renting my friend Tony's spare room trying to get together the deposit for a flat – I've found a couple of places, but the agents want more than £800 which isn't easy to come by. So although I'm now employed full-time, I take extra shifts with Oceania where they're available, working at other projects in the area.

So after leaving work proper, I head off to The Gregor Samsa Building. It's pretty much the same as Emmanuel Goldstein – just a bit smaller, with only 40-odd residents. But they say a change is as good as a rest. (They're wrong about that, sadly.)

I've been called in because Gregor Samsa has an imminent Supporting People inspection, so it's all hands to the pump in checking, checking and re-checking all the pointless paperwork they've filed in the last year or so to prove that they have told unlistening members of the underclass how to go about signing on and how not to knock up their on-off girlfriend and her best mate.

Things are in a worse state than normal at the Samsa, because a number of the regular staff have recently been fired for getting drunk and having sex with residents. The drinking I can understand – I may be a teetotaller, but I do have muscle memory – but how on earth anyone normal could bring themselves to sleep with the horrors wandering around these places I cannot.

So there are six relief support workers, a further team of three administrative staff and also three managers, all busily verifying that lots of signatures are in the right place, and that hundreds and thousands of sheets of paper are dated and numbered correctly. There must be £300,000 in annual salaries being expended on this rubbish: it's no wonder the country's in a financial black hole.

We sit there in the office and an overspill room, beavering away to satisfy external State bureaucrats, while upside the residents languish in their State-sponsored bedsits, getting high, drinking, missing appointments at the Jobcentre, fighting and impregnating each other. It's almost the definition of a modern tragi-comedy.

Suddenly one of the managers wanders over.

'Winston,' he says, 'we've got a bit of a problem. It doesn't look like the last Client Involvement Officer hit her QAF performance indicators on client involvement. So we need to arrange a quick meeting with some of them and record their views on how the Project can be run better. Can I borrow you for it?'

Pure insanity.

'Sure,' I say.

Within an hour or so, a motley crew of 10 or 12 residents have been rounded up and bribed with boxes of Snappy Tomato Pizza to sit in the common room and give us the benefit of their insights.

'First off,' says the manager, 'we want to know how you think we could make living here more fun.'

More *fun*? How much *more* fun can you get than lying in bed all day, playing *Command and Conquer* and getting smashed?

I sit back in my chair and close my eyes, making sure to adopt a thoughtful expression, as though I'm carefully considering the nonsense suggested. Of course, the manager *is* carefully considering the nonsense suggested, and by the end of the session he has committed to a Karaoke night, a weekly DVD evening and the purchasing of a communal Nintendo Wii.

Never mind that the whole charade has taken place during the day, when these young adults should have been working or training: by getting a few of them to agree to stick up some posters advertising a prosaic activity like watching films together, he is able to tick a box entitled 'resident involvement'. It all helps to keep the funds flowing in to the Project. Nice work if you can get it, and nice to know that some of the money the country is currently borrowing from the Chinese, or the international bond market, or wherever they get it from, is being spent on such laudable and worthwhile initiatives.

Later on, I witness an act of such waste and profligacy that it could really only occur when it is other people's money that is being spent.

The 40 or so residents who live in this complex of small flats share four kitchens between them. The kitchens are better-equipped and way bigger than the one I'm sharing with Tony, and each contains a large fridge-freezer.

The freezers all work fine, apart from the fact that they look, to my eye, as though they have never been cleaned or defrosted. This is pretty much par for the course with a good proportion of these young people: they seem to think that tiresome tasks like that are someone else's job. I can understand the confusion; there are already several cleaners employed to do most of that kind of work around the Project.

To say the kitchens are a 'shared space' kind of conjures up images of disadvantaged youths working in busy solidarity with each other to cook cheap and nutritious meals, dividing up the responsibilities of provision, preparation and cooking in an equitable fashion.

This is not the reality, or anything like it, for the simple fact that substantial numbers of the young people I work with are profoundly solipsistic in their motivations.

That's not to say that they don't share food; it's just that the way in which they 'share' it is different to my understanding of the word.

In their understanding, it tends to involve taking whatever you fancy from the fridge without bothering to ask the person who bought it if that's OK.

Surprisingly, several relatively new residents have started taking issue with this perfectly reasonable system. They don't seem to understand that an egalitarian distributive food-sharing scheme of this type can work perfectly, even though it seems contrary to common sense. If only they would look to great nations like North Korea, where no-one ever goes hungry and nature's bounty is available to all, one spoonful of gruel at a time.

Here's how it works. On the day you receive your jobseeker's allowance, or income support, or disability living allowance, or any combination of benefit payments, you make your two most important visits, to the dealer who provides your super-strong skunk weed and to the off-licence where you purchase a gallon or two of cheap alcohol. Once these vital tasks are completed, you then make your way around to the local Iceland and stock up on nutritionless, artery-clogging, frozen ready meals which you will later cram into the fridge-freezers until they are groaning under the weight.

Of course, you make these purchases in the knowledge that your fellow residents will be eating most of what you buy. But the fact that they also shop in Iceland means that you can be relaxed about this; you are almost guaranteed that you will get the food you want when *you* are 'sharing' *theirs*.

As long as you are quick about it, that is. Because while, at first sight, it might seem that this model ought to work well, it sadly breaks down. I suppose that as long as everyone buys some food and is open to sharing, a sort of self-sustaining, non-hierarchical process of exchange is possible. With elements of an unfettered free market, where Adam Smith's invisible hand is hard at work in the pantries and refrigerators of unemployed young adults, it could even appeal to both far left anarchists and economic liberals: a rare system indeed.

But as Robert Burns tells us, the best laid schemes o' mice and men gang aft a'gley, and leave us naught but grief and pain for promised joy. The reason for this ganging a'gley is that thorny issue of inequality; individual food requirements are dissimilar (some residents require more than others, by an order of magnitude), and not everyone is prepared to make contributions which reflect their consumption.

Thus, Mr A might buy seven pizzas a week and eat twelve; Miss Z might buy seven and find five have been snaffled.

And as soon as even one resident questions the system, or uses words like 'stolen' and 'mine', the whole thing implodes. Complaints of this type tend to arise with benefits a day or two distant, when Miss Z approaches the fridges and finds them denuded of the comestibles which she had purchased a few days earlier and which she was expecting to enjoy; to her horror, she discovers that they have been 'shared' by Mr A.

As with many ostensibly perfect economic models, human beings and their behaviour intervene and impede.

As I say, several new residents have complained that they are being robbed by innocent sharers.

I walk into the manager's office as he is responding to this. He's on the telephone, and I hear him say, 'So you can deliver them tomorrow? That's great, thanks. Just ask for me.'

He puts the phone down and looks at me. 'I've sorted the problem with the food-sharing,' he says. 'I'm ordering everyone an individual fridge.'

The following day, 31 brand new Amica fridges, complete with giant-pizza-sized iceboxes, arrive, bought at a cost of roughly £4,000 of taxpayers' dough. Additionally, a further £1,800 has been spent on purchasing seven large freezer units. The large fridge-freezers – which work just fine, and need nothing more than a clean – are discarded.

Is this money well-spent? I can't say, because I'm trying to be a lot less judgmental about things these days. I keep being told that judging (a.k.a having an opinion based on standards) is 'negative'.

But one thing I don't understand is this: won't the residents still steal each other's frozen goods from the brand new communal freezers? Did management not consider this when they were deciding how to waste thousands of pounds on how to police the shared pantries and kitchens of our young discarded on to the welfare state?

The shift ends with a bit of a drama. It's around 3pm, when a racket suddenly erupts upstairs. One of the other keyworkers runs in.

'Sean's just smashed up his room and now he's smashing up the whole place,' she says, eyes wide.

The manager runs in, and all three of us start look at the CCTV screen: the monitor is divided up into eight images, and as I watch Sean – an 18-year-old ne'er-do-well – comes round the corner on the top left image. Clearly shouting at the top of his voice, he kicks every door in the corridor, very hard, before picking up a fire extinguisher and hurling it through a window. A couple of residents run down the stairs, shouting that he has attacked them, too. They look scared.

'He's completely off his fucking face,' says one.

I wonder whether I should go and stop him, but then I remember what Oceania pay me: is it enough to risk being pushed down a flight of stairs or kung fu-kicked in the face? I hesitate.

The manager perhaps senses my dilemma. 'The best thing we can do is let him work it off,' he says. 'We don't want to escalate things. Let's keep our body language non-aggressive, let's take a non-interventionist approach here. The police have been called, so let's let them deal with it when they get here.'

So we watch as he inflicts thousands of pounds of damage on the fixtures, fittings and fabric of a building created to provide shelter to 'vulnerable young people at risk of homelessness'.

Eventually, he appears in reception – bored with attacking his fellow residents and smashing things – and storms outside. This changes things a bit, so I follow him: sure enough, he has decided to share his rage with the wider community. He runs across the street in front of the Project and attempts to pull an elderly man from a bike as he cycles by. At this point, I decide to abandon our official policy of de-escalation and leap on him, dragging him to the ground and holding him there, arms behind his back, until the cops eventually show up.

They haul him off – I never find out what happens to him, but I think it's a fixed penalty notice or a caution – and the following day he claims to remember nothing of the incident. He isn't evicted: instead, the good people at The Gregor Samsa Building 'work to understand his issues', while the taxpayer repairs the damage.

IT'S EASIER TO EXECUTE PEOPLE IN THE USA THAN FOR US TO EVICT ABUSIVE DRUNKS

TODAY IS MARTINA'S appeal hearing with the area business manager.

Here's how the appeals process works.

A keyworker issues you with notice of eviction after you have used up all your warnings. (You'll have gathered that there can be a very large number of these, and that it can take months to get to this stage – not least because you can appeal each warning individually as well.) The reasons for the eviction will have been discussed and explained to the project manager, who will have signed it off.

The project manager then writes formally to the resident, explaining that he or she has a right to appeal to the area business manager, the regional supremo.

If the area business manager backs up the decisions of the keyworker and project manager, the resident is allowed a further appeal to the national operations director.

If the ops director likewise backs up the lower echelons, the resident has a final opportunity to appeal to the board of directors.

It is actually easier to execute people in the United States than it is to kick an abusive young druggie out of supported housing, but I am not against these appeals, *per se*. For a start, it is quite possible that the keyworker, the project manager, and the area business manager are engaged in an evil conspiracy against the blameless young person. It is also possible that the operations director is in on the malicious plot. (I think – at least, I hope – that we can assume our board is untainted by this irrational hatred of the entirely innocent.)

Our residents usually admit defeat if their first appeal is turned down, but there have been several cases where particularly troublesome types have dug their heels in and used the appeals process to extend their stay as long as possible.

In Martina's case, I'm pretty confident that Tessa – who knows Martina from her own time as manager of the Project – will rule in favour of our decision and uphold her eviction. Mind you, that's what common sense tells me and we know where that leads around here. I'll just have to wait and see.

As it was Martin who signed off the eviction order, Nicola is staying out of it. It's just me – standing in for Brendan, who's on a much-needed holiday – Tessa and Martina.

Tessa arrives, and walks into the office. Martina has been pacing up and down outside the office like a caged hippo, and she barges straight in after her, ignoring as usual the sign that says 'Please knock and wait to be invited'. She grabs a chair and plonks herself down.

'Hi, Martina,' says Tessa, enthusiastically. 'How are you? Keepin' OK, I hope?'

Ah. Common sense may not be about to prevail.

'Yeah, OK,' says Martina.

'OK, so your appeal,' says Tessa. 'Well, I'll get down to that in a moment. I just need to have a pee first.'

She sort of squats a little and gyrates her hips, illustrating what 'having a pee' involves, just in case Martina and I had no idea.

I groan inwardly; Tessa is always at this type of down-with-the-youth crap. I find it cringeworthy to watch.

Martina starts giggling; she seems very relaxed all of a sudden. Tessa heads off to the loo, and the atmosphere in the office cools a little; Martina is looking at me with undisguised contempt, and I'm smiling back innocently.

Tessa's back. 'Shall we do this in the meeting room?' she says. She leads us to the dark, low-ceilinged room. Once there, she engages in another minute or two of friendly banter with Martina – most of it about the oeuvres of Lily Allen and 50 Cent – before sitting down at the head of the table.

'OK,' she says, finally. 'Let's crack on.'

'It's all in there,' I say, handing her the file in which I have documented each of the many times that Martina has shouted, sworn at or threatened members of staff or other service users during the past three months. It's a pretty hefty document – five pages in total – and it's full of language that would make your average trooper blush. I also detail what provoked each outburst: usually it was down to a rent reminder, our refusal to allow her boyfriend to stay overnight or to use the office telephone, but sometimes there was no discernible reason. It was just that she felt like it.

'OK,' says Tessa. 'Let's have a read of this, then.'

'It's all lies,' says Martina. 'They've just got it in for me. I never done any of that.'

'Let me just…' says Tessa, flicking through the pages. 'Right, OK. Right, Martina, I'm going to read you the contents of this report, and then you can respond. Is that OK with you?'

'It's all lies,' repeats Martina, folding her arms defiantly.

'OK, but I can read it to you, yes?' says Tessa.

Martina nods, and Tessa starts reading.

'August 12, told the night worker to fuck off and die because he refused to allow boyfriend to stay,' says Tessa. 'August 14, told Brendan to fuck off and die because asked Martina to stop drinking in the common space. August 15, told Perry to fuck off and die and called him fucking chav scum because he was using the washing machine when she wanted to use it. Then told Winston to fuck off and die when he asked her to desist. August 17…'

It goes on for quite a while, with Martina interjecting regularly with lots of suggestions that this is 'all bollocks', or 'all lies', and a fair bit of theatrical eyebrow-raising, harrumphing and sarcastic 'yeah, right, as if'-ing.

At length, Tessa finishes. She places the report on the table, sits back and looks at Martina.

'Martina,' she says, 'I'm surprised. This isn't my memory of you at all, but it seems from this report that you have been way out of line in the way that you have been speaking to staff. What do you have to say to this?'

'The staff hate me here,' snaps Martina, 'and besides the rules are stupid and pathetic. I should be allowed to have my boyfriend to stay overnight. Why can't I?'

I break in. 'Martina, *no-one* hates you,' I say. 'It's not about you. The rules are the same for everyone. You've received warnings for not paying rent and you've lost your overnight guest privileges as a result. The whole point of you living here is to prepare you for the real world, where there are consequences for not paying your bills. The only thing is that, in the real world, the bills are bigger and the consequences are more immediate and severe. And people will not put up with being spoken to how we put up with it.'

Instead of backing me up, though, Tessa says, 'Well, it's important for Martina to feel she can express how she feels about the rules, and for us to listen. However, Martina, you can't continue to speak to staff in the manner that you have done.'

What the hell is wrong with Tessa? I think to myself. *Why is it important to listen to Martina's feelings on the rules? The rules just are.*

But as we're not in the real world, Martina divulges her feelings. 'The staff are rude when I try to talk to them,' she says. 'They never listen. They don't understand how hard it is not being able to have my boyfriend stay over. They're only interested in rent and rules... they see us as numbers, not people. And I especially hate him.' She points at me with a glare of contempt. Tessa follows her glare and looks at me, questioningly.

'Martina,' I say, suddenly starting to wonder whether I'm the one under investigation. 'That is not true. Speaking personally, I've listened to you on many occasions. Everyone else does, too – we don't have a lot of choice. The problem is not that people don't *listen* to you, the problem is that we don't *agree* with you. You think it's unfair that your boyfriend can't stay. I listen to the words you're saying, but I have explained to you that that is the consequence of spending your dole money on beer and cigarettes, as opposed to paying the rent. Sometimes life is hard.'

It all seems pretty open and shut to me, but I have a nagging feeling – based on body language and her relaxed style of chat – that Tessa is going to overrule the decision of the staff and project manager, and give Martina another chance. The girl hasn't shown a shred of contrition throughout the meeting, but she has spent a good deal of the time laughing at Tessa's little jokes.

'Martina,' says Tessa, 'what do you think you would need to be able to turn this situation around? Do you think there is some kind of support we could give you to help you deal with your rent arrears and prevent further behavioural problems?'

There's a possibility I'm going to have a stroke when I hear this: I picture myself dying on the floor, with Martina leaning over me, laughing. What a way to go.

'Tessa,' I say. 'What you're implying here is that we haven't done enough for Martina already. When the fact is, for months various members of staff have tried to help her deal with her rent and address her behaviour.'

But I might as well not be there.

'I don't like my keyworker, Brendan,' says Martina. 'He's rude and he doesn't help me. Perhaps if someone helped me do a budgeting plan I could be better at paying my rent. I don't really get the support I need here.'

This is a blatant lie; to my knowledge, Brendan has had several conversations with her about budgeting. Somewhere in her file is the budget plan the two of them agreed, and with which she utterly failed to comply. Her anger at Brendan actually stems from the fact that he initiated the formal rent warning process, which led to her losing the overnight guest privilege.

'Right,' says Tessa. 'I think I've heard enough. I'm going to suspend your notice for a trial period of two weeks. I'll allocate you a new keyworker of your choice who will help you do up an action plan to pay your rent and the arrears you've accrued. You must meet with her or him every week. In this period of time, you must refrain from abusing staff. If, after two weeks, you have done these things I will allow you to have your boyfriend stay over one night a week. I understand it must be hard for you not having him stay. After a month, if you have abided by all these conditions and are in the regular habit of paying off your rent arrears as well as the rent I will revoke the eviction notice completely.'

I want to bang my head on the desk. I really don't understand this place. Martina has been given all the chances, help and support she needs and much more; at the same time, her behaviour and attitude have become even more aggressive, abusive and belligerent. What about those of us who have to put up with her vitriol? Don't we count?

I have one last stab. 'This idea of putting together an action plan for Martina to pay her rent is an insult to her intelligence, and ours,' I say. 'It's not like she has learning difficulties. Brendan's been over this with her and they have already produced an action plan for it – though God knows why that should be necessary. She gets JSA of £46.85 a week. She needs to subtract a tenner from that, to make a £7.50 contribution to her rent and a £2.50 contribution to her arrears. Why would you need to draw up a new action plan for this?'

But Tessa isn't listening; Martina gives me a smirk that somewhere between contemptuous and triumphant.

'OK,' I say, accepting defeat. 'But I'll just say this. Martina, you need to stop blaming other people for the problems you're now facing. They are entirely of your own making. You were offered lots of support here and failed to engage. I am going to speak to you very plainly now. You have two options and two sets of consequences. Take your pick. Option A is pay your rent, obey the rules and live contentedly here at the Project. Option B, the one you have been taking so far, spending your dole on booze, not paying your rent, abusing staff… maybe not today, but one day that will end in eviction. It's up to you to choose which one you want from here. You're really lucky you've been given another chance.'

I'm trying to hide how angry and disappointed I am at what has gone on. This suspension – and possible revocation – will send out a demoralising message to my colleagues, and a corrupting one to Martina's fellow residents: that you can refrain from paying rent for several months, and abuse the staff, with almost no consequences. Worst of all, there are bound to be kids in the town who could really do with a room like hers, but they're going to have to wait longer.

Tessa has moved away from work on the ground now, so she no longer has to deal with it all, which is a fundamental flaw in the system. It's the staff in the Project who should have the final say, but as in schools – where head teachers usually cannot decide on expulsions – the rights of the malefactor take precedence over those of decent residents and staff.

'Winston will draw up an acceptable behaviour contract for you and we'll take it from there,' says Tessa.

Later on, as I sit bathed in the greenish strip light of my office, I see Martina leaving the building for a night on the town. I bend my head and start writing, laboriously. What I produce is, predictably, no more than a longwinded way, printed on our headed paper, of telling Martina to subtract £10 every week from her weekly income of £46.85 and bring it to the office in order that she can pay her rent and knock a little off her arrears. For good measure, my plan also advises her not to swear or scream at staff, or kick any of the fixtures or fittings.

Given that this is all part of what she agreed when she moved in here, I can't see the point of the exercise; a simple verbal agreement should surely suffice. But 'simple' isn't part of the culture in supported housing. Everything must be written down, even the utterly obvious. Still, the report will look nice in Martina's file, and the fact that we have produced it and given her a copy can be written up as evidence of 'support' in her 'support plan' – something which will keep the government auditors happy. In the slightly surreal world in which I work, it's 'evidence' like this that counts.

It doesn't matter if the support isn't working, or isn't even wanted or needed, and residents have to be forced to turn up for it; what's important is that we have a paper record of having delivered it. That's a job well done, and will ensure that the salaries keep getting paid.

LET'S TALK ABOUT IT TOMORROW

ON TONIGHT'S KEYWORK agenda for Kenny are: rent arrears (as always), steps to find employment and his looming fatherhood by his ex-girlfriend.

The latter doesn't seem to bother him much. He never talks about it unless I bring it up – the fact that he is about to assume theoretical responsibility for another living human being is just so much background noise in the never-ending drama that is his life. He has already moved on to another girlfriend; what's done is done, and best forgotten.

I decide to tackle the issue of rent arrears first.

I print off a copy of his rent account from the computer.

'OK, Kenny,' I say. 'Let's talk cash first.'

'Sure.'

'Now, on the upside, after that chat we had and after me writing out a new application for you, your housing benefit situation is finally sorted out, and they've paid of most of your arrears. So your notice has been revoked.'

He nods. 'Yep. Cool.'

'However, just looking here, I notice that the weekly payments of £7.50 that you're supposed to pay on top of your housing benefit haven't actually been paid.'

'They haven't?'

'Well, you should know – you're the one not paying them. The total now stands at £67.50 which is… let me see… nine weeks.'

'Really?'

He raises his eyebrows, but I don't think his surprise is fake: Kenny *never* knows how much rent he owes. I mean, he knows it's somewhere between quite a bit and a hell of a lot, but to the penny, or even the tenner? No chance.

'Look, Ken,' I say. 'We need to sort out a repayment plan for these remaining arrears and we also need to ensure that, from now on, you pay your weekly share of the rent, agreed?'

'Yeah, of course. That sounds reasonable enough.'

I am not confident however; over what sometimes seems like the last decade, I have witnessed Kenny agree to many reasonable proposals involving the paying of rent.

'Let me see. You get £93.70 a fortnight on JSA, is that right?'

'Yeah.'

'How much do you spend on food?'

'I dunno. Thirty quid?'

'OK, so that leaves £63.70. If you pay your share of the rent, that's only fifteen quid every fortnight. If you stick another tenner on top of that, making it £25 every two weeks, is that doable? It would still leave you with nearly forty quid in your pocket.'

'Sounds fair and reasonable to me,' says Kenny. 'Yeah, that's cool.'

I know he's lulling me into false security here, but it's so seductive, the notion that this time he might comply with the plan, unlike all the other times and other plans. He always tries it, and I always fall for it. I'm just feeling my face widen into a grin, when he shatters my illusion.

'Can I just have one exception to this repayment plan?' he says.

'What might that be?' I ask, disappointment flooding my soul.

'Well, the next two instalments I'm good for,' he says. 'But the one after that, would it be all right if I don't pay that week? Only it's my birthday?'

He asks in a very confident way, like he expects me to say Yes.

'Oh, right,' I say. 'Because you want to go out on the beer with your mates, yeah?'

'That's the one,' he chuckles. 'It's gonna be mega.'

'I can't agree that it's OK to do that, Kenny,' I say. He looks completely bemused, nonplussed. 'Look, our whole job here is to help you on the road to independent living. When you're living independently, you can't drink your rent money. The real world doesn't work like that. If you spend your mortgage repayments on beer the bank manager will take your damn house off you. He doesn't care whether you were celebrating your birthday or not. You live in enough of a cocoon already, Ken. The hassles with your rent to date would have seen you made homeless in the private sector within a month. So no, you can't drink the rent on your birthday.'

He is giggling away to himself at this stage, and isn't looking me in the face. I'm not sure whether this is through embarrassment, or whether he is laughing at me and my weird ideas. I know he will be out on the piss on his birthday, come what may, and that he'll avoid me for several days afterwards.

'Did you sort that thing with the guy from the finance company?' I say.

'Which guy?'

'You know… he came round with a letter while you were playing *Command and Conquer.*'

'Ah that,' he says. 'Nah, I just binned it.'

'You know they're not going to go away,' I say.

He shrugs. 'And? What they gonna do?'

I don't have an answer for him here. The loan company might take him to court, but a County Court Judgment on his credit record isn't going to worry him too much. Their lookout for giving him the dosh, I suppose.

'Can we talk about this new baby?' I say.

'Ah mate,' he says. 'Not just now. I'm too busy. I'm off out. Let's talk about it tomorrow?'

And he's gone.

* * * * *

Later, Brendan walks into the office as I'm hunched over my keyboard, dumping his canvas satchel on the desk with a sigh

'Busy?' he says.

To the casual observer, I probably look busy. Perhaps I'm working my way feverishly through a series of action plans to see which goals and objectives have been reached and which have not. But why would I? I know with a good degree of certainty which residents will have reached which goals and which will have missed them hopelessly.

'Not really,' I say. 'To be honest, I'm reading the *Society* section of *guardianonline*, wondering where they get their writers from.'

This is something I often wonder about. They seem like nice people with their hearts in exactly the right places, but they often don't seem to me to have much hands-on experience of that about which they write.

'Did you get that stupid email from head office?' says Brendan. 'It's doing my head in, this shite.'

Brendan is a qualified youth worker who has spent more than seven years working in this place. Whereas you might say I am cynical and curmudgeonly by nature, Brendan is an upbeat, positive kind of bloke, very 'proactive' in his approach to working with young people. Well, he used to be: lately he's becoming more and more like me. As the years have gone by, and the 'Supporting People' ethos has infected every aspect of the place, his once enthusiastic approach has started to wane.

'Which email?' I say. We get quite a few.

'It was from some manager in head office telling us that from now on we are no longer to refer to the residents as residents but instead we need to start calling them "clients". I mean, what is the difference?'

'Hmmm… I don't think I got that one,' I say. 'Or if I did, I don't think I read it.'

'You know,' he says, 'I got pulled up last week for having failed to number some of the pages in my support plans, as well as having forgot to get the resident to sign next to all of the support that I'd written up. I put my heart and soul in to the work I do, and instead of getting some thanks for that I get criticised for how my files look, and the fact I don't have nice cover sheets at the front of them.'

He throws himself down on the office sofa, looking thoroughly pissed off.

'God, I miss the days before Supporting People,' he says. This is before my time he's talking about, when we were owned by a different housing association and before the government launched the Supporting People project. 'It was just a completely different ethos back then.'

'In what way?' I say, looking away from Polly Toynbee.

'The project manager had much more power. We had the final say on who we accepted – none of this coercion and bullying by Connexions – so we didn't get the kind of people we're taking in now. Don't get me wrong, we got kids with problems and there was the normal, low-level teenage disruption here and there. But it rarely got out of hand and if it did, and someone needed evicting, they just got evicted. I mean, with immediate effect – no right to appeal. Our word was trusted, it was worth something. So the times when we got serious shit off anyone… I could count them on the fingers of one hand.'

'Sounds a lot better than it is today,' I say.

'Oh, loads,' says Brendan. 'We used to see the young people progress much more in those days. Like, between 9am and 5pm Monday to Friday, the rule was that they *had* to be out of the building. What they did with their time during those hours was up to them

– they could go to work, or get themselves on a course, or just be more active – but what they *couldn't* do was sit around all day in their bedrooms, smoking weed and playing *Grand Theft Auto*.'

'And you guys used to enforce that rule?' I say.

'You're damned right we did,' he says. 'The manager would go around making sure everyone was up and out, and guess what? We had a greater proportion of residents in meaningful activity. Then along came Supporting People, and the QAFs, and "client involvement", and the emphasis on rights, and… well, the proof of the pudding is in the eating, isn't it?'

'Sounds like a kind of nirvana,' I say, reflecting on the anger, abuse and contempt directed at us now.

'You know Winston,' says Brendan. 'I'd just be happy to retire early from all this nonsense and spend my time working on my car if I could afford it.'

Brendan's a classic car buff – he buys them in shocking condition, does them up and flogs them at a profit.

'Still got that old Morris thing?' I say.

'No, I've just bought an Alvis TD21 Drophead Coupé,' he says. 'It's in a state at the moment, but when I've finished it it'll be worth a fair bit. Probably twice what I earn here in a year. Trouble is, in order to afford to renovate it I need to carry on at the Project.'

He sinks into the sofa with a sigh, and closes his eyes. I feel sorry for him: he really wants to help young people, but feels constrained by a system that focuses on bureaucratic compliance to the exclusion of just about everything else. Is Kyle on a course? Yes he is, so we can tick that box – job done. Is Kyle actually bothering to attend his course and learn anything of value? No. But that isn't the point, is it?

Brendan isn't an isolated case. Although many of the people I have met and worked with seem to be convinced of the efficacy of the work they do – in the face of clear evidence to the contrary – I've also met many professionals throughout the housing, youth work, youth offending and social services sectors who privately hold pretty reactionary views in relation to the problems they experience. These are not the knee-jerk reactions of the toff from Tunbridge Wells or the Little Englander from Lytham St Annes. Believe me, very few right-wingers go into these lines of work; I'd say that, like me, most probably come from left-wing backgrounds. Most came into the job determined to help and understand people whom they believe to be vulnerable and underprivileged. The question that they start to ask themselves is, *Is what I am doing actually working?* The answer, far from the theories of the management and academia and grounded in the reality of youth re-offending rates, persistently high rates of teenage pregnancies and the huge numbers of young people not in education, employment or training, is often No.

'Anyway,' I say. 'Work to do. I need to nip up and have a word with Kirsty about the state of her kitchen. It's absolutely filthy.'

* * * * *

Kirsty is Kenny Mulligan's current girlfriend: in fairness, she shares the kitchen with several others so it's not all her mess, but I've already spoken to them. I'm not looking for Michelin restaurant standards of cleanliness – I'm just trying to ensure it that we don't get to the stage where we have another maggot infestation in the Project.

It's 3pm on a Wednesday, but she's not in employment, education or training, or looking particularly hard to be in any of them; instead, she's in her room, reading a magazine and listening to music.

'Can I just have a chat with you about the bins and the cooker and stuff?' I say.

I can see her eyes glaze over; this happened with the others, too, and I know my advice about washing up and emptying the bins will probably go nowhere. But it's my duty to tell her, so I drone on for a few minutes.

Lecture over, I decide to ask Kirsty about Kenny's ex, and the impending arrival of her baby by the rat-faced ne'er-do-well.

'So where's Ken?' I say. 'I was hoping to get a word with him about the new baby. Is it here yet?'

Kirsty doesn't look best pleased at the change of topic. I think she'd rather talk grease and dirt.

'No,' she spits. 'His ex had like a miscarriage the first time, innit. So it ain't due till next year.'

'Oh, right,' I say. Then I realise what she's said. 'Hang on a minute, Kirsty, I'm a bit confused. What do you mean, she had a miscarriage "the first time"? Are you saying she lost that baby but then he went and got her pregnant again?'

'Er, *der*,' she says, sarcastically. 'That's what I said, didn't I?'

'But how did that happen?' I say. 'I mean, not biologically but... logically?'

'Well, you know,' she says, 'me and Kenny was on a break and that, yeah? It was a few months ago for like a couple of weeks. Well, he slept with her again that time, innit? And he got her pregnant again. Or so *she* says.'

Her tone suggests she thinks this second pregnancy might have been dreamed up by the other girl to lure Kenny back as a ruse; personally, I'd imagine he *has* got her up the duff again. Some of our most fertile males seem to come from the dregs of society, a fact which scares me a bit, in a Darwinian sort of way. Eejits like Kenny are breeding at twice the rate of the rest of the country, and this has to have some sort of implication for the gene pool.

Either way, why two young women would be jealous of the affections of this utter waster is beyond me. OK, Brad Pitt isn't about to walk into their lives but there are plenty of decent lads in the town. It's weird.

Later on, I catch sight of the great impregnator loping through reception like a walking ad for Kappa.

'Hey, Kenny,' I say. 'Can I have a word?'

'Sure man,' he says. 'If it's about me rent...'

For once, I'm not interested in his rent. 'Is it right that your ex lost the baby but you then went and got her pregnant a second time?' I say.

'Oh,' he says, looking relieved. '*That*. Yeah, s'true, man. Yeah, what can I say? Another accident. I don't like them condoms, and you know how it is.'

With that, off he strolls again, without a care in the world.

I'M A BORING PRICK SOMETIMES

IT'S THE THIRD WEEK in December and I'm in the office alone, trying to work out my costs for the month. What with moving into a shared house in the New Year, and a trip home to Dublin at Christmas, I'm just about going to break even. (I've given up on the idea of renting my own place, it's just too expensive). For a while, I sit pondering the general crapness of being in my mid-thirties in a badly-paid job that doesn't afford me a wage with which I can even rent my own flat. Then an obese and uncouth female storms in to the office. It's Kirsty.

She immediately starts shouting. 'This place is a fucking joke,' she yells.

'I can't disagree with you there, Kirsty,' I say. 'I'm not sure we'd agree on *why*, though. Calm down. Let's get off on the right foot, eh? Firstly, please don't walk into the office on the offensive, and please remember that you should…'

She finishes my sentence for me: '…*always knock and wait to be invited*, yes, I *know*. God, you're a boring *prick* sometimes, Winston, you know that?'

'If I wanted to talk to you,' I say, 'I'd knock on your door and wait until you opened it, wouldn't I? The least you could do is show me the same courtesy.'

She ignores me, and continues her rant. 'Where's Brendan?' she demands. 'I want to talk to him.'

'He's keyworking someone.'

'Well, I put in a request for a fucking wake-up call with the night worker,' she says. 'I know they wrote it in the book because I seen them do it. But Brendan only called me once and because of that I overslept. I had a job interview this morning, and now I've missed it and it's this place's fault I missed it. I *specifically* said I wanted to be called three times between eight and eight-thirty.'

'Are you serious?' I say. 'You specified *three* times?'

'Of course I'm fucking serious,' she says. 'Do I look like I'm fucking joking?'

'For a start,' I say, 'this is not a hotel. The night worker is not a night porter, and I'm not a conçierge. There's nothing in your licence agreement to say we have a duty to provide you with wake-up calls. If you'd asked me, I'd have told you to use the alarm on your mobile phone.'

She stares at me, nostrils flaring like a bull about to charge.

'But out of the kindness of his heart, Brendan obviously did give you a call this morning, and you chose to turn over and go back to sleep. So you missed your important appointment. Maybe this will teach you a lesson.'

I make a big deal of opening a folder of support plans, hoping she'll get the hint. Obviously, she doesn't.

'I've got a fucking disorder,' she says. 'I don't find it easy to get up in the morning. I have to be woken several times or I just fall back to sleep. I've told my doctor about it… give her a call if you don't believe me.'

I didn't know being lazy and stupid was a medical disorder, but there you go. Maybe she's also suffering from Repetitive Shoving of Pie and Chips Down Your Gullet Syndrome.

'I'm not going to call your doctor,' I say. 'I'm busy – can't you see that? But if I did, I very much doubt that she would back you up on this one.'

I'm not sure I'm right in this: many in the medical fraternity seem to believe lots of things I'd call the result of conscious decisions are in fact down to illnesses. The number of these new conditions seems to increase every year, too; the fact that this snowball of ill-health creates yet more work, money and status for the self-same medical fraternity is surely a coincidence.

'If she did, I think you'd find that half the country, including myself, suffer from the very same illness. Except the rest of us don't have keyworkers to beg us to get up.'

Steam starts coming out of her ears. 'You lot are supposed to help us,' she barks. 'Instead, you just hassle us over shit, and when we ask you for help you don't give it. Thanks to this place, I've lost that job.'

'No,' I say, calmly. 'Thanks to *you*.'

And you only missed the interview anyway, I think. *Unless they were looking for a fat, foul-mouthed, lazy narcissist you'd probably have been shit out of luck.*

She shrieks in frustration. 'I'm putting in a fucking complaint form about this,' she says, wobbling out of the office in her tracksuit. 'It's not on.'

You do that Kirsty, I think. *It's your right, after all.* As our Complaints Charter states:

> *We treat all complaints about the services we provide, the conduct of our staff and any other matter extremely seriously… We aim to ensure that all our service users are able to make, and feel comfortable making, complaints about our services. To do this we will provide as many different options to make complaints as possible, including text, telephone, in writing, email and in person.*

With policies like that, it's no wonder we get bullshit like this. What's worse, management will dignify it with a written response and we might have to answer for our failure.

* * * * *

The festive season is a week away, and the place is dripping with bargain booze, Pound Shop tinsel and Iceland mince pies as the majority of our residents gear up for the seasonal orgy of crass materialism and drunkenness that (to be fair to them) most of the rest of society also seems to enjoy.

Like the Scrooge I am, I'm trying to ignore it and am concentrating on my personal life which mainly consists of changing the ring tone on my mobile. I'm just fiddling with it when Nicola comes out of the project manager's office to borrow a stapler. And as I'm hunting through our drawers, Kacey – an 18-year-old lad who's been with us for a few months – joins us, carrying two huge plastic bags brimming over with presents. He's not the first I've seen weighed down like a pack horse recently: in the past few days, I've seen stacks of our residents walk in to the Project with bags and boxes of expensive goodies – all, and I hate to sound bitter, costing way more than I could afford. The few who are working, and those on the various types of fairly lucrative top-up benefit payments, can probably afford to indulge themselves. But most of them are on standard JSA or low levels of income support, so I just can't see how they pay for this stuff.

'Chuck us that Sellotape so I can wrap Paige's presents,' he says. Paige is his girlfriend.

Not a 'please' in sight. Nicola reaches across a desk for the tape and hands it to him. Not a 'thank you', either.

'When do you plan on bringing it back?' I say. 'Or were you going to borrow it like you borrowed that pen and notepad last week, and didn't return them? You should set aside some of your benefits for stuff like tape and pens.'

'Oh, for fuck's sake,' he replies. 'It's just a couple of things. Relax.'

Maybe I overdid the sarcasm. 'It's the principle,' I say. 'And I'd prefer it if you didn't swear in the office. This is a place of work. You wouldn't swear at your doctor or lecturer, would you?'

This is a pretty stupid question; of *course* he'd swear at the doctors or at college. He'd swear at anyone, any place, any time, if he felt in any way aggrieved. He's never been taught any discipline or manners and he struggles with self-regulation. But my preachy little speech has brought disapproving glances from Nicola, who finds my approach old-fashioned and authoritarian.

'Out of curiosity, Kacey,' I say, 'how much did you spend in total on those presents?'

I'm really interested in where he got the cash. He's on a part-time plumbing course at the local college (which, to be fair, he's almost completed) but only gets just over £50 a week in income support, and from that he has to pay £7.50 towards his rent (the rest being covered by housing benefit). Given that he's buying like a depressed shopaholic, it's odd.

'A couple of hundred quid or thereabouts,' he says, carelessly. 'I got twenty quid off me dad and another twenty off me uncle for Christmas, and I nicked a few bits and pieces as well. Only the things I couldn't afford, and only from the bigger shops. I don't do the small ones nowadays.'

I don't know how many of our residents are involved in low level crime, but quite a few – like Stella earlier – are happy to admit to it openly. There's rarely any indication of shame or contrition: it's as if they really don't know that it's wrong.

'Kacey, I'm worried to hear you say that,' I say. 'If you're caught this will have serious repercussions for you, never mind the damage it causes to businesses. You haven't been convicted of an offence since you turned 18, but if they nick you now you'll go to court as an adult and they take things a bit more seriously once you're over 18. If you carry on with this, you're going to see the inside of a prison cell.'

'Oh, it's just a bit of shoplifting, it's no big deal,' he says. 'I ain't gonna get caught, and if I do they'll just give me a ticket, or something. Anyway, it ain't my fault I'm short of cash. Why shouldn't my missus have a great Christmas like yours will?'

'I'm not with my girlfriend any more,' I say, 'and if I was she wouldn't be getting a quarter of that.'

'Besides,' he continues, 'I used to be way worse when I was under 18. I done burglaries and breaking and entering and getting drunk nearly every night and I was always in trouble with the old bill. I've come a long way from that. I don't burgle no more, and I only get pissed on Fridays and Saturdays. I've only been nicked once in the past few months and that was only a little drunk and disorderly thing which they gave me a fixed penalty for.'

He looks at Nicola for support, and adds, 'You're having a right go at me here, Winston. I feel very judged.'

In the social housing sector, judgmentalism is, naturally, a far worse offence than theft or bad behaviour. Accordingly, Nicola is quick to defend Kacey from any shameful feelings that might arise were he to be forced to view his behaviour in moral terms.

'No-one is judging you, Kacey,' she says. 'I think Winston's just concerned that you may get in to more trouble. Of course, we acknowledge that you have done remarkably well and improved so much during the last year. Well done on that score... we'd just like to see you do even better, that's all.'

Why is she congratulating this youth for refraining from breaking in to people's homes and businesses? There so many people like Nicola in this sector who think like this, that we should tread on eggshells when talking to young offenders about their anti-social behaviour. I'm not advocating shouting and being really confrontational, and I wouldn't want kids like Kacey to be mired in shame for the rest of their lives, but I do want them to grow into functioning human beings and decent members of the community. Apart from anything else, it's my job to try to help them like that.

'I've got news for you both,' I say. 'God forbid, but I *am* being judgmental of your behaviour, Kacey. It's atrocious. And we need to get rid of the hypersensitivity around this word, if only for the simple reason that it won't help you one bit. If you're caught stealing you will be arrested and taken to court and placed before a man who is so judgmental he's actually *called* a judge. It's his *job* to judge you, and I don't think he'll waste much time congratulating you, or praising you for progressing from burglaries and breaking and entering to just stealing from chain stores and large corporations. He will not take in to account the fact that you have developed an ethical framework to decide who deserves to be stolen from.'

'I don't see anything wrong with stealing from big shops,' retorts Kacey. 'They can afford it.'

'If everyone thought like that there'd be no shops to steal from. Anyway, the big shops just pass on the cost of what they lose from thieves to people who work for a living. So you're just creating higher prices for law-abiding citizens. Most people that can't afford to pay for something outright either buy it on credit or, better still, go without. It's time you copped on to yourself.'

Kacey says nothing. He picks up his two bags of mixed stolen-and-bought goods and the Sellotape, and retires to his room, hopefully feeling judged sufficiently enough to get him to question the current trajectory of his life.

Nicola looks at me. 'Well done, Winston,' she says, in a voice loaded with sarcasm. 'That was really helpful, wasn't it?'

She goes back into her office, stapler in hand, leaving me wondering what it's all about.

FATUOUS EXERCISES TO PLEASE GOVERNMENT AUDITORS

IT'S NEW YEAR'S DAY and the Project is pretty empty – most of our residents are either staying with the families from whom they are supposedly irreconcilable or round at mates' houses – so I get on with my favourite job of all, dishing out the annual client survey forms.

This is a fatuous exercise which involves housing associations like ours pretending that they care about our 'customers' being delivered a high quality of service. The truth, of course, is that the survey's existence has more to do with ensuring the chequebook-bearing government auditors are happy, rather than anyone *really* caring what the residents think.

I'm sitting under the harsh, greeny-yellow strip light in the office, looking at the damned thing.

Apparently, residents at various projects around the UK were involved in formulating it. Sounds to me like someone somewhere put a giant-sized tick in his 'client involvement' box with that one.

It's a glossy, full-colour, 12-page document, and 66 of them have been sent, first class, from Head Office down in London, to our project alone. Given that my housing association provides accommodation for several thousand people nationwide, I wouldn't like to hazard a guess at the cost of designing, printing and posting all these surveys. It wouldn't exactly be cheap, though. But then, it's not Oceania's money, is it?

This already almost criminal waste is exacerbated by the fact that the majority of residents don't even read the damn things, much less fill them in. When I handed them round last year, I'd say 90 per cent of the people I gave them to just binned them after a glance, and some didn't even bother with a glance.

I imagine it will be the same this year and while I don't claim to be Mystic Meg I wouldn't be surprised if the pattern is replicated up and down the country at the majority of our projects. It would be quicker and less time-consuming, and better for the environment, if we had just burnt the money it all cost in a field somewhere.

I look at the survey, and notice that – ironically – the first question is:

Why bother filling the survey in?

In case you cannot think of an answer to this question, and I confess I cannot, there is a helpful little paragraph below, written in *Janet and John*-level prose:

> *Most of our clients tell us that they think we are good. But we know that we are not perfect. We want to be as good as we can, so we really want you to complete this survey, to tell us what you think about us.*
>
> *The survey was designed by our staff with the help of a group of your fellow clients. The clients made a lot of really helpful suggestions to help us make the survey better for you.*

My spider sense is tingling for what's coming next, and I think it might involve cash.

> *Even better, everyone who fills in a survey will go into a prize draw to win one of ten prizes of £50 Argos vouchers.*

Yep, that sounds about right. We're bribing people who live off the hard work of others, with money produced by the hard work of others, to tell us whether they feel that the free accommodation that they get, including bills paid and a personal assistant to 'support' them in accessing their free money, is all tickety-boo. Through the red mist, and with a slight migraine starting to throb, I read some of the questions.

Do you get the support service that you want?

Because what *you* want is *all* that counts. And if you're not happy, don't worry – we're going to give you the chance to tell us where we're going wrong. And we guarantee to listen, no matter how vile you are and how ridiculous your suggestions, because what's important is that we 'involve' you and you feel 'listened to'.

How do you feel when you use our services?

Hard done by, I'd say. Plus 'hassled', 'discriminated against' and generally pissed off, for being expected to obey some basic rules and ensure that you sort out your Housing Benefit and pay some rent. I would bet my house – if I had one – that not one single resident in the entire nationwide survey will use the box provided to write:

> *I feel grateful to live in a country that has such a generous welfare system, and humbled that selfless people* [I don't include myself in this, admittedly; I'm talking about the rest of the staff] *are prepared to dedicate their lives to helping me move toward independence.*

The next question looks like fun.

Do staff understand your needs?

See, 'need' has a different meaning in here to the meaning it has outside. I can tell you now what many of our residents *think* they need, but what they think they need and the staff think they need are often very different things. For instance, here are a few things I feel the residents need.

Bianca needs not to have got pregnant, as she can't look after herself, never mind an infant.

Kenny needs not to have knocked his ex-girlfriend up twice 'by accident', and now that he has, he needs to man up and provide for his kid and the mother.

Gavin needs to stop swearing at staff when asked to stop having loud and violent domestic disputes with Julian.

Perry needs to stop smoking dope all day, as well as stealing; actually, this goes for quite a few of our residents.

Most of them need to look for work or take responsibility for their own benefits and stop relying on staff to remind them to sign on, drop in documents and attend meetings with the Jobcentre or Housing Benefit section at the council.

A few of them need to be locked up.

Can you influence how the service is run? What do you think about your level of involvement in the running of the service?

Do you feel you are involved enough in the running of the service?

What could we do to help you be more involved?

My Lord, imagine if – one day – a load of them decided to take this seriously! The very fact that the question is put to a group of people who – taking the average – could not run a bath shows how naïve our bosses are. Luckily, very few of the residents ever show any interest whatsoever in getting involved or 'influencing how the service is run'. Those who do are already able to sit in on interviews for new staff; lately there is talk of involving them in monthly staff appraisals. If that's brought in, I'm giving my notice: I'd rather sweep the streets or stack shelves in Tesco.

When you made a complaint, how did you feel about the way we handled it?

How come staff never get sent surveys asking:

When complaints are made, would you generally rate them as:
a) Ludicrous
b) Absurd
c) Unfounded
or
d) Laughable?

It might be because, unlike the residents, who at all times have the absolute right to be listened to and taken seriously, we're just cannon fodder.

The next question takes on a slightly pious tone:

Are your religious and cultural needs treated with sensitivity?

Religious and cultural needs are pretty thin on the ground around here – we don't have too many believers. I'm an agnostic myself, but if anyone asked for support in this area I'd have to deliver it, though you might think they'd be better off speaking to one of the learned preachers at the church, mosque, synagogue or other meeting place of their choice. Quite why the State should involve itself in a person's private beliefs – unless those beliefs are infringing on the rights of others – is a bit beyond me.

The survey also asks the residents to rate the following:

Standard of decoration in your room (because if it's not good enough, we can arrange for Lawrence Llewellyn-Bowen to pop round?)

Furniture provided in the room (ditto, except we'll send Terence Conran.)

Cleanliness of the communal areas (we provide paid cleaners, as I've said; there is no chance of most of our residents cleaning up after themselves.)

Equipment we provide in the communal areas (Perhaps the TV and DVD are not of the brand of your liking? Or are you irritated by the fact that we only provide eight computers with free broadband access when it would be more convenient for you if we gave you each one for your rooms?)

The standard of repair work and the attitude of those who carried it out (it's obviously not good enough that you get free accommodation and free repairs; you should also be able to demand that the working person who carries out your maintenance does so in a servile manner.)

The best question is the final one:

Do you get good value for the money you pay?

Excuse me? The money *they* pay? I rip the survey up and chuck it away. It's just another expensive example of how the admirable aims of William Beveridge have become perverted and distorted down the decades. The questionnaire demonstrates a compliance with the government's Quality Assessment Framework, but it has the unintended consequence of deepening the already entrenched sense of entitlement and something-for-nothing culture amongst residents.

GIVING FEEDBACK TO SERVICE USERS

IT'S 9AM ON Monday, and I've just come on shift.

Knackered from a dodgy night's sleep, I yawn and open the logbook. Ah. It seems from what Posy the night worker has written that things didn't run entirely smoothly.

> *Some residents up most of night making noise and messing about. Julian and Kirsty seem to be ringleaders. 5am – several have pupils like saucers + odd behaviour = Ecstasy?? Haven't raised it yet.*

I read on. Seems Stella got herself into a bit of trouble, too.

> *Middle-aged man appeared on premises at 3am demanding entry. Said was going to 'sort Stella out'.*

I hope he has more luck with her than we've had, but then I doubt his methods would have been quite as soft.

> *Said Stella had pulled clump of hair out of his daughter's head and given her a few thumps as well. Demanded we hand Stella over to him. When said No he left.*

There's nothing else of note, so I close the logbook. *Maybe all's well that ends well*, I think, picking up my tea and sitting at my desk. *Maybe we'll hear no more about it?*

Five minutes later, at what is for her an ungodly hour, Stella appears in reception and walks into the office.

'I need some laundry tokens,' she says, swigging from a can of Coke, wiping her mouth with the back of her hand and belching loudly.

She looks very much the worse for wear, and if past experience is any guide I'd say she knocked back her week's worth of recommended units in the Starz club in town last night. She chugs back more Coke. From the way she's going at it, I'd guess she's a mite dehydrated. But then it could be worse – she could be starting off the day with a beer, as some of her peers are wont to do.

'Not at work today?' I say.

'Day off,' she says.'

I take the money and hand over the tokens. 'You know there was a man here looking for you last night?' I say, conversationally.

'Yeah, I heard him shouting and screaming outside,' she says. 'So what, I pulled her hair out and slapped her? She won't fucking mess with me again, that's for sure.'

I sigh. I bet you Jeremy Kyle doesn't have to deal with this kind of thing at 9.15 on a Monday morning.

'Listen,' I start, and then I stop. It's too early for this, I don't have the energy and she won't listen anyway. She's impervious to any advice – a granite boulder to our soft rainwater. Some people just don't want to change. The government can have teams of keyworkers trying to 'support' them, but unless there's some kind of two-way interest you're pissing in the wind.

'So Stella, apart from the fight you had a good night did you?' I say, keeping my tone light and breezy. 'You look very hung over today, that's for sure.'

'Yeah,' she says. 'Fucking brilliant night. I was so smashed, I got off with a girl and I snogged a gay bloke as well. Mental, innit? Anyway I'm off, see you later.'

If I let her, she'd be quite happy to discuss the intimate details of her evening with me, even though – on a personal level – I'm a complete stranger. There is a term for this within the counselling profession: collapsed boundaries. Don't get me wrong: she's an adult, and she can do what she likes, with whom. I just don't want to hear about it.

Sadly, even younger girls than Stella will casually and openly try to discuss their sex lives in front of staff and other residents. I don't think I'm a prude, but it's enough to make you cringe; I make a point of informing the resident that I'm not comfortable with the chat, that it's inappropriate to talk to me about this stuff and that if they have any issues regarding sex that they need to discuss then they'd best do so with a female member of staff.

* * * * *

Not long afterward, I find myself flicking through our Complaints Charter, shaking my head bitterly. My heart is pumping and my hands are quivering with adrenaline.

The reason for the elevated pulse is that I've just been grabbed and threatened by Julian.

I'm looking at the Charter because he and several others are shouting about making a complaint against me, and I'm bitter about it because there's nothing in the bloody thing about *staff* making complaints.

The reason we have the Charter in the first place is to demonstrate to Supporting People compliance with the Quality Assessment Framework. As well as giving residents the means by which to complain, it is very clear that we must respond and take prompt action.

Take this excerpt from a Supporting People document that outlines how to meet your QAF targets with regards to whining hoodies and whinging layabouts:

> *Examples of good practice: Complaints logs and service user files should detail what responses were given with regards to complaints and where possible copies of letters should also be retained on service user files and in complaint files. Feedback given to service users in response to complaints should indicate what specific actions the provider has taken to prevent similar complaints arising in the future e.g. changes to policies.*

Another portion of the document highlights the importance of ensuring that residents are made aware of the fact that they can complain. However, we are told to ensure that this is done using:

> *Language and presentation of the procedure that promotes understanding by the majority of the service users.*

In other words, avoid using any word that contains more than two syllables and, where possible, use pictures. Ah… you think I'm being sarcastic. Think again. Here's what the document actually says:

> *So it is accessible providers have put the procedure in to a number of formats including: large print, posters, tenant handbooks, pocket books, other languages and pictorial.*

I'm not quite sure *how* you might use pictures to convey that it is possible to complain about being asked for the fifth time in a fortnight whether you would mind paying the rent you earlier swore on your life you'd pay.

Personally, I'd scrap the whole thing and just institute a system where the keyworkers ring round all the residents every day and just ask them what they'd like to complain about. It would save so much hassle.

Unsurprisingly, the Complaints Charter encourages the residents to moan incessantly. It also undermines our ability to carry out other aspects of our job, like trying to promote a drug-free environment.

This whole drama started about an hour ago when Kirsty walked through reception while I was putting up some mindless new poster.

'Hey, Kirsty,' I said. 'Can I just have a word about last night's logbook please?'

Sighing, she turned and waited. I walked over to her: her eyes were still showing the tell-tale signs.

'You look to me like you've taken some E,' I said. 'Your pupils are huge.'

Instantly, her face was alive with indignation and anger. 'You can't accuse me of that!' she shouted. 'You've got a fucking nerve! You don't know what you're fucking talking about!'

She may have taken Ecstasy, but she certainly wasn't loved up.

'Whooah,' I said. 'Kirsty, calm down, I only said you *look* like it. The night worker says you were up all night partying and making a noise, and your pupils are massive… what else am I supposed to think? I'm not saying I'm going to do anything about it… I can't, unless I catch you in the act. That said, I would advise you that if you *are* taking any drugs on the premises to be very careful and be aware what could happen if you do get caught. Remember, the police watch this place for obvious reasons. Now, about the noise…'

I got no further than that: she turned on her heel and stormed off upstairs. A few minutes later she came back down with Julian in tow. He proceeded to berate me for my 'fucking cheek' and started threatening that he was going to kick my head in. He started pushing me backwards and I think he'd have taken a swing if Brendan had not intervened and pulled him away.

Most of them have cleared off to bed now – well, it *is* 11am on a weekday – and I'm sitting here basically wondering whether they'll complain and what will happen if they do.

I make a mental note to speak to Nicola the new manager next time I see her. Since my relationship has ended, and since the cost of living in this area is prohibitive for a single person on my salary, I'm thinking of resigning and heading elsewhere. There's nothing particular keeping me in this area, or at The Emmanuel Goldstein Project. I'm getting close to jacking it in.

*****

It's the following week. Julian was issued with 48 hours' notice for his physical threats towards me and, naturally, he is appealing. Naturally, too, we are taking his appeal seriously – even though two members of staff witnessed the assault and have made statements to that effect, and even though we've now also included the issue of his violent attacks on his partner, Gavin.

The basis of Julian's complaint seems to be that I have no right to question his behaviour or suggest that I think he has taken drugs. In fact, he claims this whole thing is all a violation of *his* rights.

Tessa is in to hear the appeal, but she's asked if she can speak to me first. I think this might be because of my chat with Nicola, during which I said I was thinking of leaving. I have no job to go to, but I don't care – I can't put up with this much longer. There's the constant, cumulative bollocks, and now Julian has been trying to intimidate me. Ever since our confrontation, he's been hanging around the building making further threats to me, usually quietly enough that only I can hear. He's not a particularly frightening individual, but he is unpredictable: working with the knowledge that he could attack me at any time – and maybe with a weapon – is wearing. I'm also worried that I myself might snap. I'm a pretty placid person, but with every nasty remark and menacing stare he gives me, I can feel my own anger bubbling up. If I were to respond physically, that would end my career working with young people and while I think I've had it with this project I still feel I have something to give, somewhere.

I go into the office, sit down opposite Tessa and hand over the file I've completed. One part of it documents Julian's ongoing violent and aggressive behaviour towards Gavin, as well as various other behavioural issues, and how we have tried to support him in 'discontinuing his negative behaviours'. The second part focuses on incidents of abuse and intimidation towards myself and other members of staff.

As I thought she might, before she hears Julian's appeal Tessa tries an appeal of her own.

'Look, Winston,' she says, 'I hear from Nicola that you're talking about handing in your notice and we really don't want you to leave. We're here to support you and help you work through it.'

It doesn't feel like anyone's supporting me much, I think. *You've never talked to me about how I feel about stuff before.*

'You're a really excellent project worker,' she says, appealing to my ego.

And she's right, I *am* excellent – at filling in endless reams of paperwork and stating the obvious to young people who pay no heed to me. But then it's hardly the most challenging of roles.

I can't help but feel cynical about this sudden charm offensive. I can't help but think that trying to placate me like this is more to do with the hassle of recruiting another willing victim to fill my position. With nothing to lose, I decide to lay my cards on the table.

'Listen Tessa,' I say. 'No offence, but it's not really about Julian. He's a pain, but I can live with that. It's more the fact that I shouldn't *have* to live with it, and that's all part of the real problem – I don't believe anything we do here actually helps any of these young people.'

She's nodding and looking thoughtful. I feel a bit like I'm talking to a shrink.

'Very few of them use this place to change, and those who do change usually just do it off their own bat, with little or no input from us. All we really do is sit here in our offices, filling in forms and ticking boxes to indicate how we are supporting the residents. There's too much paperwork and too much emphasis on recording and measuring everything. We don't seem to stop to think about whether what we're recording and measuring is of any use. And as a result, most of their lives are going nowhere. I simply can't do it anymore. I don't believe in it. It's just dishonest.'

'I hear what you're saying,' she says. 'I understand.'

Does she? I doubt it.

'This whole appeal with Julian, it's just a farce,' I say. 'He physically attacked me in front of witnesses. What's to appeal? When we have a resident like him, someone we want to get rid of, the entire process is geared in favour of the offender. And with all due respect, the higher echelons of management don't seem to even know how the appeals process works – they lose essential paperwork and don't bother to hear the appeals on the few occasions it goes as high up as them.'

Wow, it feels good, telling it like it is. All the stuff I normally keep bottled up inside comes spilling out: it's very cathartic, and I wish I'd done it in all the crap jobs I've had.

I delve into the complaints folder. 'This is the kind of thing I'm talking about,' I say, pulling out a letter from Kirsty to Nicola, in which she complains that I have unjustly accused her of taking drugs, and the manager's reply, which is attached. Nicola's reply thanks Kirsty profusely for her complaint – the QAF encourages us to seek complaints and see them as 'a means by which we can improve our service.'

I have spoken to Winston, it says, *and there shouldn't be any more instances like this in the future.*

'The clear impression here is that I've been given a thorough dressing down,' I say. 'What actually happened was Nicola mentioned in passing that Kirsty had written to object about what I'd said, but told me that she wasn't taking it seriously and that I had done the right thing in raising my suspicions. OK, Kirsty will drop it now, which means Nicola's workload is kept down. But that letter will sit in the file, waiting for a future review by someone from Supporting People. I don't care two hoots what they say about it, but it's the corrupting influence of all the bureaucracy I hate – why let a little thing like the truth and supporting your staff get in the way of complying with the paperwork diktat and avoiding confrontation with the unpleasant inhabitants of the underclass? As long as the file demonstrates that compliance with the QAF, everything's cushtie.'

I'm expecting Tessa to jump to the defence of Oceania, but she surprises me.

'What can I say?' she says. 'You're right. These places don't work. They fail the people they're supposed to help. I agree, there's way too much paperwork and the appeals process is a joke. Every day when I come to work I feel like I've stepped on to the set of *The Jeremy Kyle Show*.'

I'm stunned: she's a relatively senior manager in this housing association. This is like sitting in Moscow in 1945 and hearing a member of the KGB openly denouncing Stalinism. If she knows where we're going wrong, why doesn't she say something to the people who count? I think I know the answer to this. There are those in the industry who delude themselves that it's all going swimmingly, and judge success in terms of DVD nights and Cook and Eat workshops. But lots of project workers and managers will admit that the system is broken – it's just that they will only say this privately. I think the majority don't wish to rock the boat for one simple reason – their wages. This industry is no different from any other – how often have *you* spoken out about the cock-ups, bullshit and incompetence that undoubtedly exist in *your* line of work?

I sit there, open-mouthed.

'Will you at least have a think before you do anything?' she says.

I nod.

Tessa hears Julian's appeal, upholds his eviction and he leaves that day.

GOING, GOING, GONE

I'VE SPENT A FEW nights thinking over my situation, and in the end I've decided to go.

I don't have anywhere to go, job-wise, but in a way it's quite exciting: earning as little as I do is actually quite freeing, because it's not a lot to kiss goodbye. I've got friends on the south coast, so I think I'll head down there and have a mooch around for a bit. There's plenty of work like this in other projects, so even in the current climate I shouldn't be out of work for long. Obviously, I don't expect things to be much different elsewhere, but I can hope.

Today's my last day at the Emmanuel Goldstein Project and I can safely say I won't miss the place one damn bit. I've had haemorrhoids I was fonder of.

I *will* miss all the staff – they're all lovely people, even the ones I don't see eye-to-eye with on everything. It might surprise you to hear that I'll miss quite a few of the residents, too, even some of the scoundrels.

I just won't miss the all-pervading aura of dishonesty – not from individuals, but from the system. Everything is built on a lie here.

I'm at the last Emmanuel Goldstein staff meeting that I will ever attend, and to be honest I am only half-listening. I'm not missing anything – it's exactly like the first staff meeting I sat in on over a year ago. Nothing has changed, but the staff continue to use the same procedures that have been failing them for years. It's almost textbook insanity.

The kitchens are mostly still abysmal, with the majority of residents complaining about the minority not cleaning up, and the staff are still writing polite letters asking people to do something about bearded fungus on rotting food and insect infestations in the carpets.

Most residents are still not paying the £7.50 share of the rent from their benefits, choosing instead to spend it on super strength cannabis and cheap booze.

Of the few who are working, several have not paid any rent for some time, and several more have been issued eviction notices for non-payment of rent or anti-social behaviour. They are all awaiting their first appeal.

If I came back here in a year, it would all be exactly the same.

As the staff meeting draws to a close, we shoot the breeze about a few of the residents.

Barry Jameson has assaulted his girlfriend again and was actually jailed for six months yesterday, which I didn't know.

'That's a result,' I say.

Someone has arranged for Sharn the Overdoser to get some proper mental health treatment, which means she'll be leaving and moving to a residential centre somewhere where they have the skills and expertise to help her. This is another result. I know a doctor who dealt with a persistent young cry-for-help/attention overdoser like Sharn. One day the kid took a few too many paracetamol, and the doctor had the unfortunate duty of telling her that, unfortunately, she had damaged her liver irreparably and really was going to die. She did, 24 hours later, tearful family at her bedside.

Bianca is moving out to a council flat ahead of the birth of her baby.

'Hey,' says Abigail. 'I meant to say, do you know who the father is? Kenny.'

I remember Bianca abusing Kenny as a 'chav bastard' and predicting that he would be a 'shit dad' to his third child, and I laugh at the irony of it.

Martina has left to shack up with a nightclub doorman in town; Laura Miller is applying to return for a third time (Margaret says we should 'consider her application sympathetically'); Gavin and Perry – amazingly, to me – are now an item.

'Did you hear,' says Sally, 'that Martin has left the Joseph K Project? Apparently he just lost it one day, started throwing files around his office and then just ran out. No-one has seen or heard from him since.'

A chuckle ripples around the table.

Brendan tells an amusing anecdote about one of the many love triangles going on between several residents. Karen, the new project manager – Nicola left suddenly last week – turns to me and says, 'You could write a book about this place, but no one would believe you.'

I might just do that.

Postscript

The purpose of this book has been to show that, in my experience, the British supported housing and social care sectors are in chaos.

The narrative is based on real events which I have witnessed during several years working in a number of supported housing and care homes at various sites around the UK. However, the timescales and chronology and the names and physical descriptions of people and places in the foregoing pages have been altered and blended together in the interests of confidentiality. Necessarily, dialogue and specific details of incidents have been likewise changed. Resemblances to living people and existing entities are coincidental: if you think you recognise yourself or someone else in these pages, or that you have visited The Emmanuel Goldstein Project, then I am flattered but you are mistaken.

However, the overall picture – of a huge State bureaucracy wasting millions of pounds working counter-productively to its proclaimed aims – is entirely accurate.

Also from Monday Books

Sick Notes / Dr Tony Copperfield
(ppbk, £8.99)

Welcome to the bizarre world of Tony Copperfield, family doctor. He spends his days fending off anxious mums, elderly sex maniacs and hopeless hypochondriacs (with his eyes peeled for the odd serious symptom). The rest of his time is taken up sparring with colleagues, battling bureaucrats and banging his head against the brick walls of the NHS.

If you've ever wondered what your GP is really thinking - and what's actually going on behind the scenes at your surgery - *SICK NOTES* is for you.

'A wonderful book, funny and insightful in equal measure'
– *Dr Phil Hammond (Private Eye's 'MD')*

'Copperfield is simply fantastic, unbelievably funny and improbably wise... everything he writes is truer than fact'
– *British Medical Journal*

'Original, funny and an incredible read' – ***The Sun***

Tony Copperfield is a Medical Journalist of the Year, has been shortlisted for UK Columnist of the Year many times and writes regularly for *The Times* and other media.

From all good bookshops, online from
www.mondaybooks.com or via 01455 221752.
All of our titles are also available as eBooks from amazon.co.uk

It's Your Time You're Wasting
– A Teacher's Tales Of Classroom Hell / Frank Chalk
(ppbk £7.99)

THE BLACKLY humorous diary of a year in a teacher's working life. Chalk confiscates porn, booze and trainers, fends off angry parents and worries about the few conscientious pupils he comes across, recording his experiences in a dry and very readable manner.

'Does for education what PC David Copperfield did for the police'

"Addictive and ghastly" – *The Times*

Wasting Police Time / **PC David Copperfield** (ppbk, £7.99)

The fascinating, hilarious and best-selling inside story of the madness of modern policing. A serving officer - writing deep under cover - reveals everything the government wants hushed up about life on the beat.

'**Very revealing**' – *The Daily Telegraph*
'**Passionate, important, interesting and genuinely revealing**' – *The Sunday Times*
'**Graphic, entertaining and sobering**' – *The Observer*
'**A huge hit… will make you laugh out loud**'
– *The Daily Mail*
'**Hilarious… should be compulsory reading for our political masters**' – *The Mail on Sunday*
'**More of a fiction than Dickens**'
– *Tony McNulty MP, former Police Minister*
(On a BBC *Panorama* programme about PC Copperfield, McNulty was later forced to admit that this statement, made in the House of Commons, was itself inaccurate)

**From all good bookshops, online from
www.mondaybooks.com or via 01455 221752.
All of our titles are also available as eBooks from amazon.co.uk**

Perverting The Course Of Justice / Inspector Gadget

(ppbk, £7.99)

A senior serving policeman picks up where PC Copperfield left off and reveals how far the insanity extends – children arrested for stealing sweets from each other while serious criminals go about their business unmolested.

'Exposes the reality of life at the sharp end'
– *The Daily Telegraph*

'No wonder they call us Plods... A frustrated inspector speaks out on the madness of modern policing'
– *The Daily Mail*

'Staggering... exposes the bloated bureaucracy that is crushing Britain' – *The Daily Express*

'You must buy this book... it is a fascinating insight'
– *Kelvin MacKenzie, The Sun*

In April 2010, Inspector Gadget was named one of the country's 'best 40 bloggers' by *The Times*.

When Science Goes Wrong / Simon LeVay
(ppbk, £7.99)

We live in times of astonishing scientific progress. But for every stunning triumph there are hundreds of cock-ups, damp squibs and disasters. Escaped anthrax spores and nuclear explosions, tiny data errors which send a spacecraft hurtling to oblivion, innocent men jailed on 'infallible' DNA evidence…just some of the fascinating and disturbing tales from the dark side of discovery.

'Spine-tingling, occasionally gruesome accounts of well-meant but disastrous scientific bungling'
– *The Los Angeles Times*

'Entertaining and thought-provoking'
– *Publisher's Weekly*

'The dark – but fascinating – side of science… an absorbing read' – *GeoTimes*

From all good bookshops, online from
www.mondaybooks.com or via 01455 221752.
All of our titles are also available as eBooks from amazon.co.uk

A Paramedic's Diary / Stuart Gray

(ppbk, £7.99)

STUART GRAY is a paramedic dealing with the worst life can throw at him. *A Paramedic's Diary* is his gripping, blow-by-blow account of a year on the streets – 12 rollercoaster months of enormous highs and tragic lows. One day he'll save a young mother's life as she gives birth, the next he might watch a young girl die on the tarmac in front of him after a hit-and-run. A gripping, entertaining and often amusing read by a talented new writer.

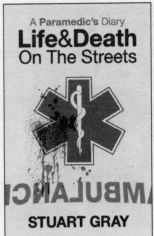

As heard on BBC Radio 4's Saturday Live and BBC Radio 5 Live's Donal McIntyre Show and Simon Mayo

In April 2010, Stuart Gray was named one of the country's 'best 40 bloggers' by *The Times*

From all good bookshops, online from www.mondaybooks.com or via 01455 221752. All of our titles are also available as eBooks from amazon.co.uk

So That's Why They Call It Great Britain / **Steve Pope**
(ppbk, £7.99)

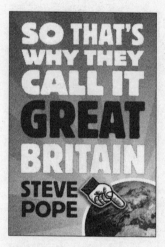

From the steam engine to the jet engine to the engine of the world wide web, to vaccination and penicillin, to Viagra, chocolate bars, the flushing loo, the G&T, ibruprofen and the telephone... this is the truly astonishing story of one tiny country and its gifts to the world.

In Foreign Fields / Dan Collins
(ppbk, £7.99)

A staggering collection of 25 true-life stories of astonishing battlefield bravery from Iraq and Afghanistan... medal-winning soldiers, Marines and RAF men, who stared death in the face, in their own words.

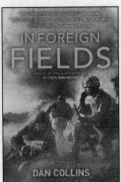

'Enthralling and awe-inspiring untold stories'
– The Daily Mail

'Astonishing feats of bravery illustrated in laconic, first-person prose' – *Independent on Sunday*

'The book everyone's talking about... a gripping account of life on the frontlines of Iraq and Afghanistan'
– News of the World

'An outstanding read' – *Soldier Magazine*

From all good bookshops, online from
www.mondaybooks.com or via 01455 221752.
All of our titles are also available as eBooks from amazon.co.uk